The Phantom of the Opera

THE GRAPHIC NOVEL

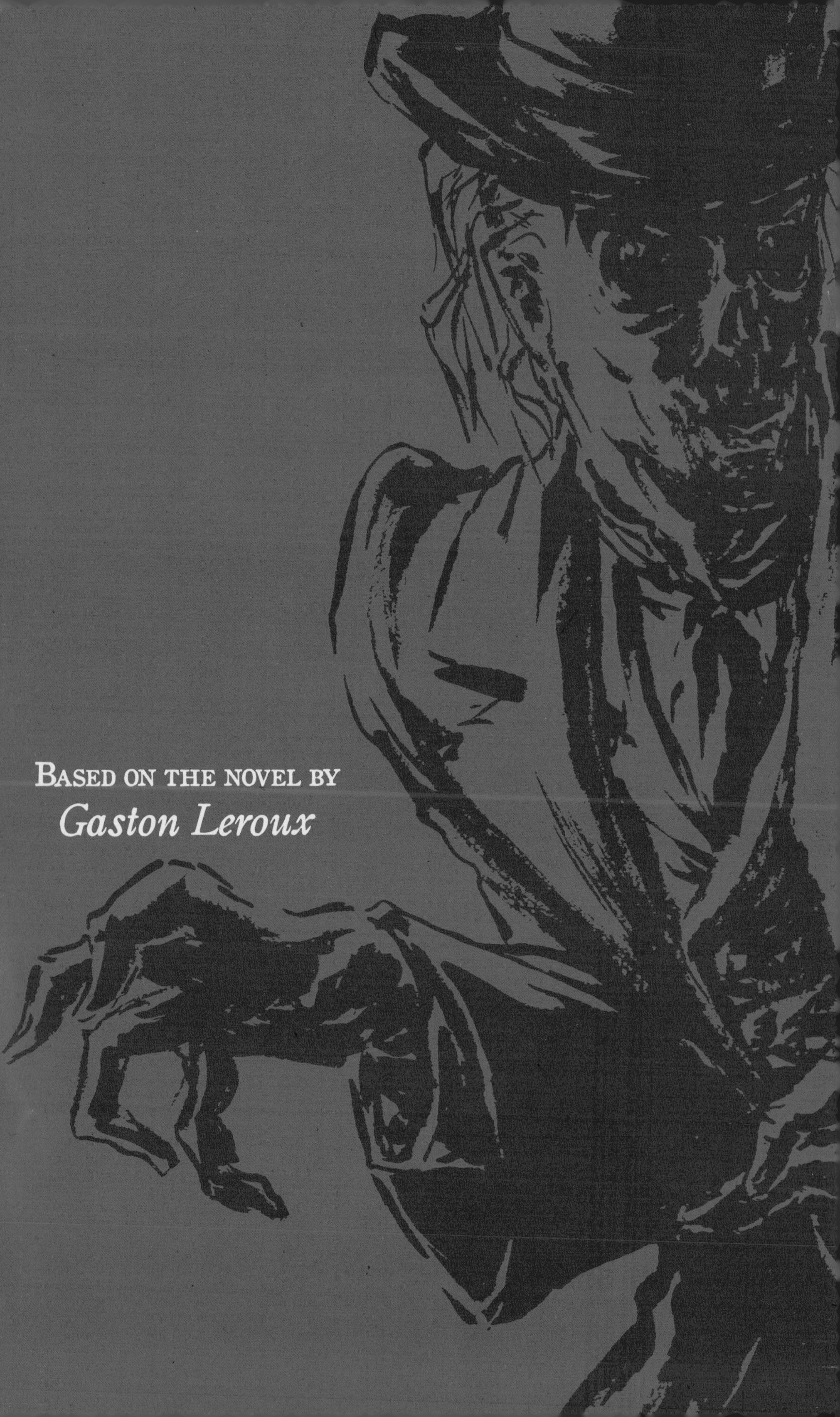

BASED ON THE NOVEL BY

Gaston Leroux

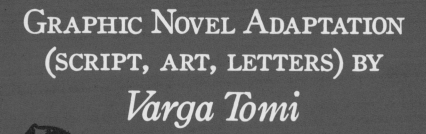

Graphic Novel Adaptation
(script, art, letters) by
Varga Tomi

Edited by
Tyler Chin-Tanner

Cover Illustration and Logo: Varga Tomi
Book and Production Design: Pete Carlsson

Tyler Chin-Tanner: Co-Publisher
Wendy Chin-Tanner: Co-Publisher
Justin Zimmerman: Director of Operations and Media
Pete Carlsson: Production Designer
Erin Beasley: Sales Manager
Jesse Post: Book Publicist
Hazel Newlevant: Social Media Coordinator

ISBN: 978-1-949518-09-2   Printed in Canada   AWBW.com

Publisher's Cataloging-In-Publication Data
(Prepared by The Donohue Group, Inc.)

Names: Tomi, Varga, author, illustrator, letterer. | Chin-Tanner, Tyler, editor. | Carlsson, Pete, designer. |
     Graphic novelization of (work): Leroux, Gaston, 1868-1927. Fantôme de l'Opéra.
Title: The phantom of the opera : the graphic novel / [graphic novel adaptation (script, art, letters)
     by Varga Tomi ; edited by Tyler Chin-Tanner ; cover illustration and logo: Vargi Tomi ; book and
     production design: Pete Carlsson].
Description: [Rhinebeck, New York] : A Wave Blue World, 2020. | "Based on the novel by Gaston Leroux."
Identifiers: ISBN 9781949518092
Subjects: LCSH: Phantom of the Opera (Fictional character)--Comic books, strips, etc. | Opera--France--
     Paris--Comic books, strips, etc. | LCGFT: Graphic novels. | Horror comics.
Classification: LCC PN6727 .V384 2020 | DDC 741.5973--dc23

Chapter One

The Opera ghost really existed.

He was not, as was long believed, a creature of the imagination of the artists, the superstition of the managers, or a product of the impressionable brains of the young ladies of the ballet.

No, he existed in flesh and blood, though he assumed the outward appearance of a real phantom; that is to say, of a shade.

From the Author's Introduction

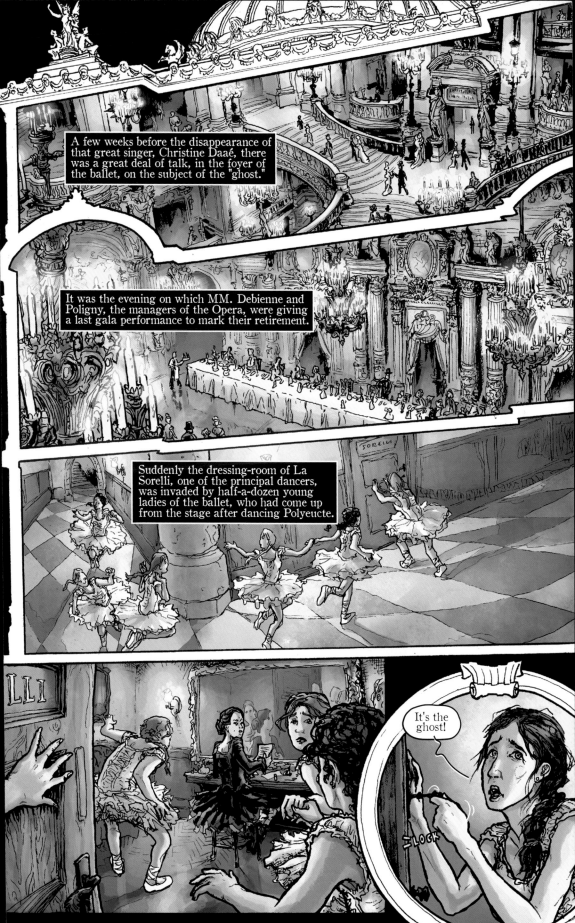

A few weeks before the disappearance of that great singer, Christine Daaé, there was a great deal of talk, in the foyer of the ballet, on the subject of the "ghost."

It was the evening on which MM. Debienne and Poligny, the managers of the Opera, were giving a last gala performance to mark their retirement.

Suddenly the dressing-room of La Sorelli, one of the principal dancers, was invaded by half-a-dozen young ladies of the ballet, who had come up from the stage after dancing Polyeucte.

It's the ghost!

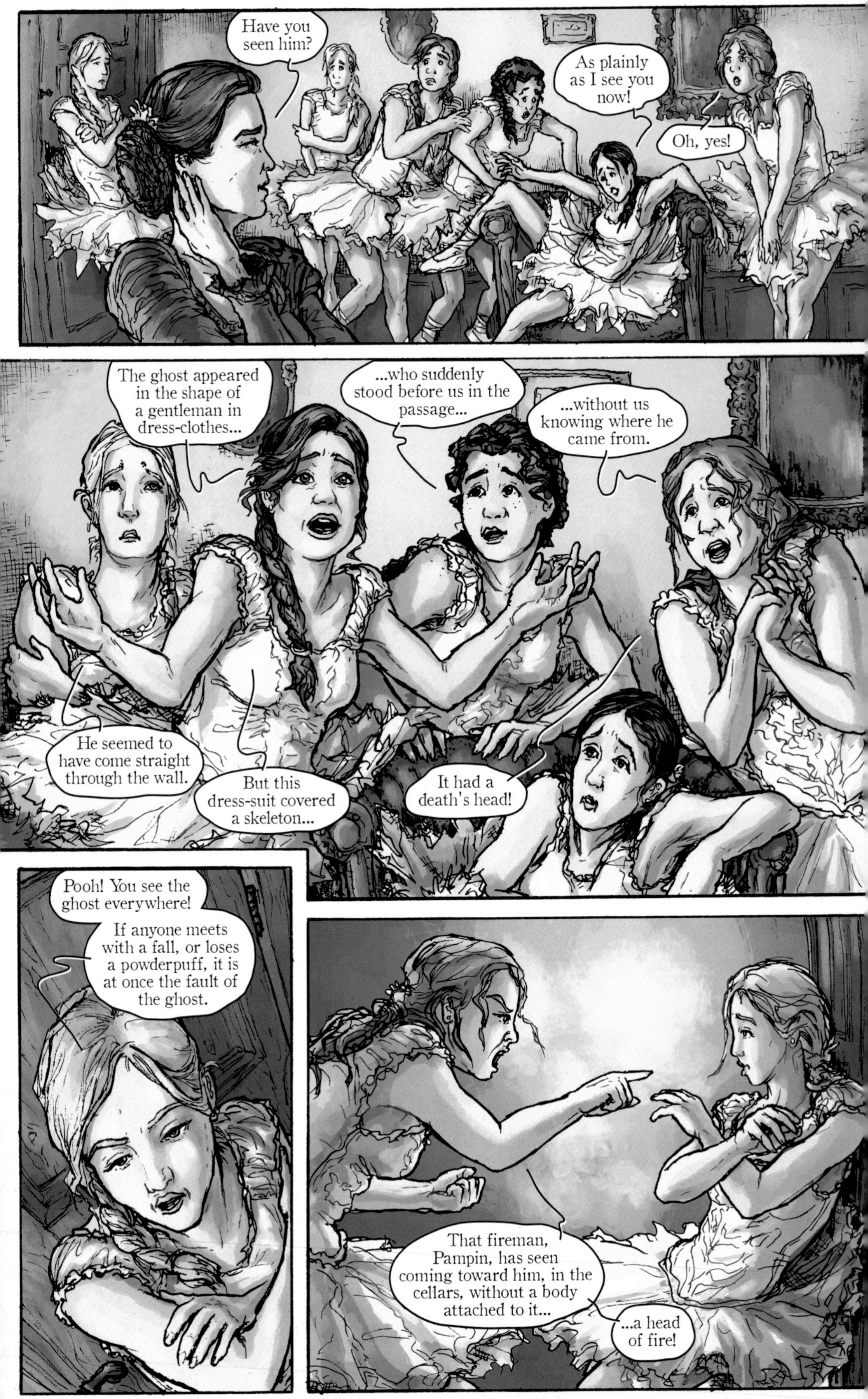
Have you seen him?
As plainly as I see you now!
Oh, yes!
The ghost appeared in the shape of a gentleman in dress-clothes...
...who suddenly stood before us in the passage...
...without us knowing where he came from.
He seemed to have come straight through the wall.
But this dress-suit covered a skeleton...
It had a death's head!
Pooh! You see the ghost everywhere!
If anyone meets with a fall, or loses a powderpuff, it is at once the fault of the ghost.
That fireman, Pampin, has seen coming toward him, in the cellars, without a body attached to it...
...a head of fire!

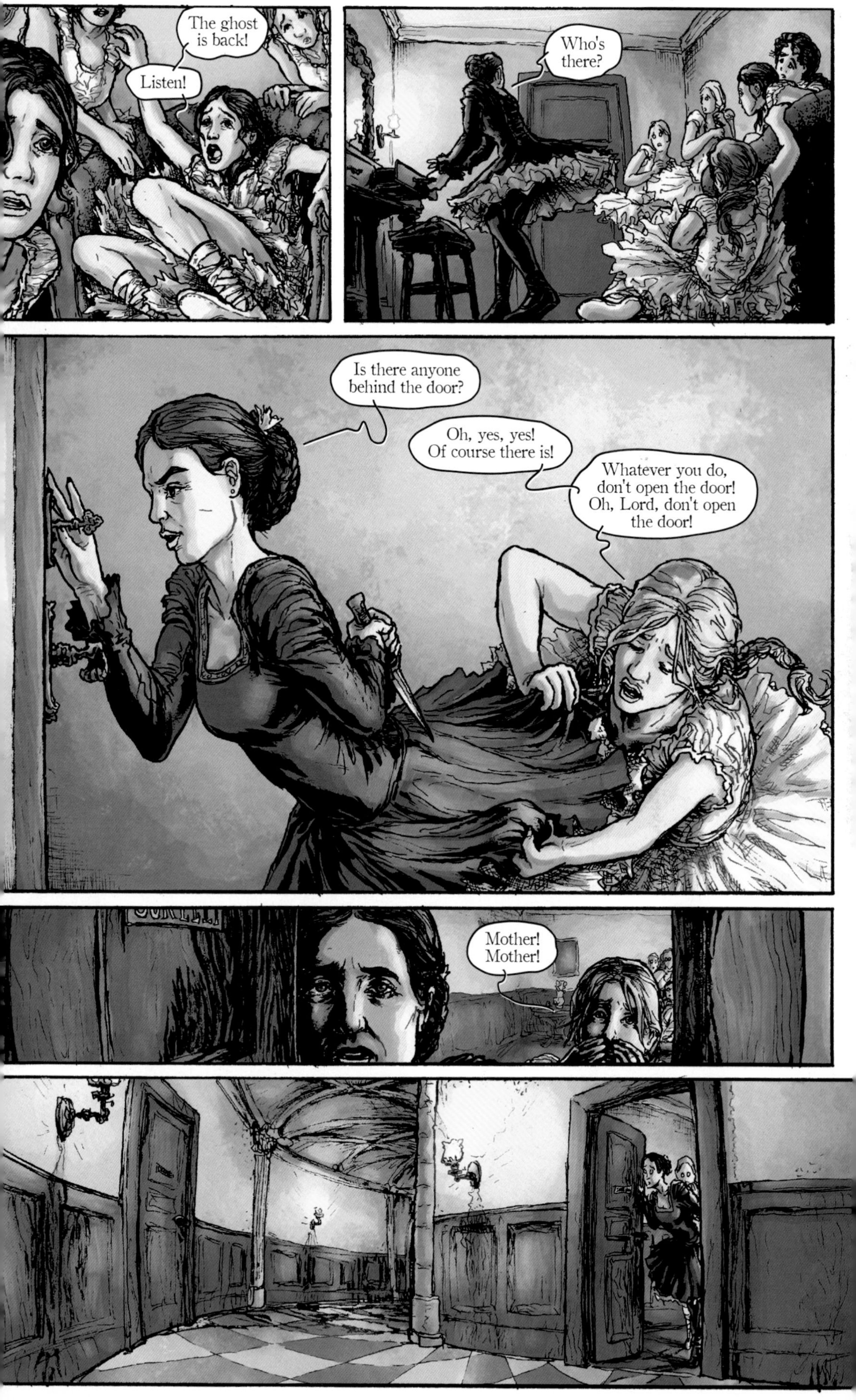
The ghost is back!
Listen!
Who's there?
Is there anyone behind the door?
Oh, yes, yes! Of course there is!
Whatever you do, don't open the door! Oh, Lord, don't open the door!
Mother! Mother!

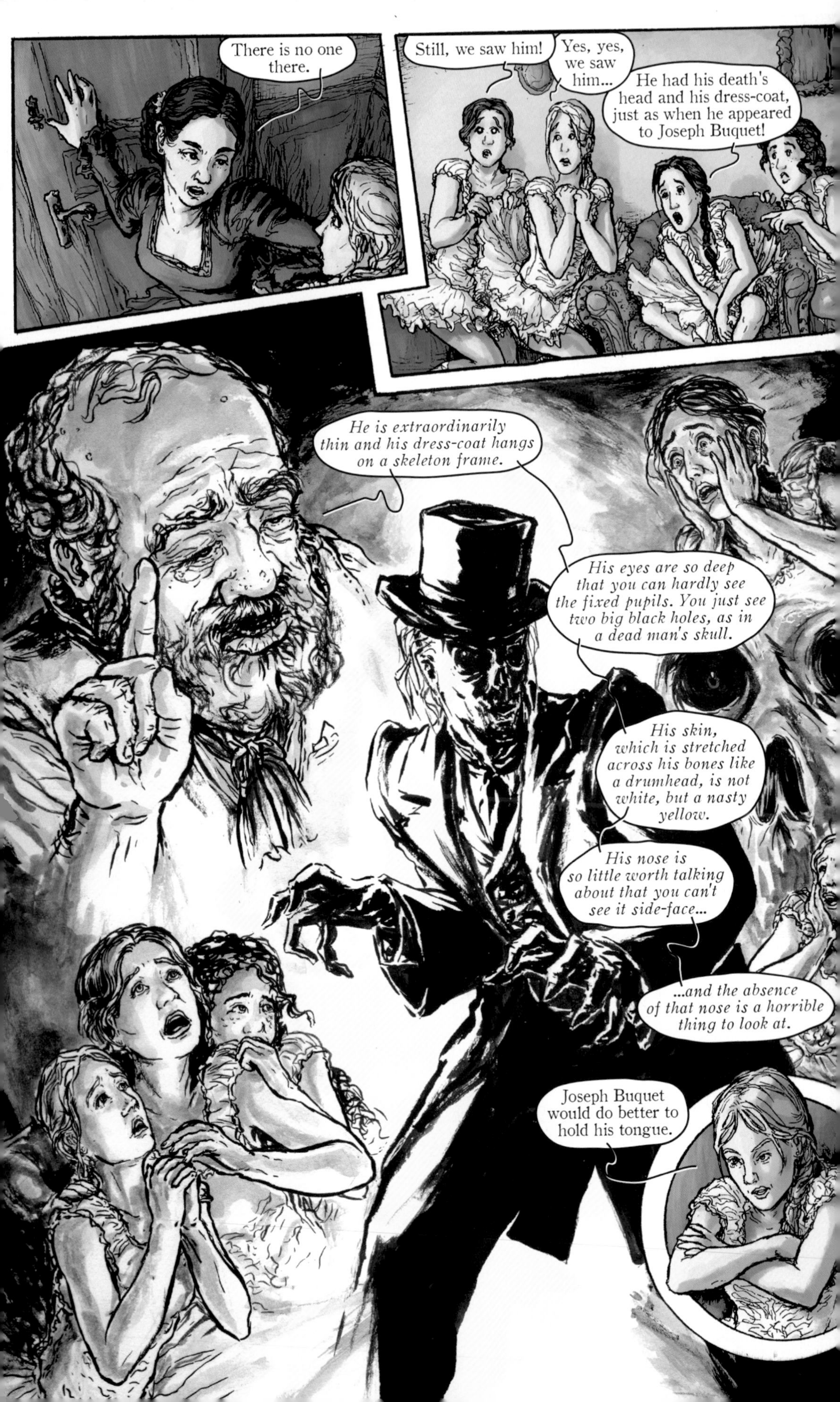

There is no one there.
Still, we saw him!
Yes, yes, we saw him...
He had his death's head and his dress-coat, just as when he appeared to Joseph Buquet!
He is extraordinarily thin and his dress-coat hangs on a skeleton frame.
His eyes are so deep that you can hardly see the fixed pupils. You just see two big black holes, as in a dead man's skull.
His skin, which is stretched across his bones like a drumhead, is not white, but a nasty yellow.
His nose is so little worth talking about that you can't see it side-face...
...and the absence of that nose is a horrible thing to look at.
Joseph Buquet would do better to hold his tongue.

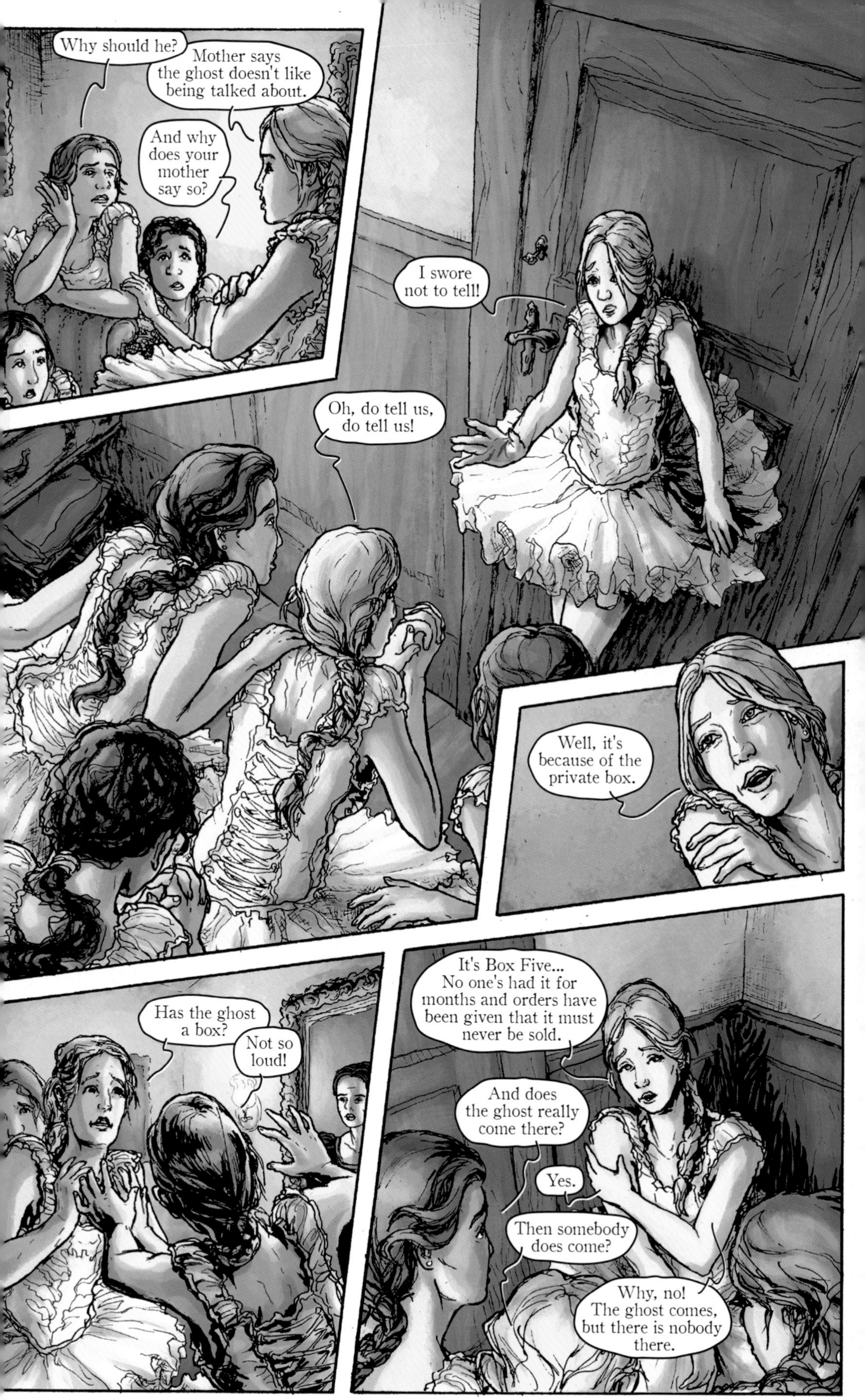
Why should he?
Mother says the ghost doesn't like being talked about.
And why does your mother say so?
I swore not to tell!
Oh, do tell us, do tell us!
Well, it's because of the private box.
Has the ghost a box?
Not so loud!
It's Box Five... No one's had it for months and orders have been given that it must never be sold.
And does the ghost really come there?
Yes.
Then somebody does come?
Why, no! The ghost comes, but there is nobody there.

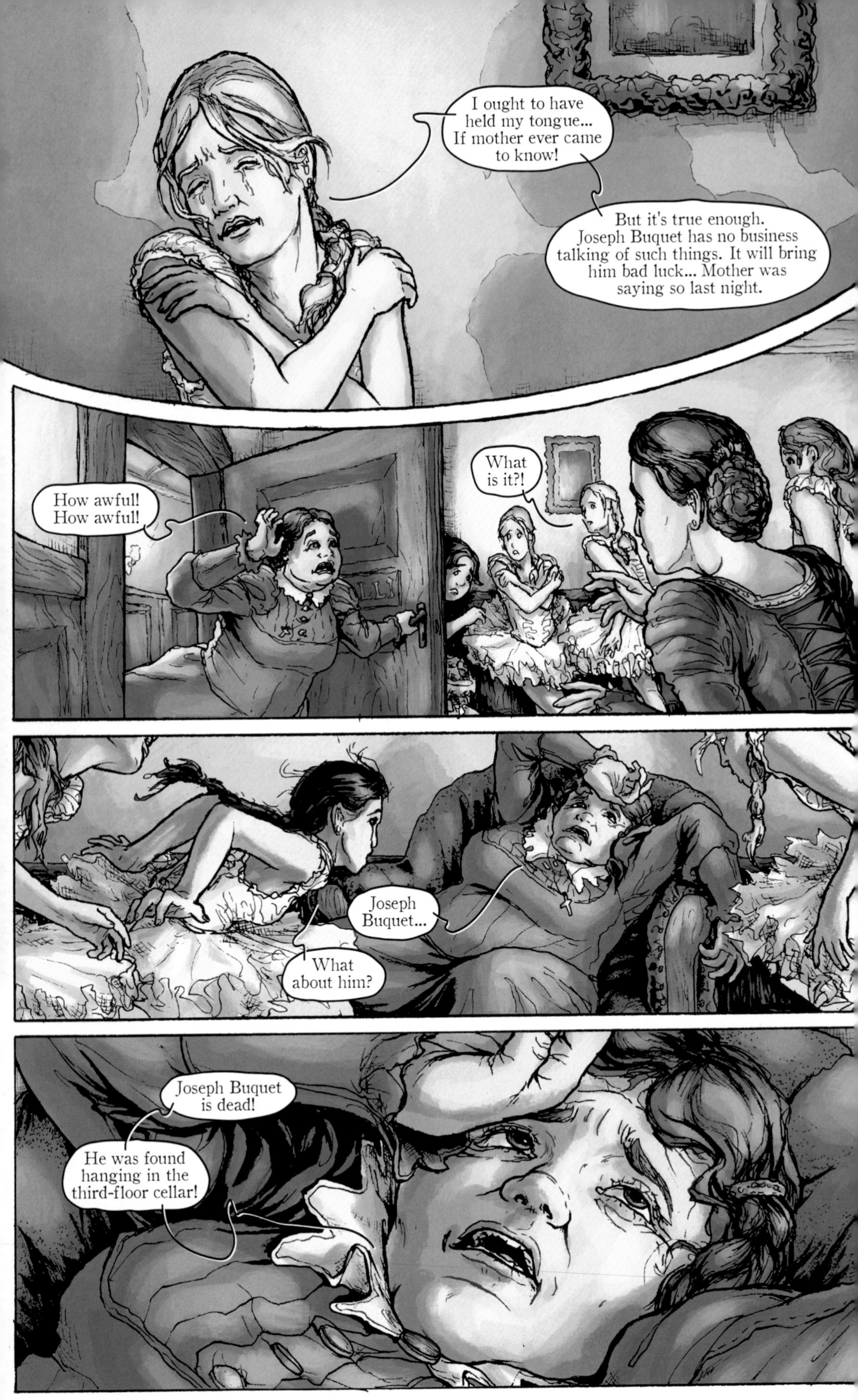
I ought to have held my tongue... If mother ever came to know!
But it's true enough. Joseph Buquet has no business talking of such things. It will bring him bad luck... Mother was saying so last night.
How awful! How awful!
What is it?!
Joseph Buquet...
What about him?
Joseph Buquet is dead!
He was found hanging in the third-floor cellar!

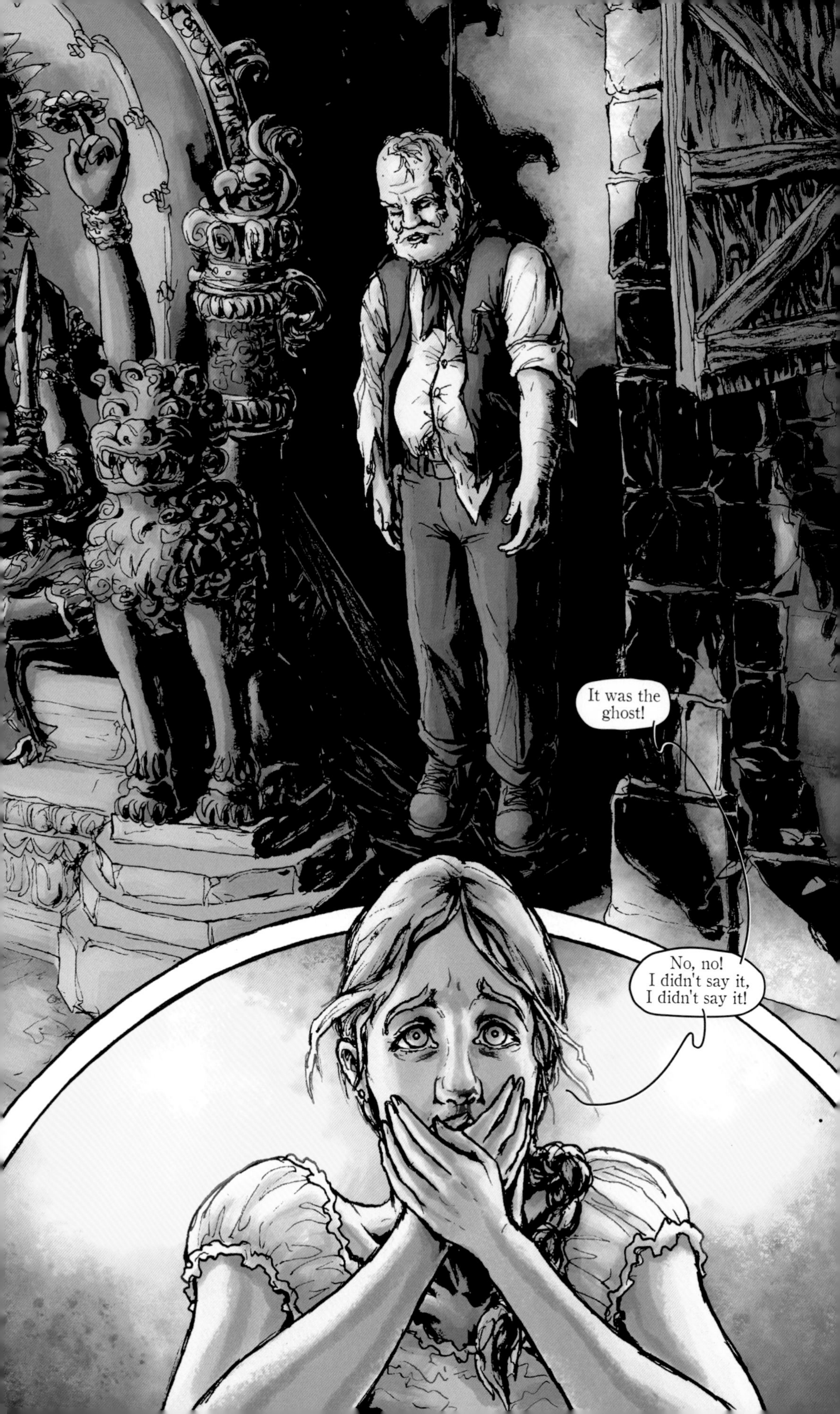
It was the ghost!
No, no! I didn't say it, I didn't say it!

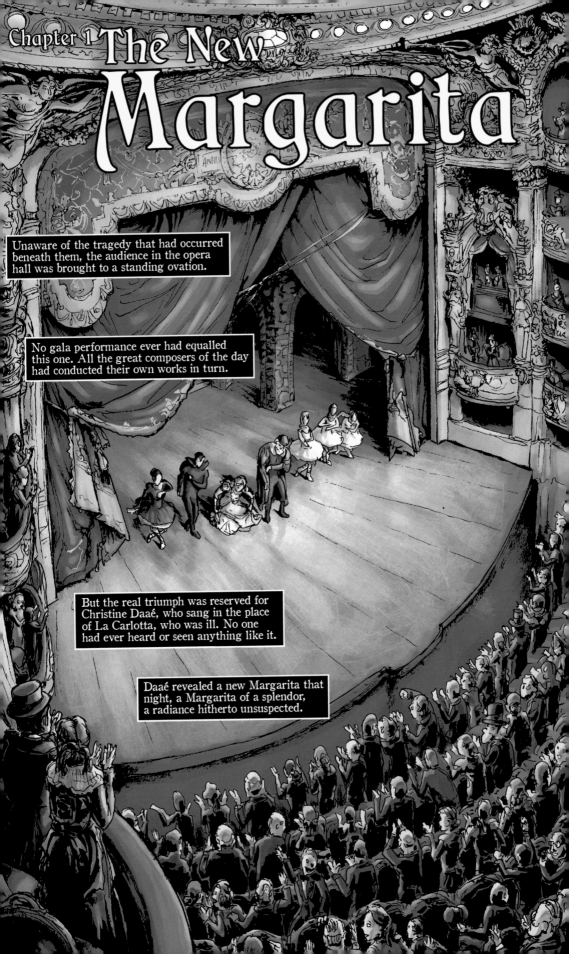

Chapter 1 The New Margarita

Unaware of the tragedy that had occurred beneath them, the audience in the opera hall was brought to a standing ovation.

No gala performance ever had equalled this one. All the great composers of the day had conducted their own works in turn.

But the real triumph was reserved for Christine Daaé, who sang in the place of La Carlotta, who was ill. No one had ever heard or seen anything like it.

Daaé revealed a new Margarita that night, a Margarita of a splendor, a radiance hitherto unsuspected.

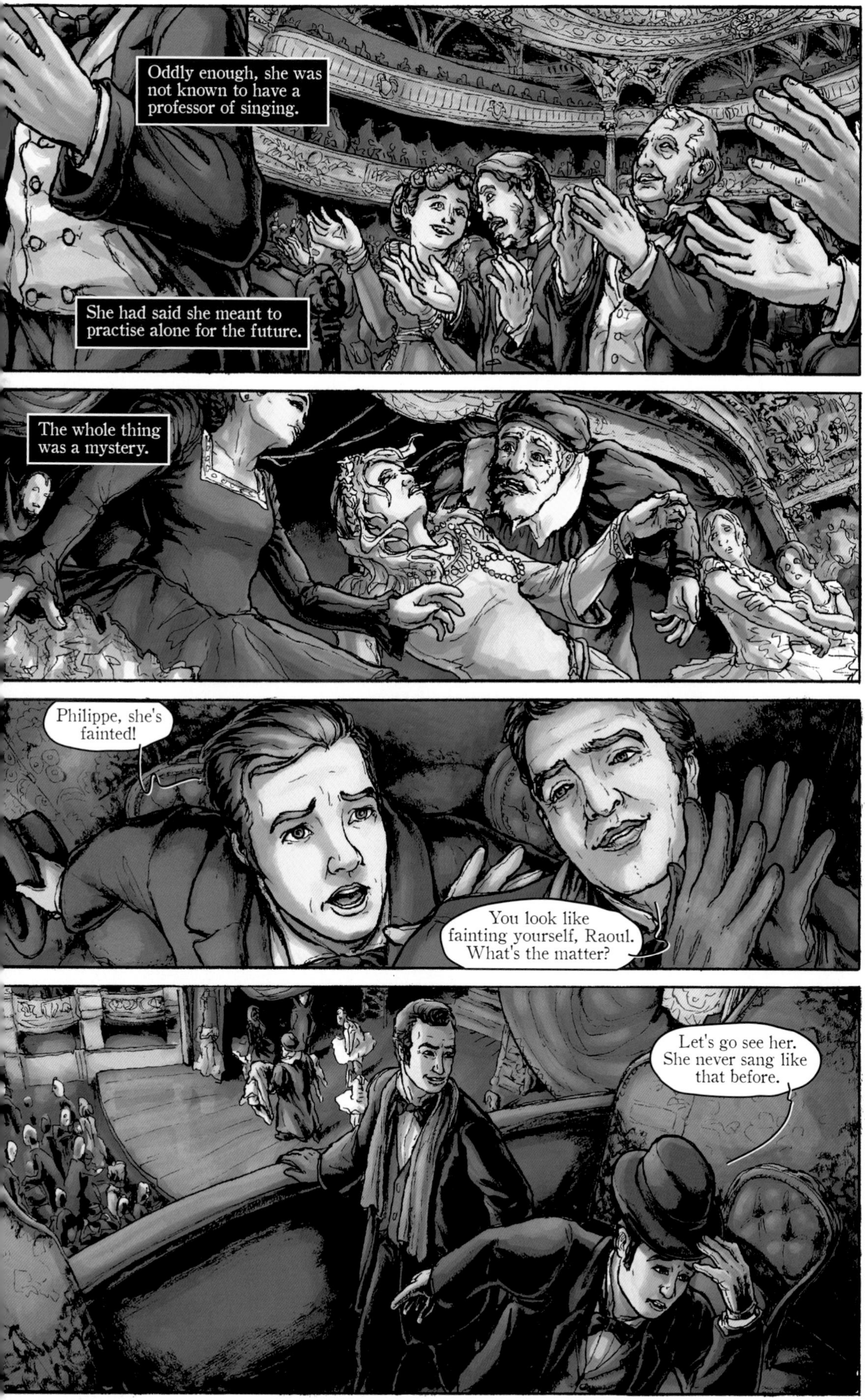

Oddly enough, she was not known to have a professor of singing.
She had said she meant to practise alone for the future.
The whole thing was a mystery.
Philippe, she's fainted!
You look like fainting yourself, Raoul. What's the matter?
Let's go see her. She never sang like that before.

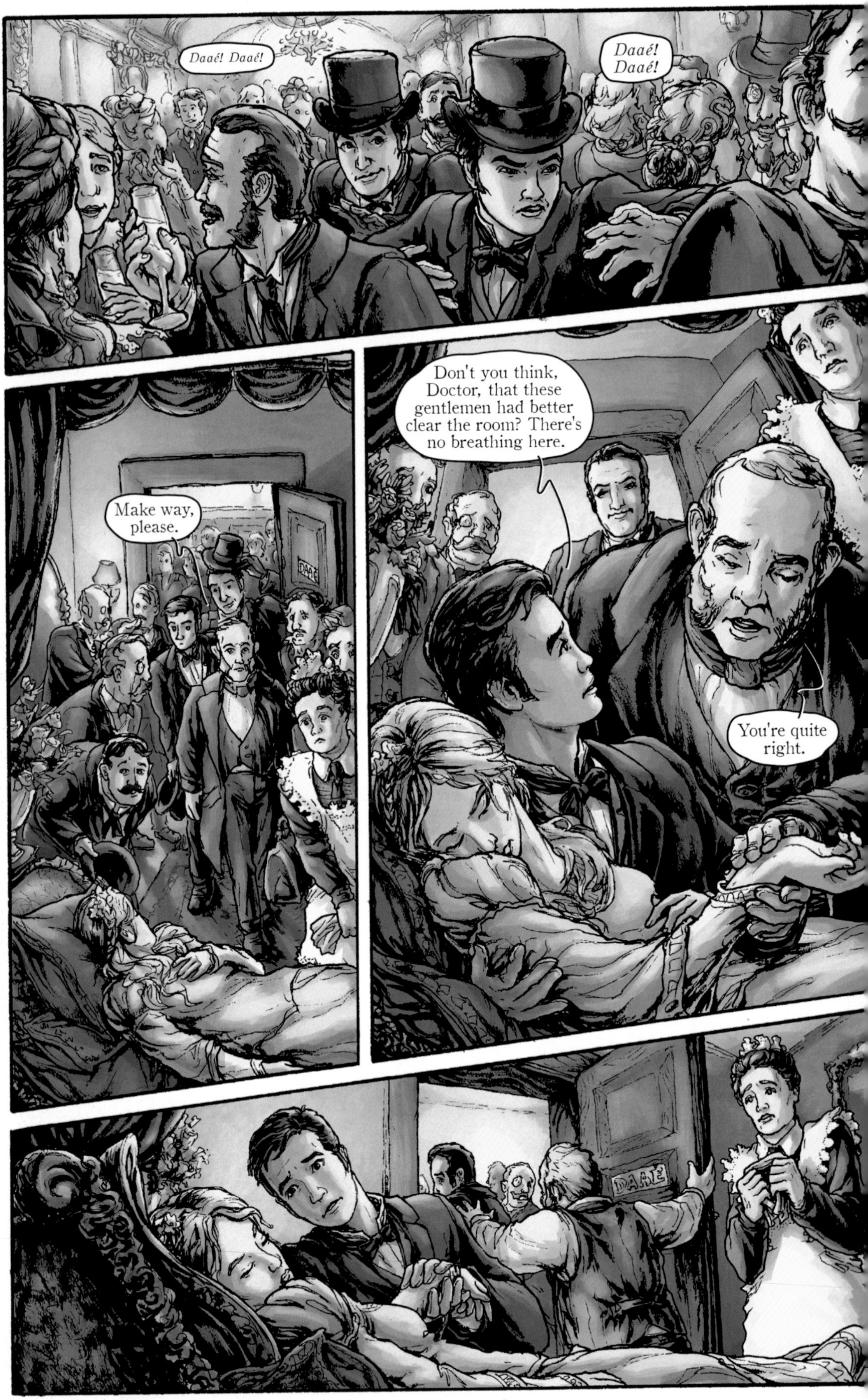
Daaé! Daaé!
Daaé! Daaé!
Make way, please.
Don't you think, Doctor, that these gentlemen had better clear the room? There's no breathing here.
You're quite right.
DAAÉ
DAAÉ

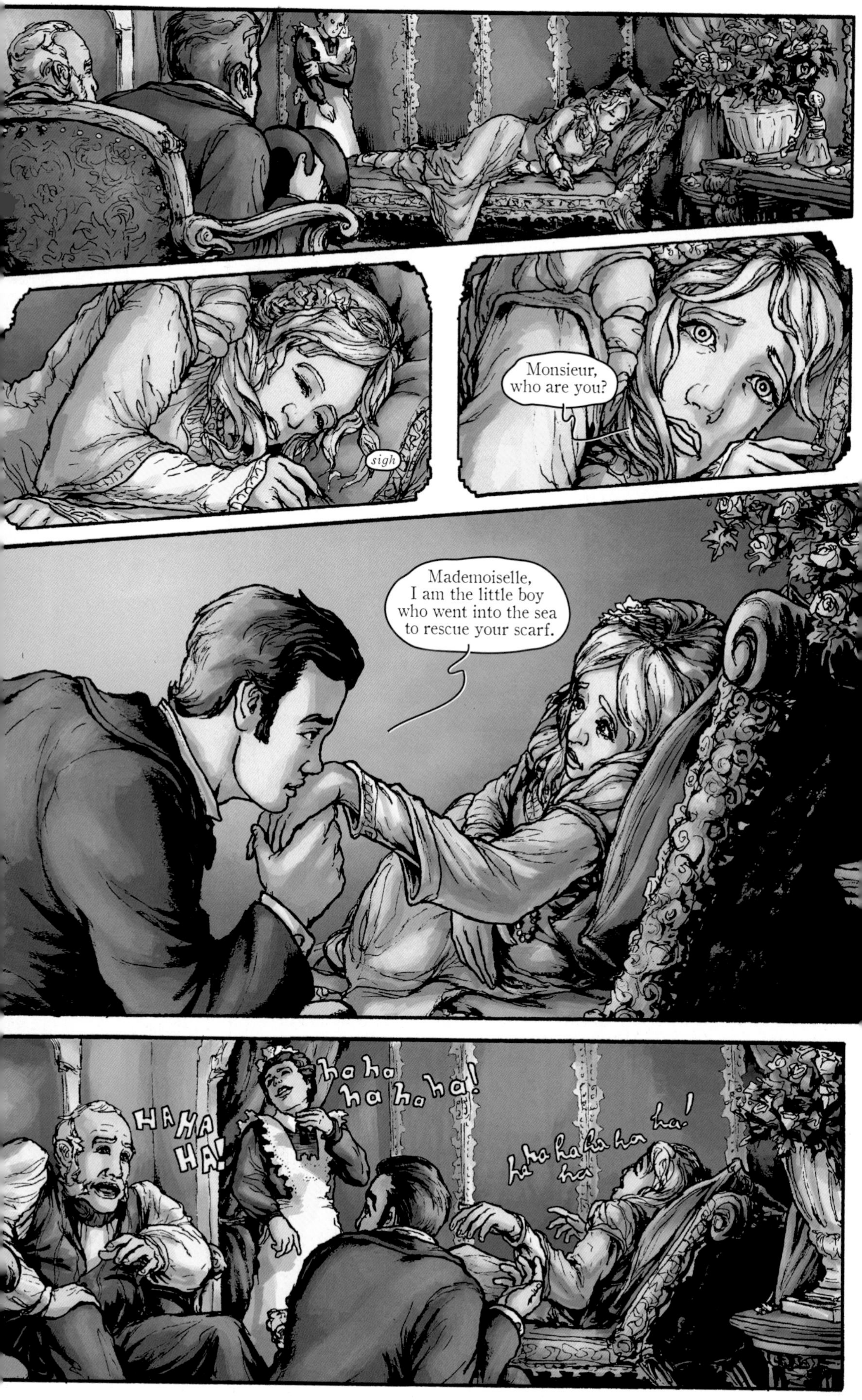
sigh
Monsieur, who are you?
Mademoiselle, I am the little boy who went into the sea to rescue your scarf.
HA HA HA HA!
ha ha ha ha ha!
ha ha ha ha ha ha ha ha!

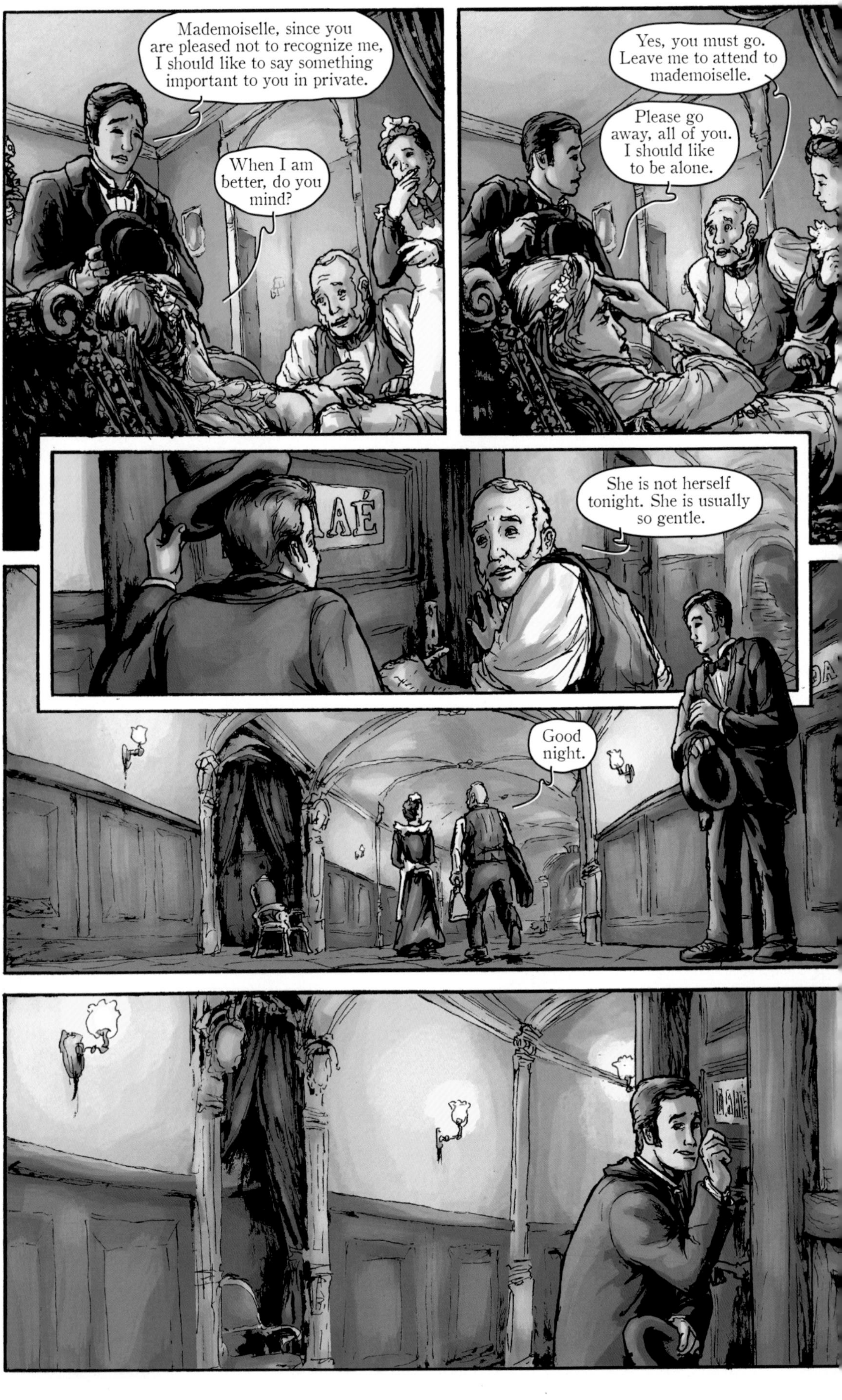
Mademoiselle, since you are pleased not to recognize me, I should like to say something important to you in private.
When I am better, do you mind?
Yes, you must go. Leave me to attend to mademoiselle.
Please go away, all of you. I should like to be alone.
She is not herself tonight. She is usually so gentle.
Good night.

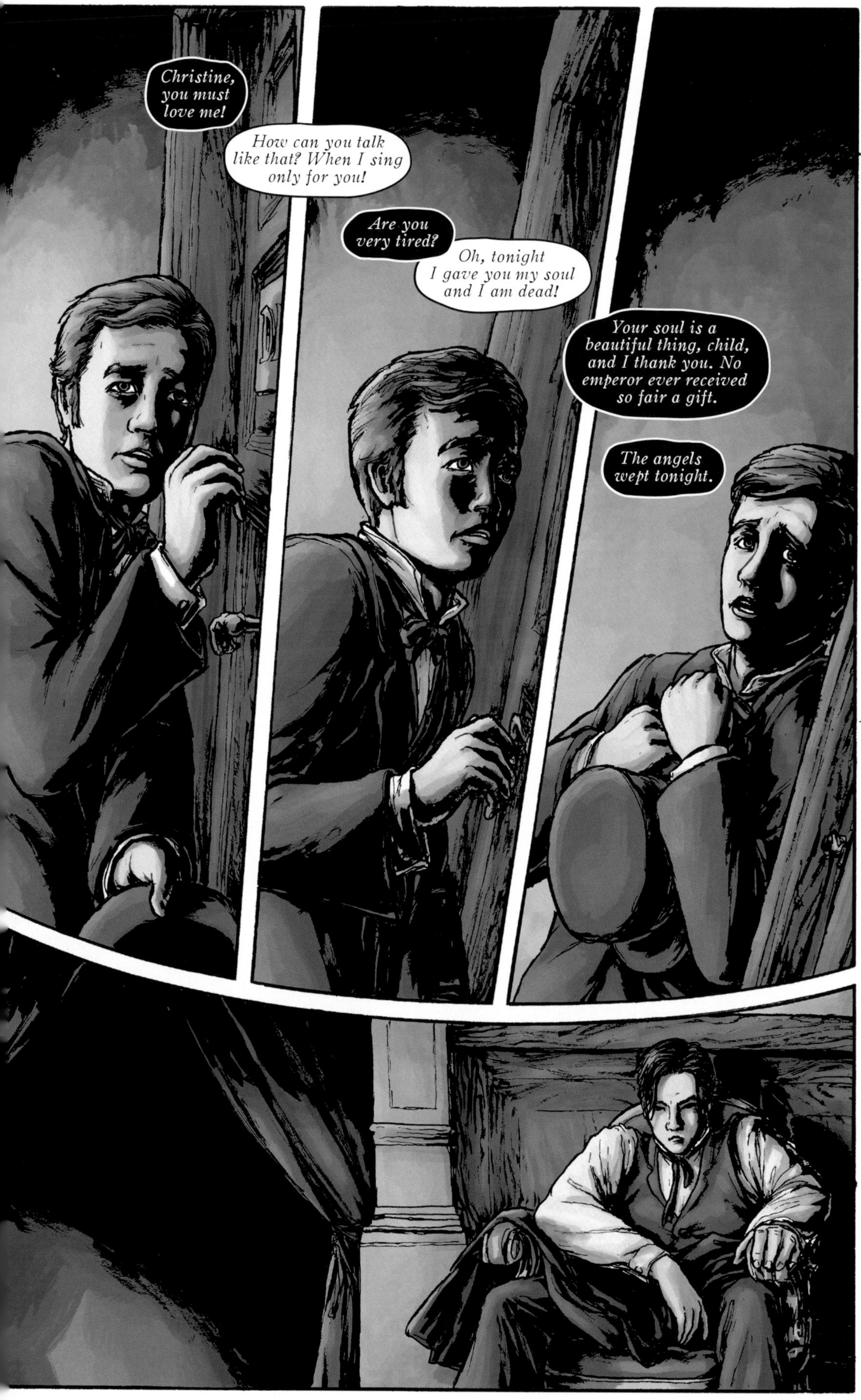
Christine, you must love me!
How can you talk like that? When I sing only for you!
Are you very tired?
Oh, tonight I gave you my soul and I am dead!
Your soul is a beautiful thing, child, and I thank you. No emperor ever received so fair a gift.
The angels wept tonight.

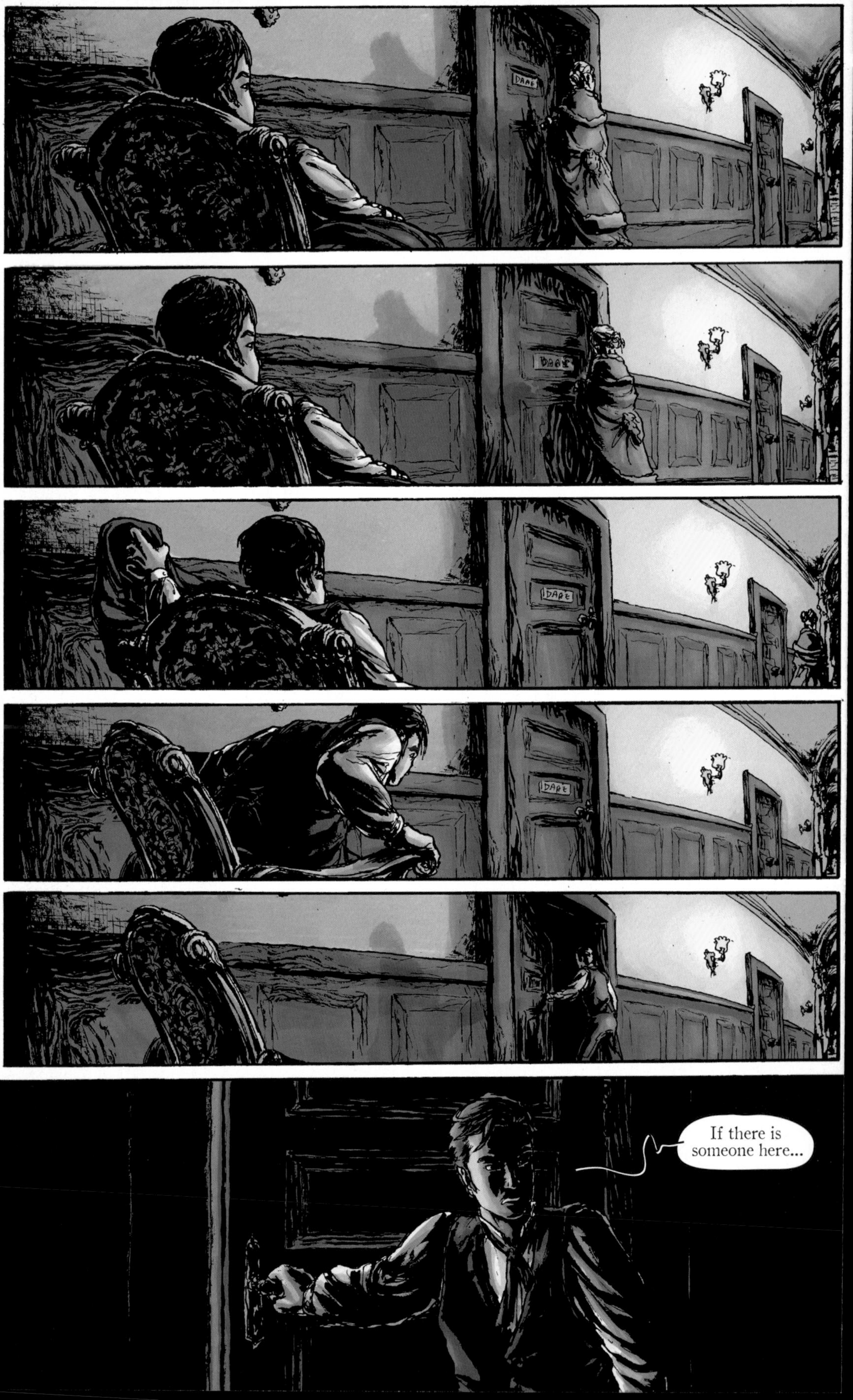
If there is someone here...

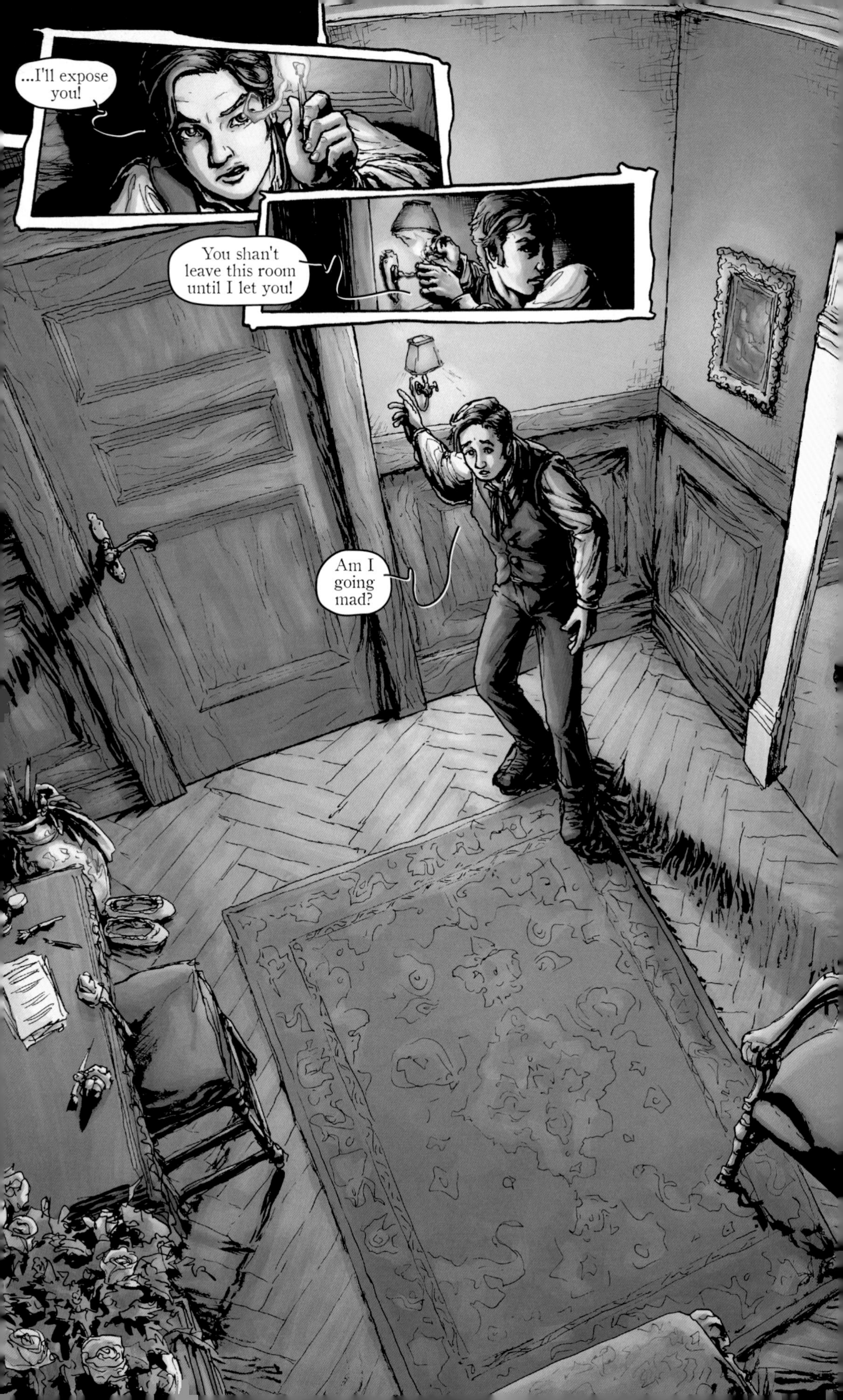
...I'll expose you!
You shan't leave this room until I let you!
Am I going mad?

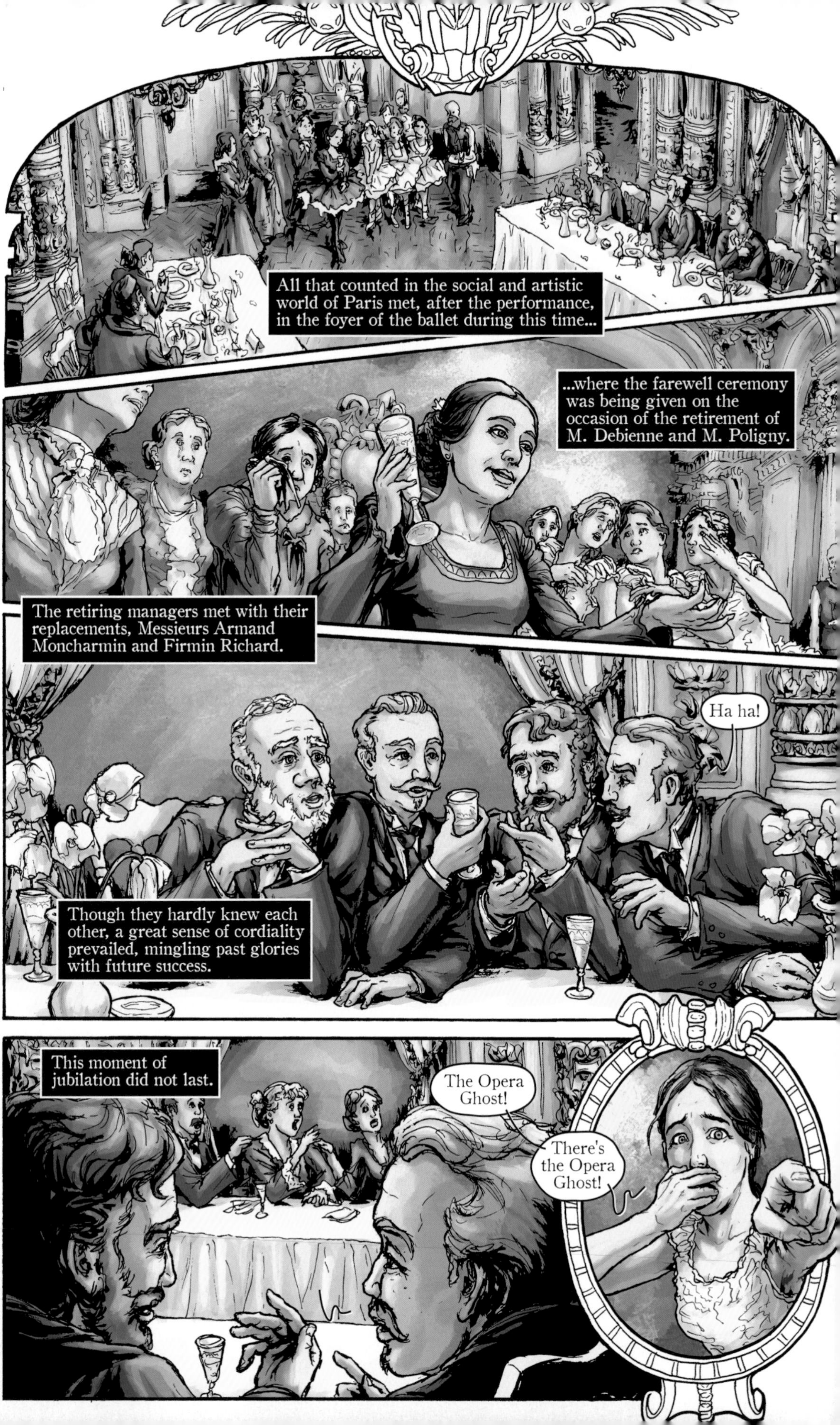
All that counted in the social and artistic world of Paris met, after the performance, in the foyer of the ballet during this time...
...where the farewell ceremony was being given on the occasion of the retirement of M. Debienne and M. Poligny.
The retiring managers met with their replacements, Messieurs Armand Moncharmin and Firmin Richard.
Ha ha!
Though they hardly knew each other, a great sense of cordiality prevailed, mingling past glories with future success.
This moment of jubilation did not last.
The Opera Ghost!
There's the Opera Ghost!

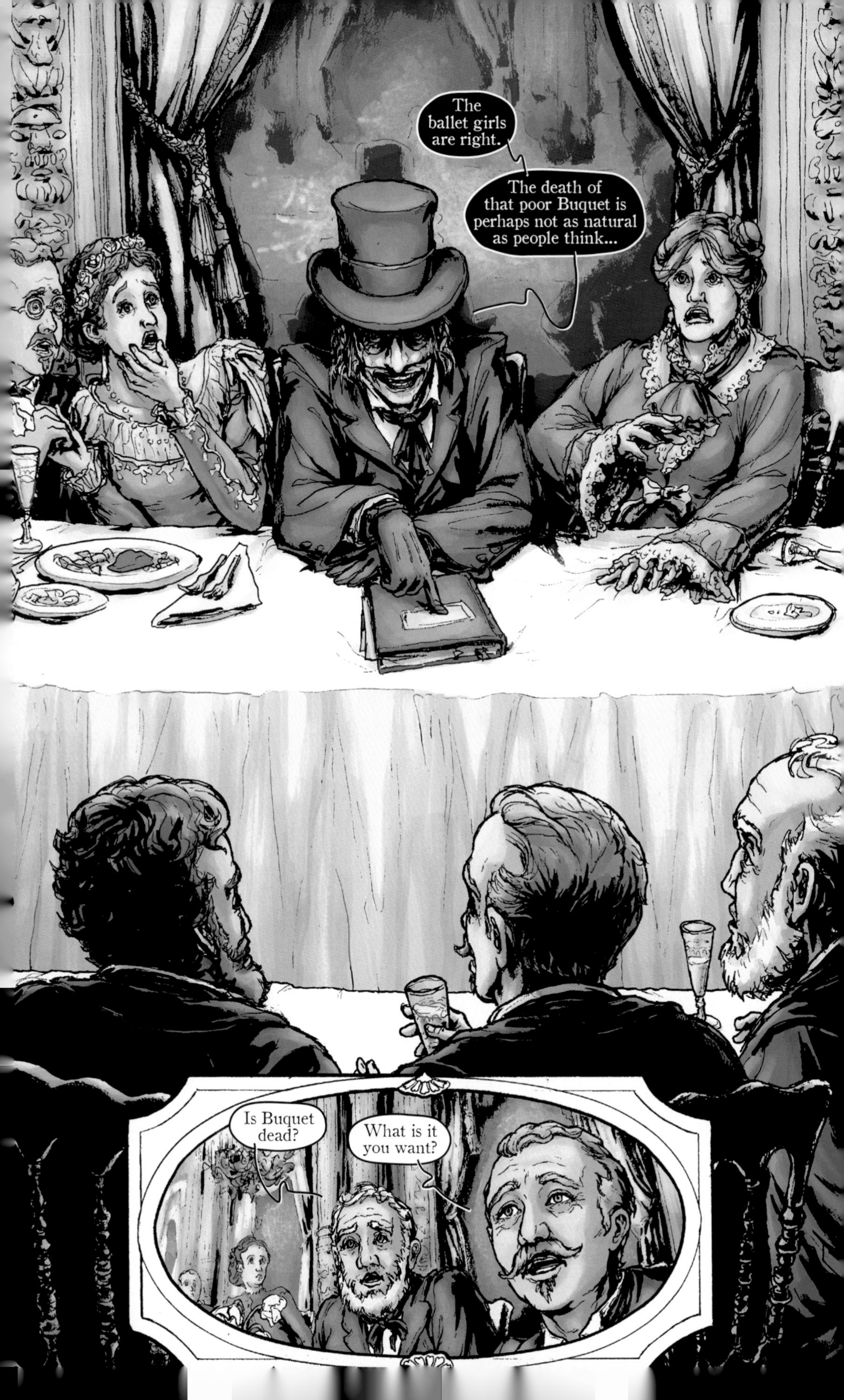
The ballet girls are right.
The death of that poor Buquet is perhaps not as natural as people think...
Is Buquet dead?
What is it you want?

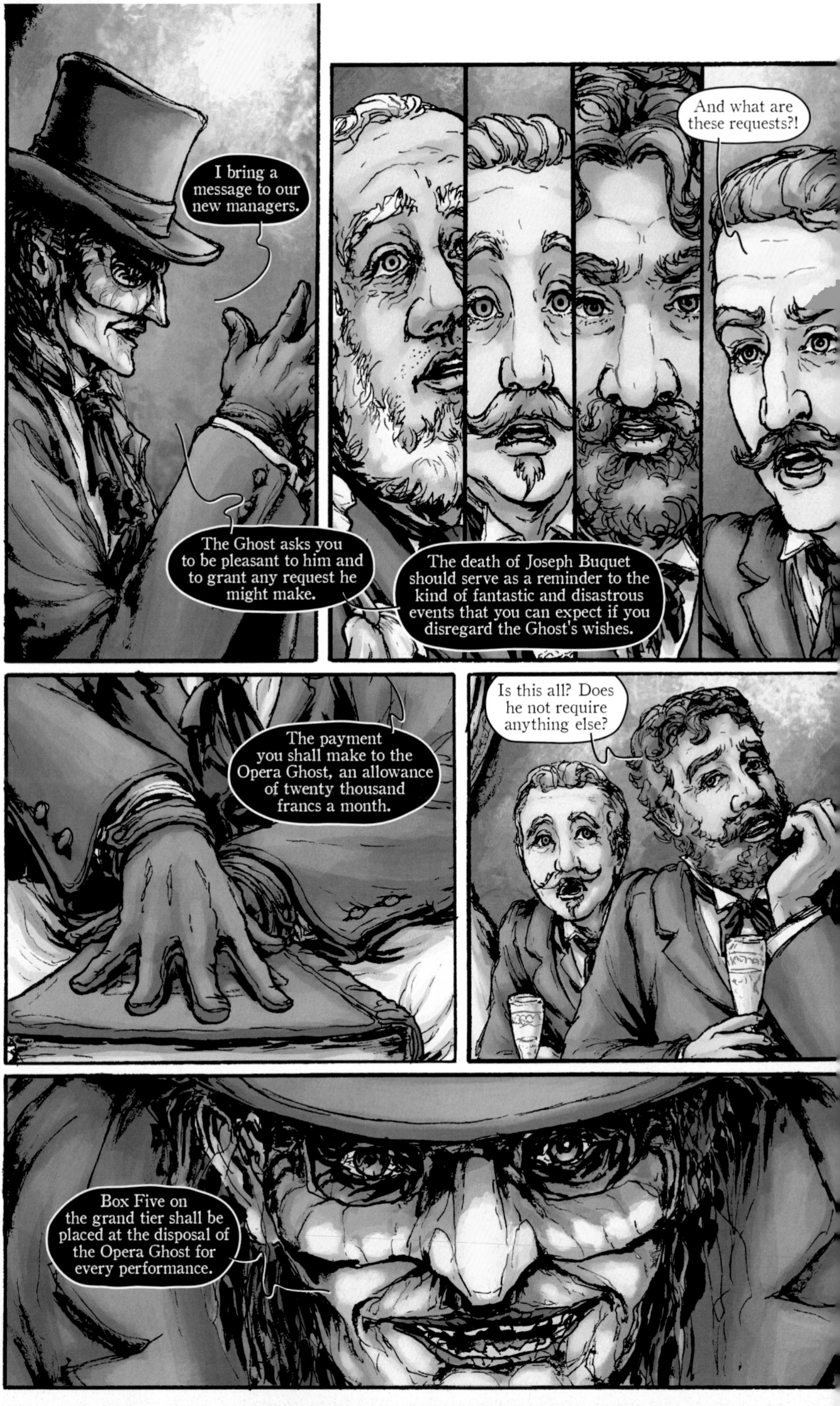
I bring a message to our new managers.
And what are these requests?!
The Ghost asks you to be pleasant to him and to grant any request he might make.
The death of Joseph Buquet should serve as a reminder to the kind of fantastic and disastrous events that you can expect if you disregard the Ghost's wishes.
The payment you shall make to the Opera Ghost, an allowance of twenty thousand francs a month.
Is this all? Does he not require anything else?
Box Five on the grand tier shall be placed at the disposal of the Opera Ghost for every performance.

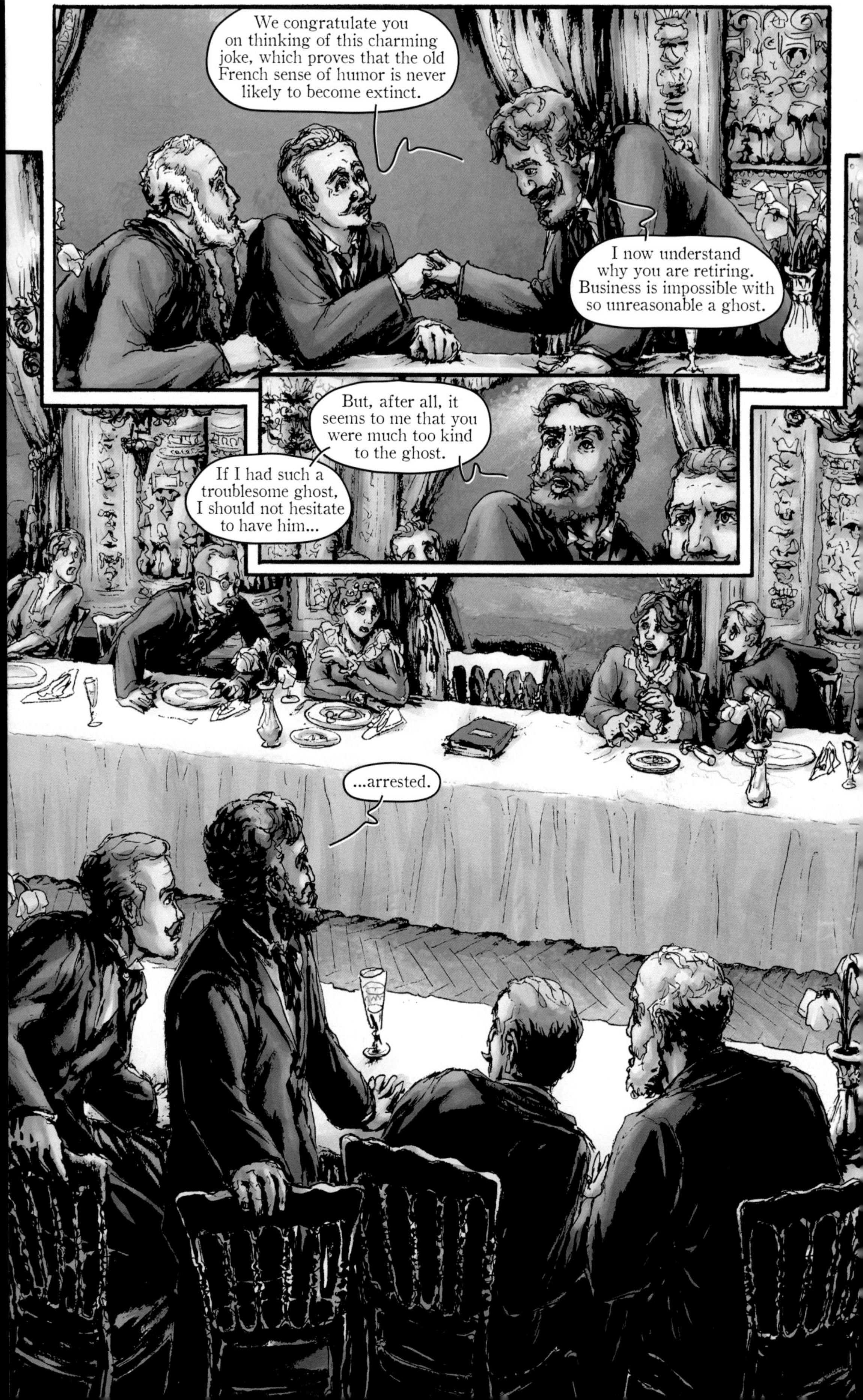
We congratulate you on thinking of this charming joke, which proves that the old French sense of humor is never likely to become extinct.
I now understand why you are retiring. Business is impossible with so unreasonable a ghost.
But, after all, it seems to me that you were much too kind to the ghost.
If I had such a troublesome ghost, I should not hesitate to have him...
...arrested.

The first few days which the partners spent at the Opera were given over to the delight of finding themselves the head of so magnificent an enterprise.

And they had forgotten all about that curious, fantastic story of the ghost.

Dear Mr. Manager:

I am sorry to have to trouble you at a time when you must be so very busy.

I should like to hear Christine Daaé this evening in the part of Siebel, as that of Margarita has been forbidden her since her triumph of the other evening; and I will ask you not to dispose of my box to-day nor on the following days. If you wish to live in peace, you must not begin by taking away my private box.

Will write you soon for the 240,000 francs of my allowance for the current year.

Your Most Humble and Obedient Servant,

OPERA GHOST.

They are keeping up the joke, but I don't call it funny.

I am not in the mood to put up with this much longer!

And that evening Box Five was sold.

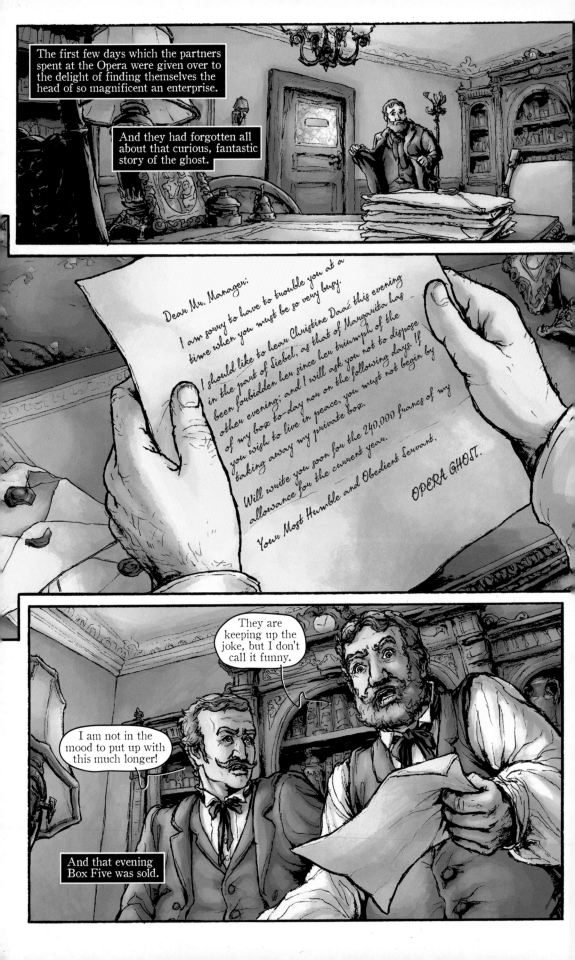

Chapter Two

Christine Daaé did not immediately continue her triumph at the Opera.

The famous gala night was the last occasion on which she was heard. She showed herself nowhere, and the Vicomte de Chagny tried in vain to meet her.

He wrote to her, but despaired of receiving a reply when, one morning, she sent him the following note:

Monsieur:

I have not forgotten the little boy who went into the sea to rescue my scarf.
I am going to Perros, in fulfilment of a sacred duty. Tomorrow is the anniversary of the death of my poor father, whom you knew and who was very fond of you.
He is buried there, with his violin, in the graveyard of the little church, beside the road where we said goodbye for the last time.

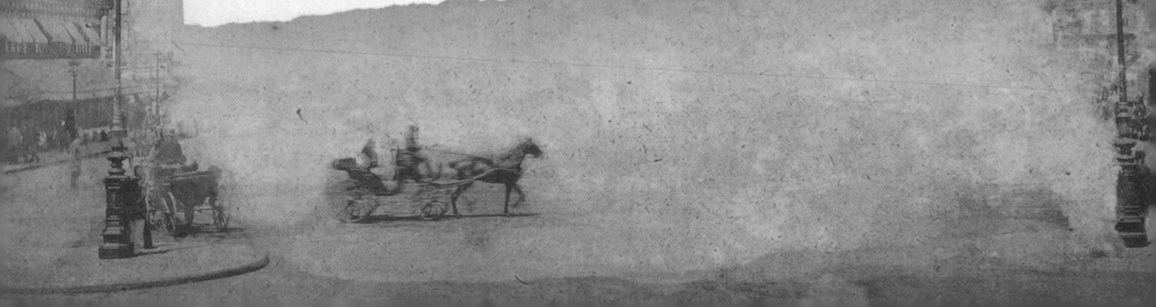

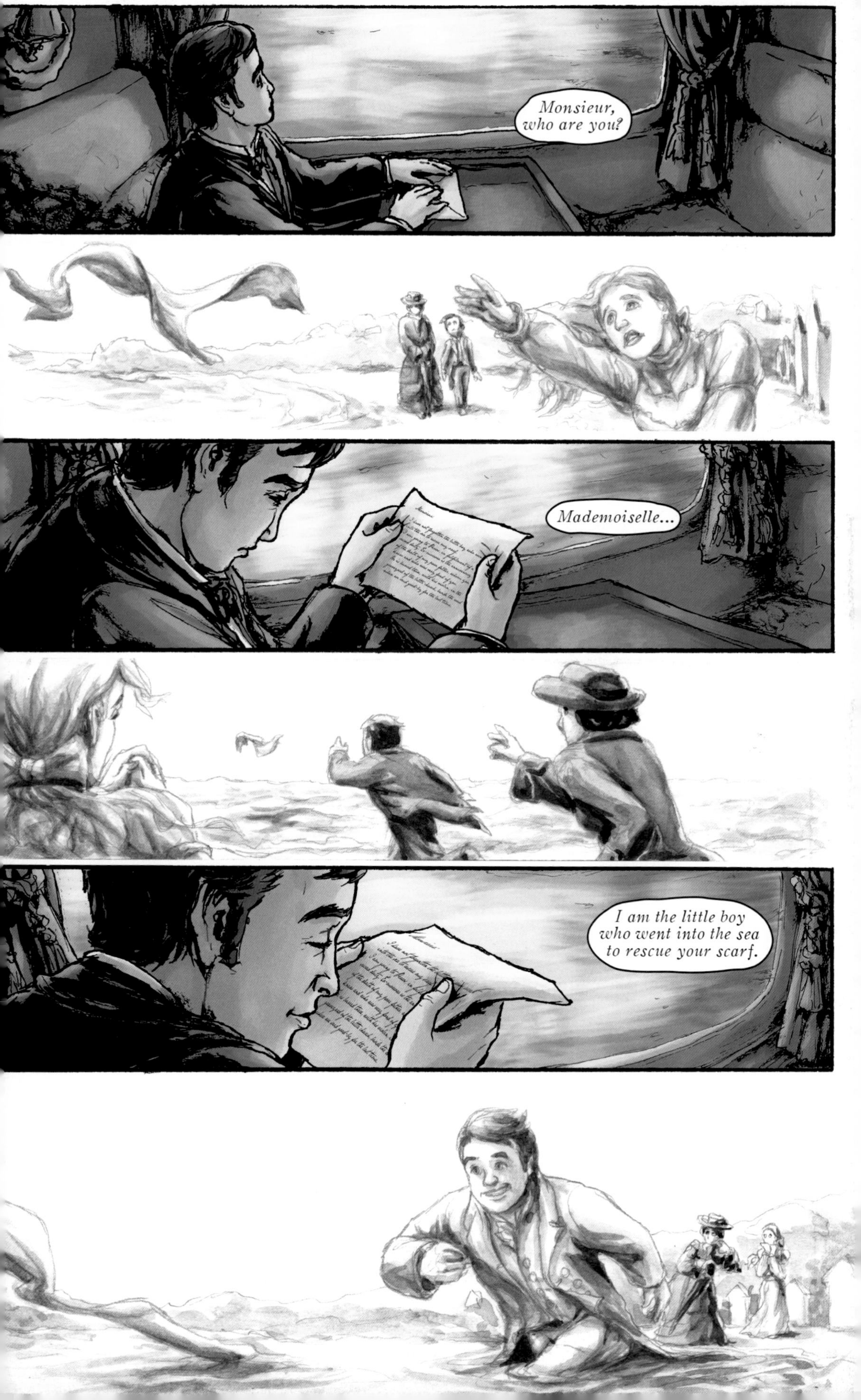
Monsieur,
who are you?
Mademoiselle...
I am the little boy
who went into the sea
to rescue your scarf.

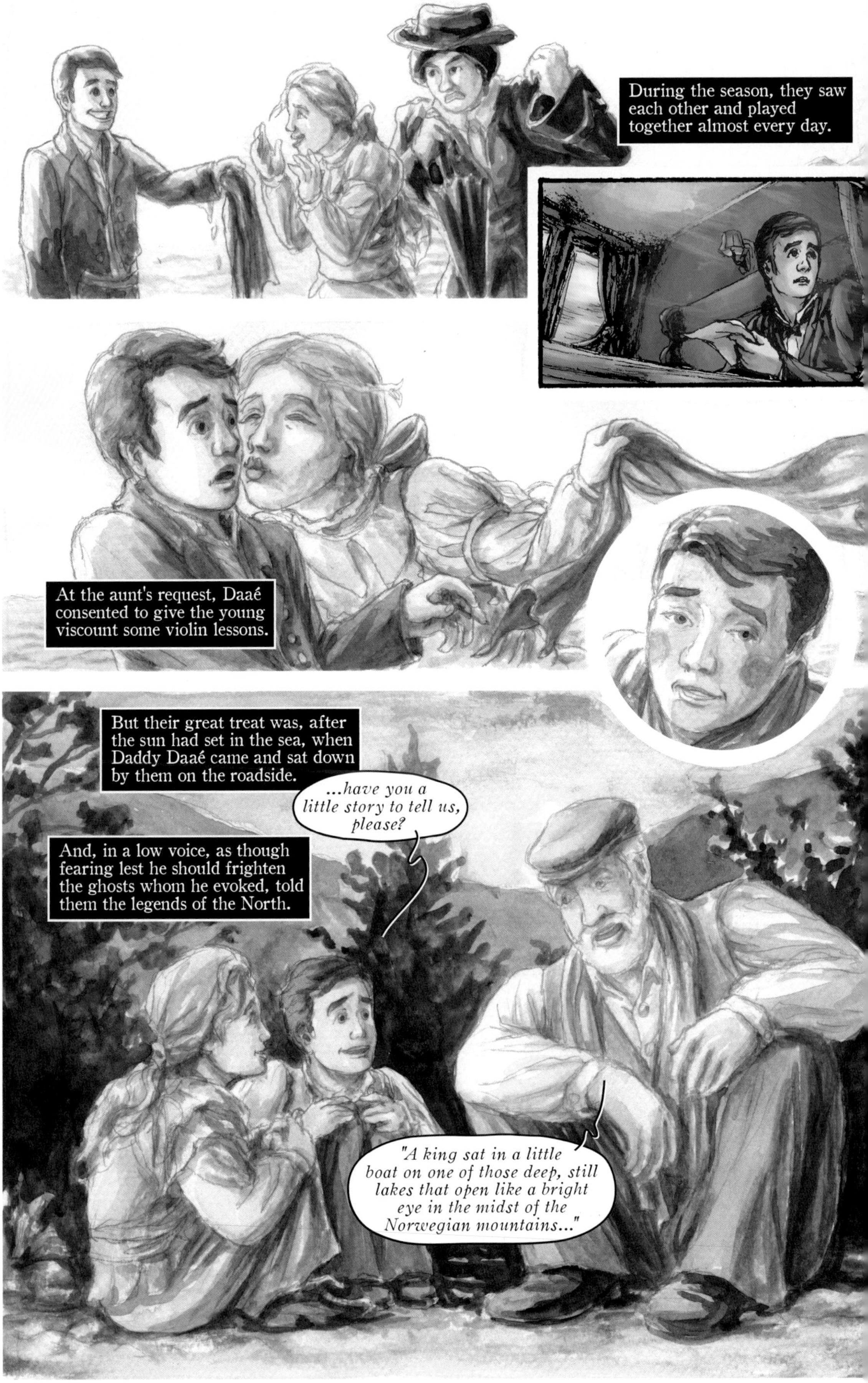
During the season, they saw each other and played together almost every day.
At the aunt's request, Daaé consented to give the young viscount some violin lessons.
But their great treat was, after the sun had set in the sea, when Daddy Daaé came and sat down by them on the roadside.
...have you a little story to tell us, please?
And, in a low voice, as though fearing lest he should frighten the ghosts whom he evoked, told them the legends of the North.
"A king sat in a little boat on one of those deep, still lakes that open like a bright eye in the midst of the Norwegian mountains..."

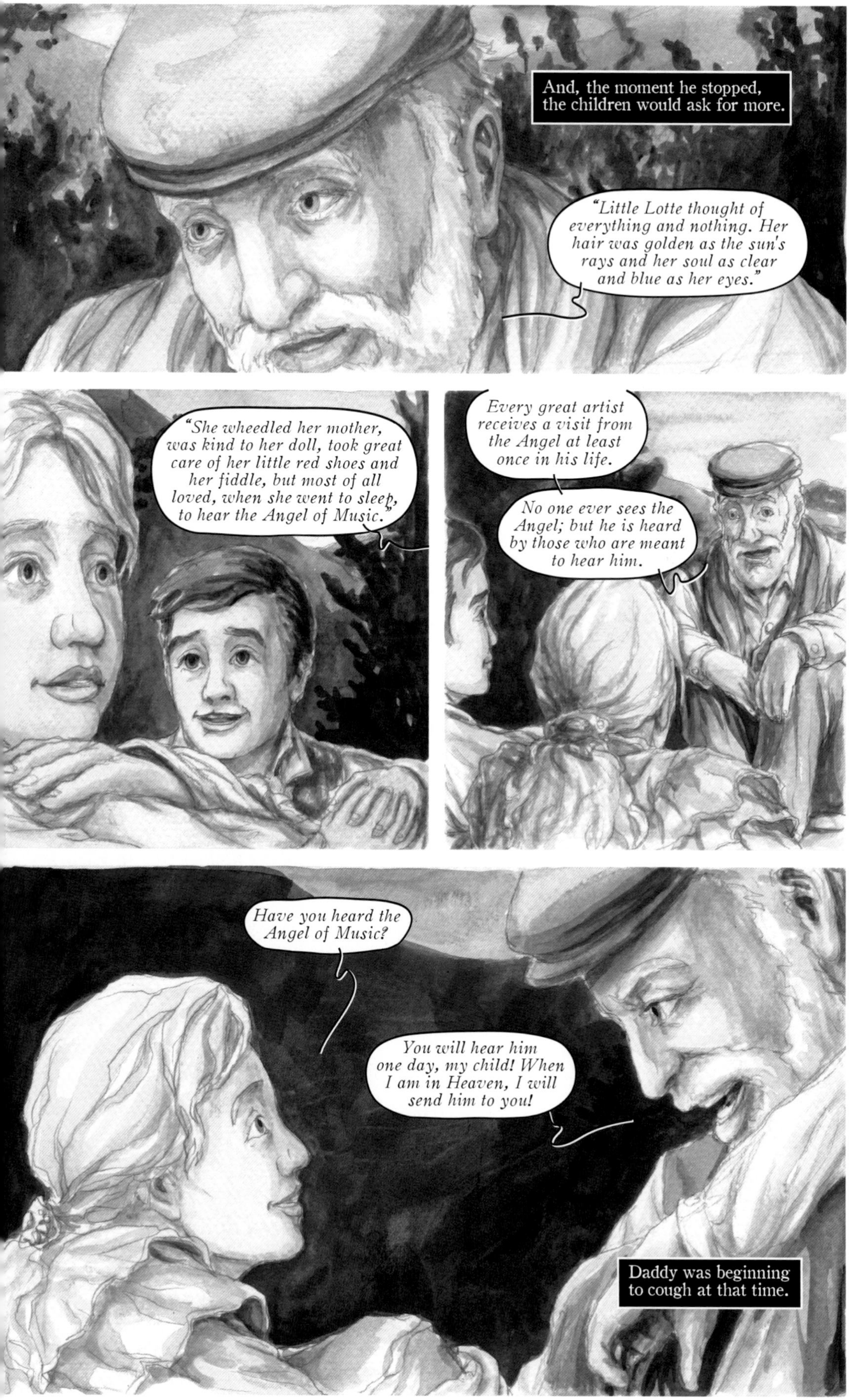
And, the moment he stopped, the children would ask for more.
"Little Lotte thought of everything and nothing. Her hair was golden as the sun's rays and her soul as clear and blue as her eyes."
"She wheedled her mother, was kind to her doll, took great care of her little red shoes and her fiddle, but most of all loved, when she went to sleep, to hear the Angel of Music."
Every great artist receives a visit from the Angel at least once in his life.
No one ever sees the Angel; but he is heard by those who are meant to hear him.
Have you heard the Angel of Music?
You will hear him one day, my child! When I am in Heaven, I will send him to you!
Daddy was beginning to cough at that time.

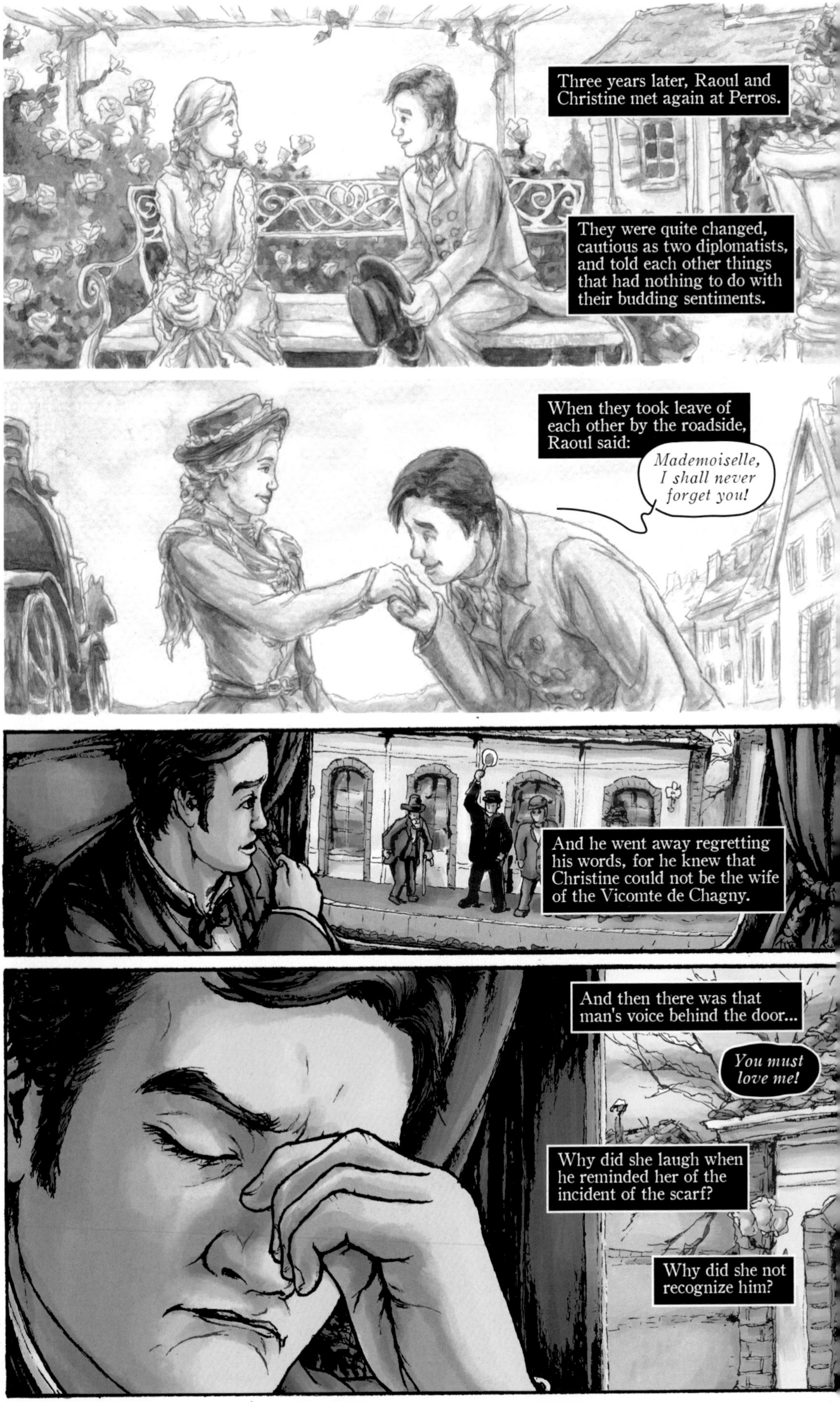
Three years later, Raoul and Christine met again at Perros.
They were quite changed, cautious as two diplomatists, and told each other things that had nothing to do with their budding sentiments.
When they took leave of each other by the roadside, Raoul said:
Mademoiselle, I shall never forget you!
And he went away regretting his words, for he knew that Christine could not be the wife of the Vicomte de Chagny.
And then there was that man's voice behind the door...
You must love me!
Why did she laugh when he reminded her of the incident of the scarf?
Why did she not recognize him?

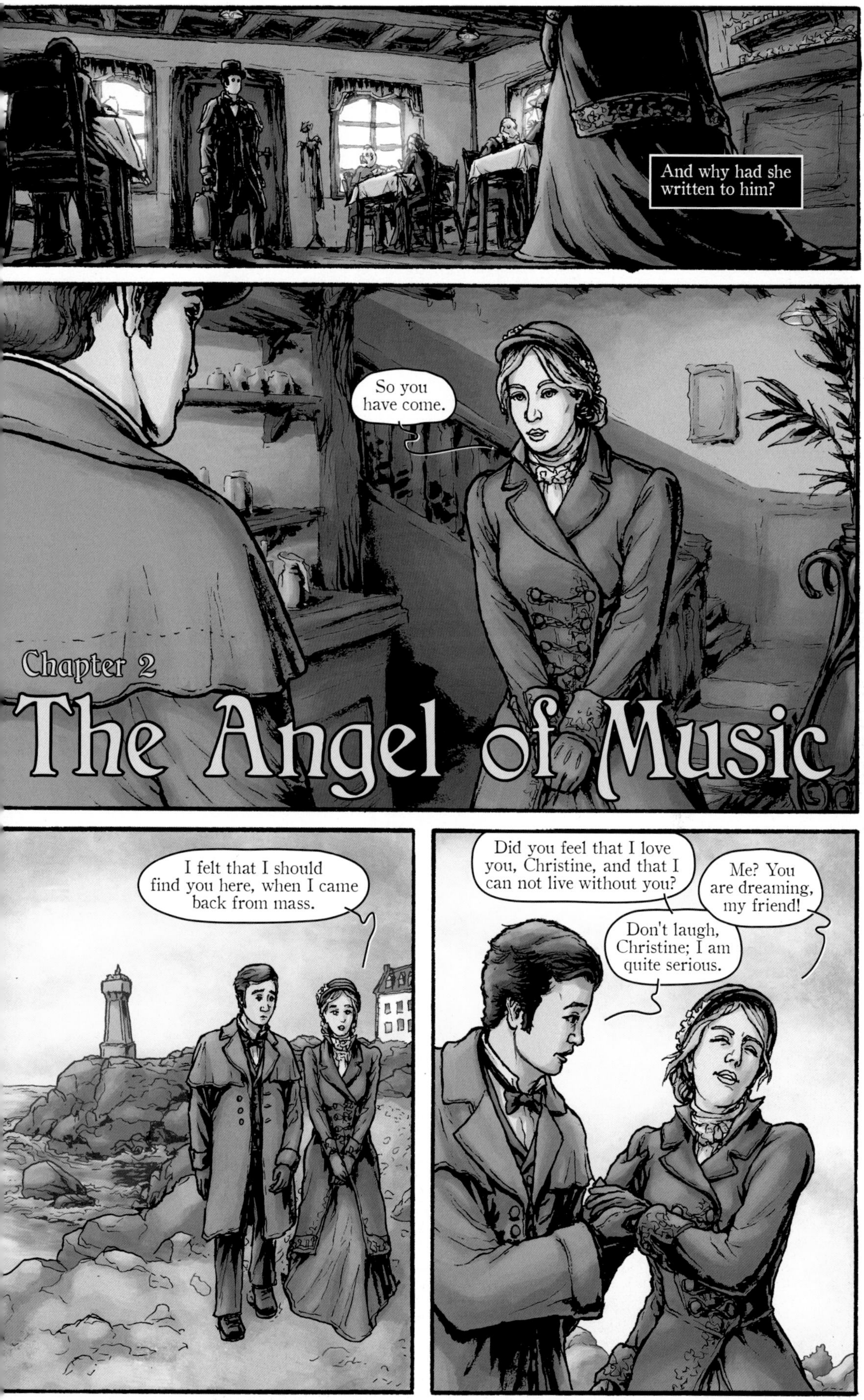
And why had she written to him?
So you have come.
Chapter 2
The Angel of Music
I felt that I should find you here, when I came back from mass.
Did you feel that I love you, Christine, and that I can not live without you?
Me? You are dreaming, my friend!
Don't laugh, Christine; I am quite serious.

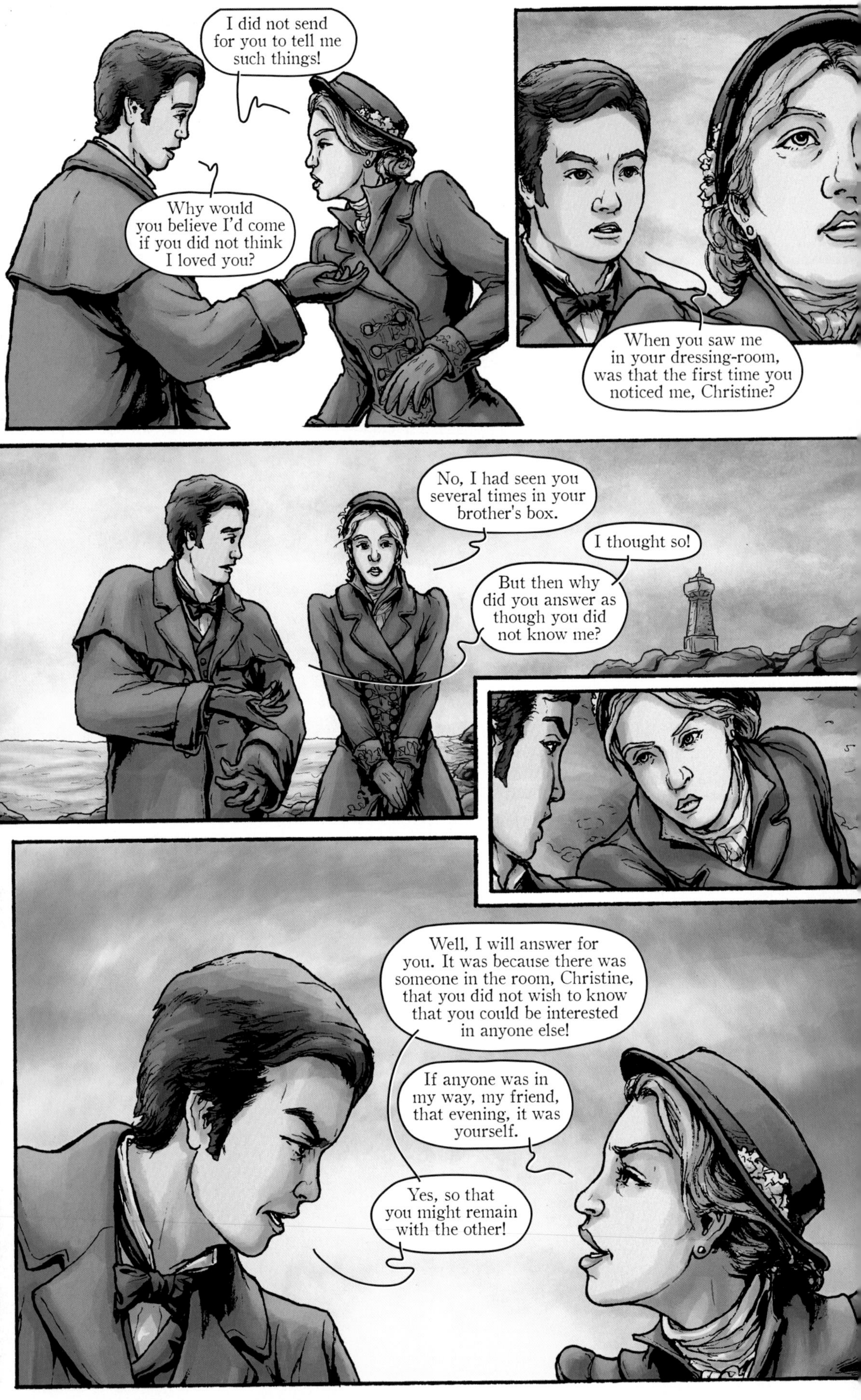
I did not send for you to tell me such things!
Why would you believe I'd come if you did not think I loved you?
When you saw me in your dressing-room, was that the first time you noticed me, Christine?
No, I had seen you several times in your brother's box.
I thought so!
But then why did you answer as though you did not know me?
Well, I will answer for you. It was because there was someone in the room, Christine, that you did not wish to know that you could be interested in anyone else!
If anyone was in my way, my friend, that evening, it was yourself.
Yes, so that you might remain with the other!

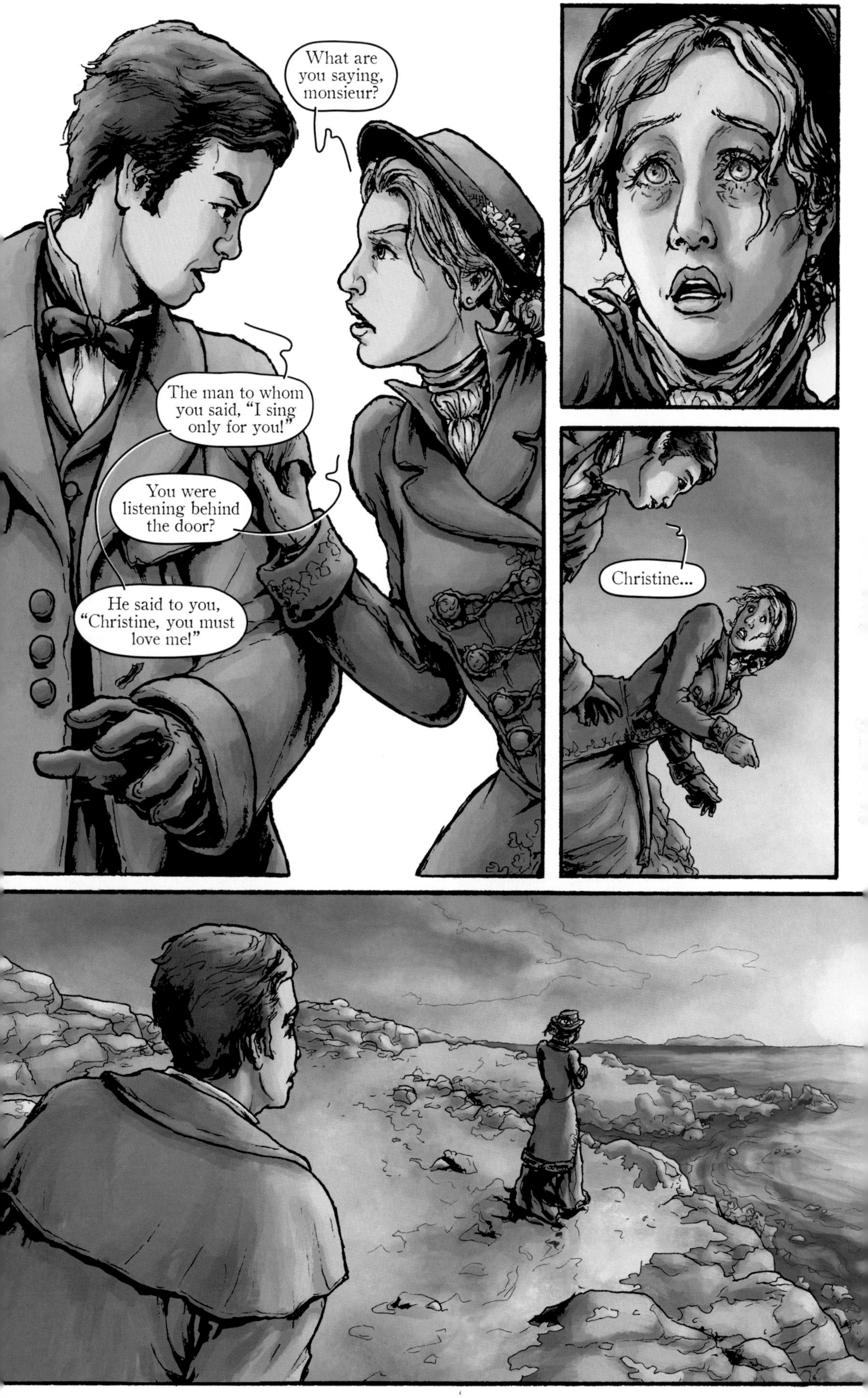
What are you saying, monsieur?
The man to whom you said, "I sing only for you!"
You were listening behind the door?
He said to you, "Christine, you must love me!"
Christine...

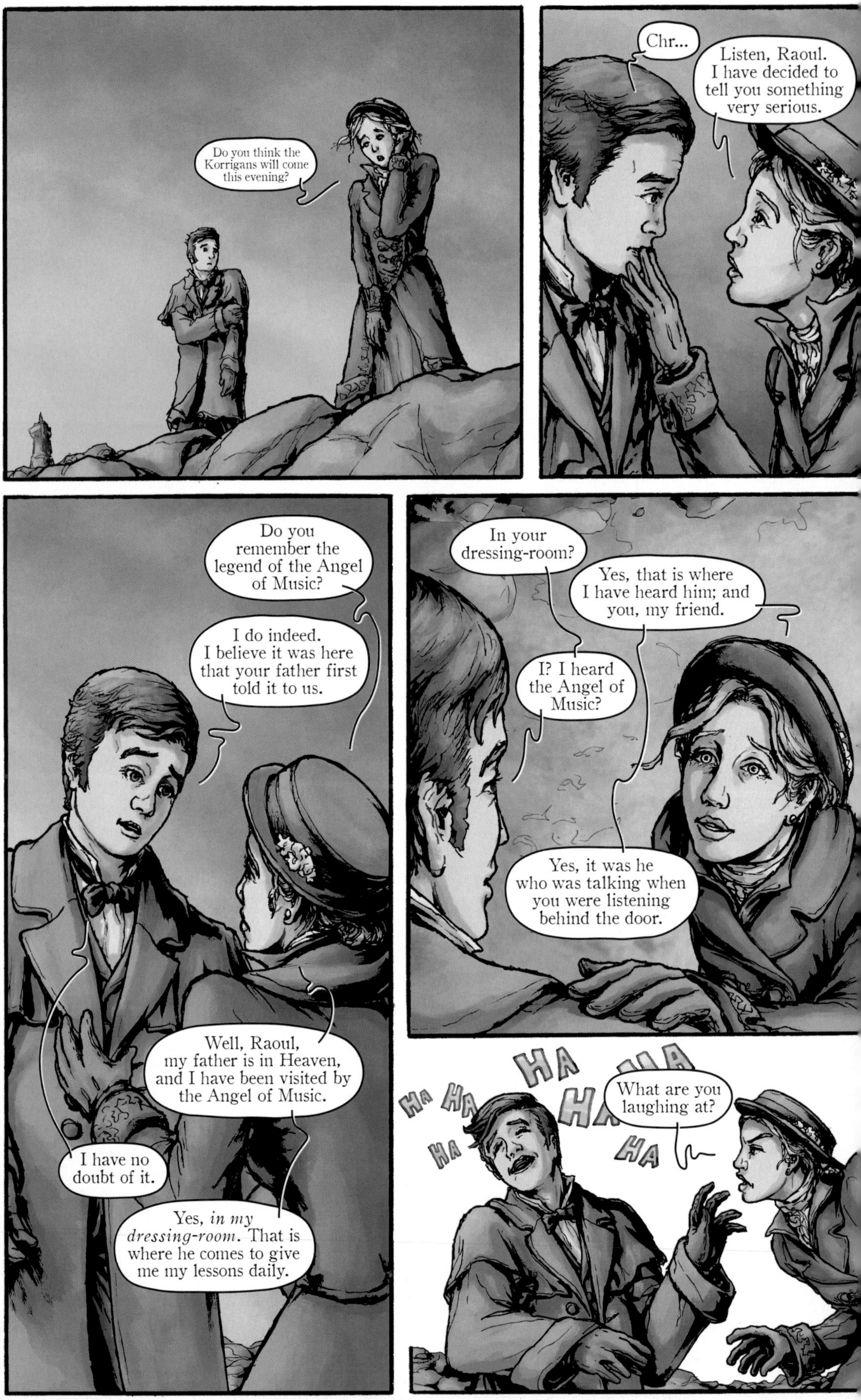
Do you think the Korrigans will come this evening?
Chr...
Listen, Raoul. I have decided to tell you something very serious.
Do you remember the legend of the Angel of Music?
I do indeed. I believe it was here that your father first told it to us.
Well, Raoul, my father is in Heaven, and I have been visited by the Angel of Music.
I have no doubt of it.
Yes, *in my dressing-room*. That is where he comes to give me my lessons daily.
In your dressing-room?
Yes, that is where I have heard him; and you, my friend.
I? I heard the Angel of Music?
Yes, it was he who was talking when you were listening behind the door.
HA HA HA HA HA HA HA HA
What are you laughing at?

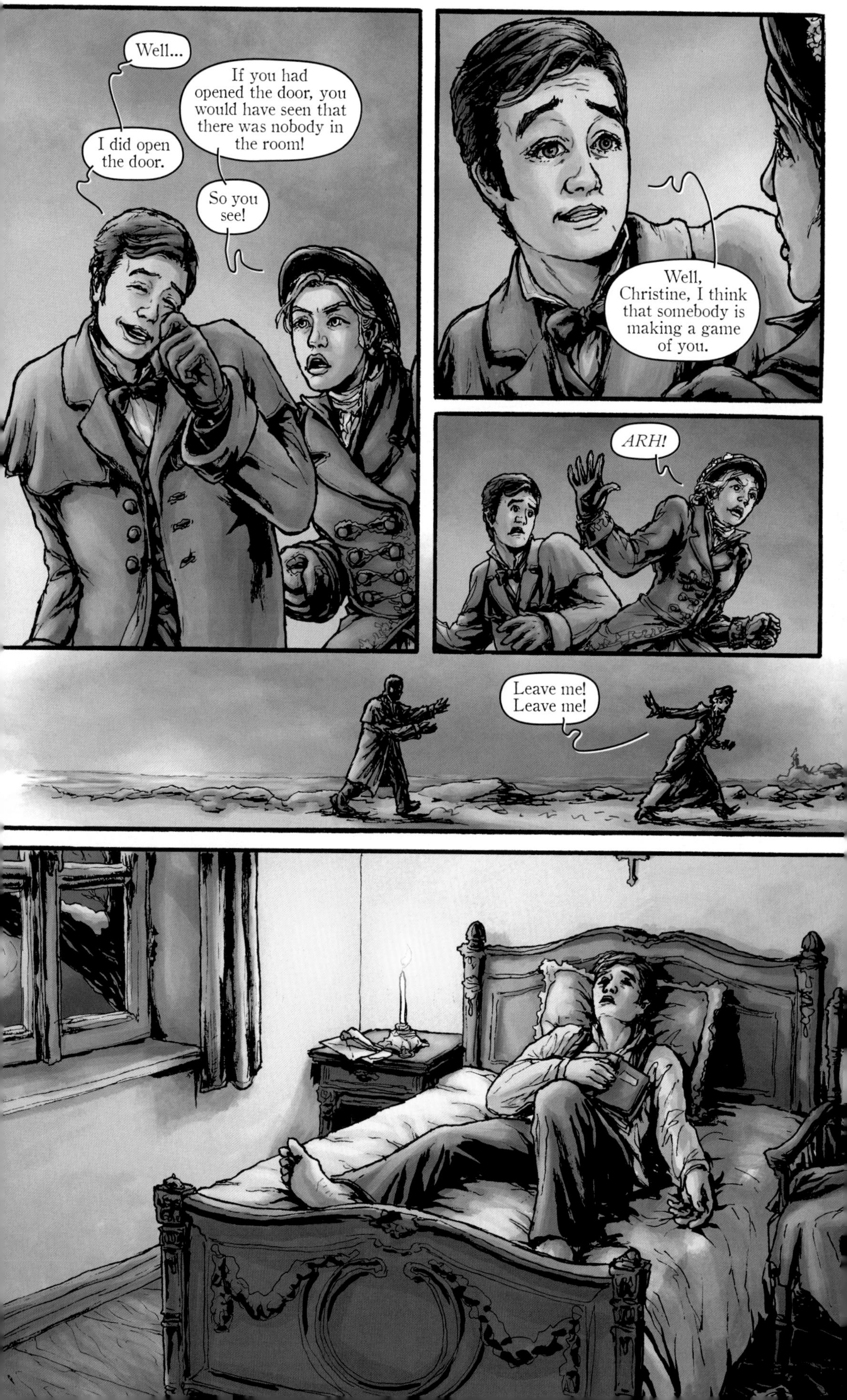
Well...
I did open the door.
If you had opened the door, you would have seen that there was nobody in the room!
So you see!
Well, Christine, I think that somebody is making a game of you.
ARH!
Leave me! Leave me!

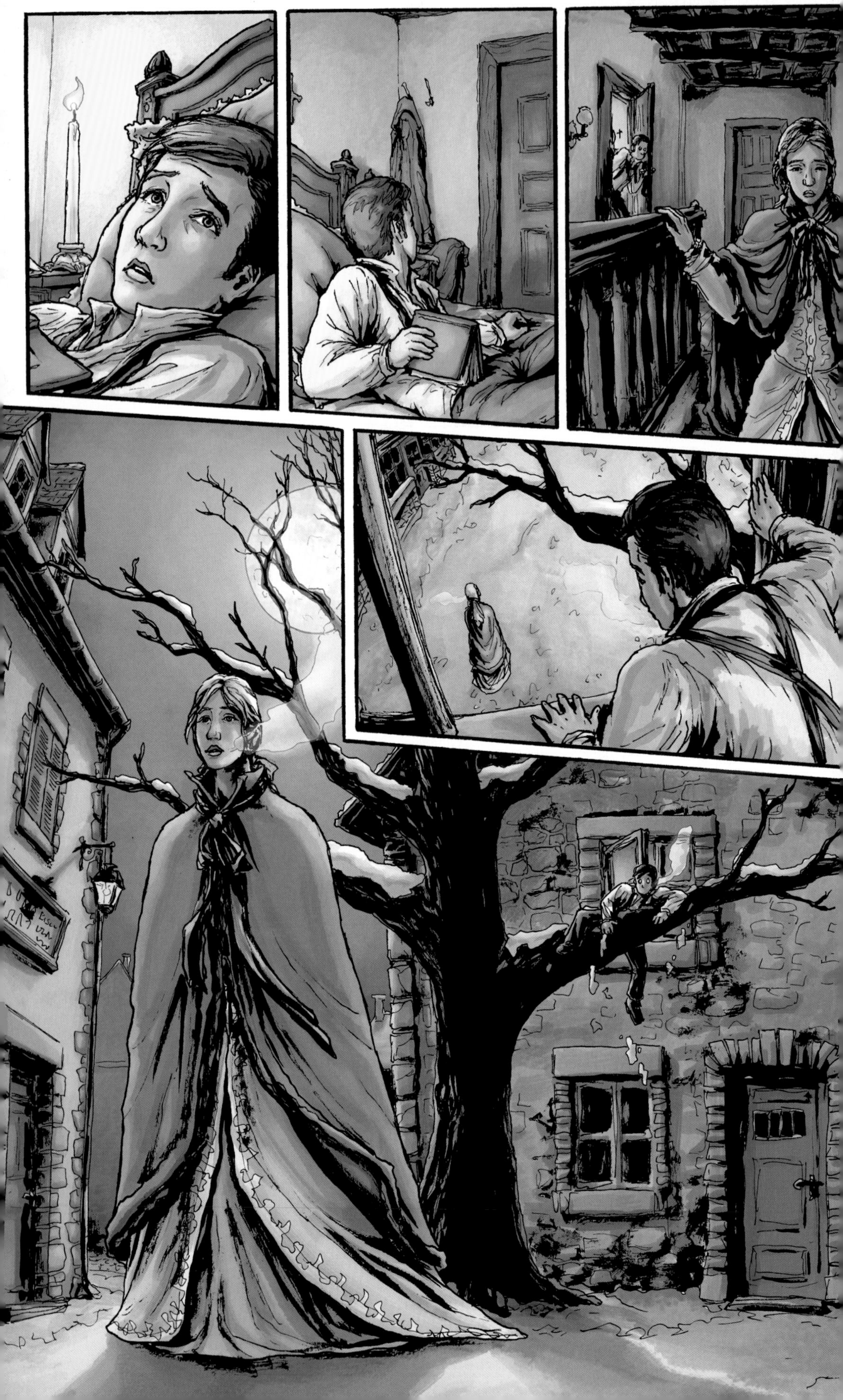

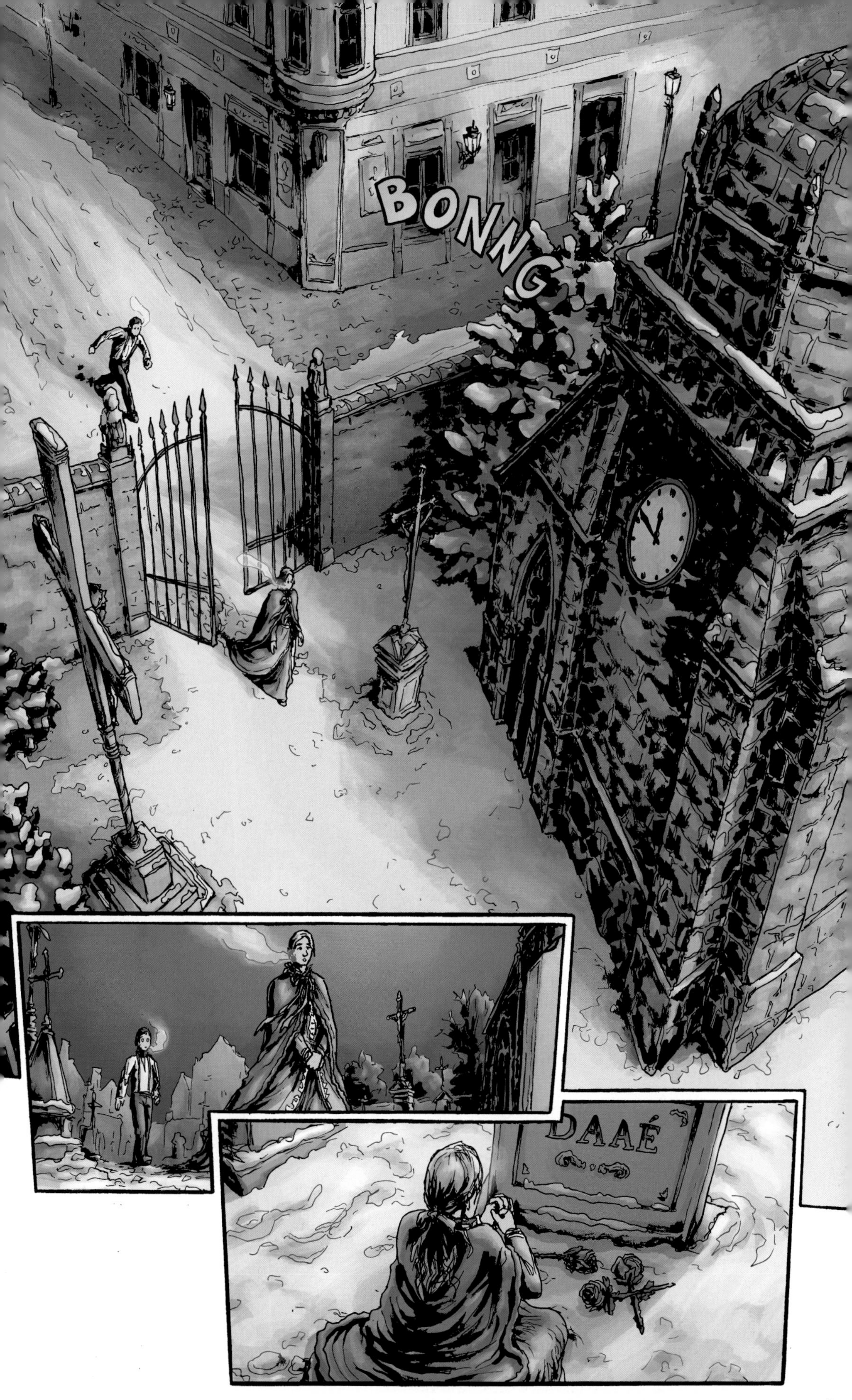
BONNG
DAAÉ

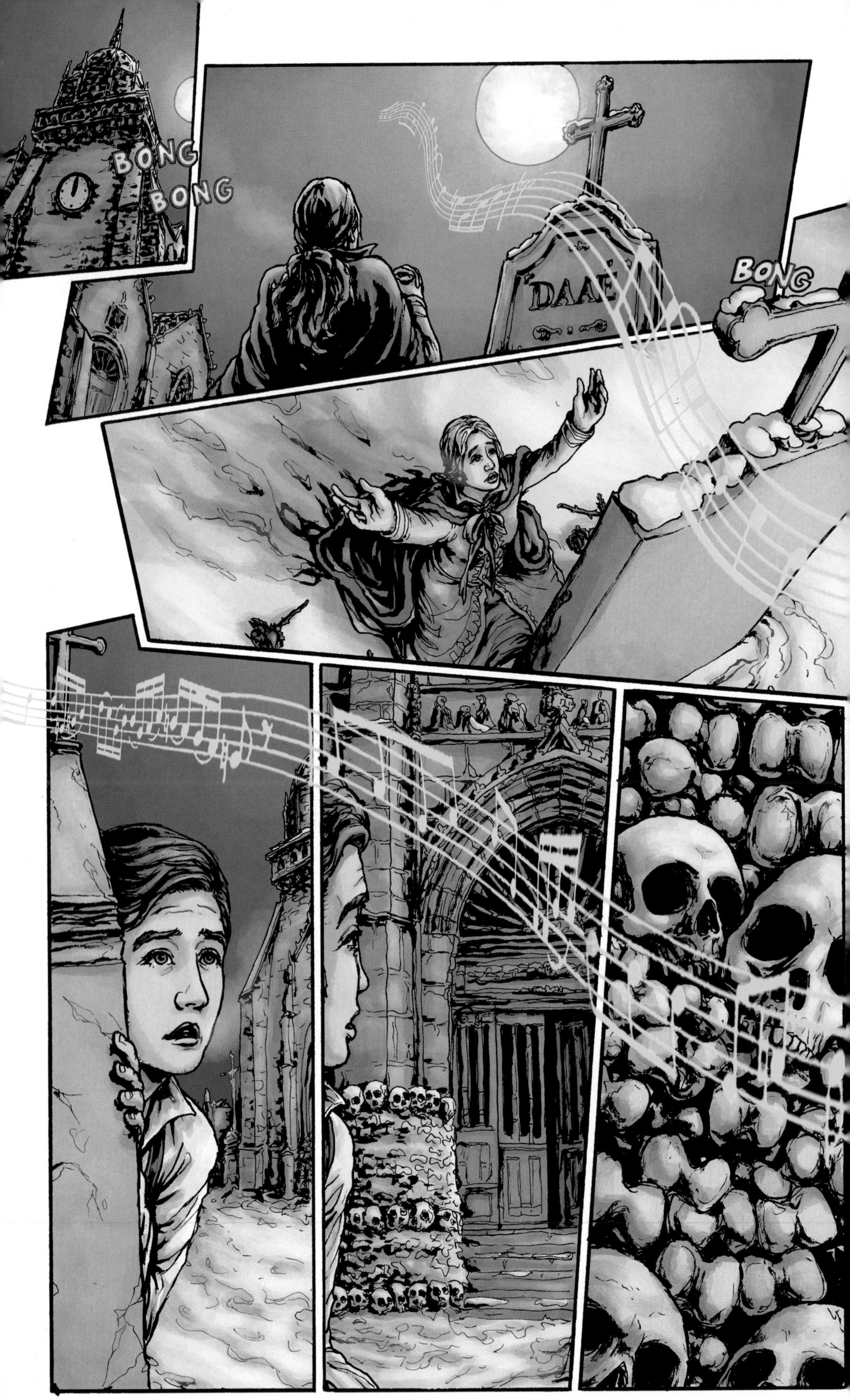

BONG
BONG
DAAÉ
BONG

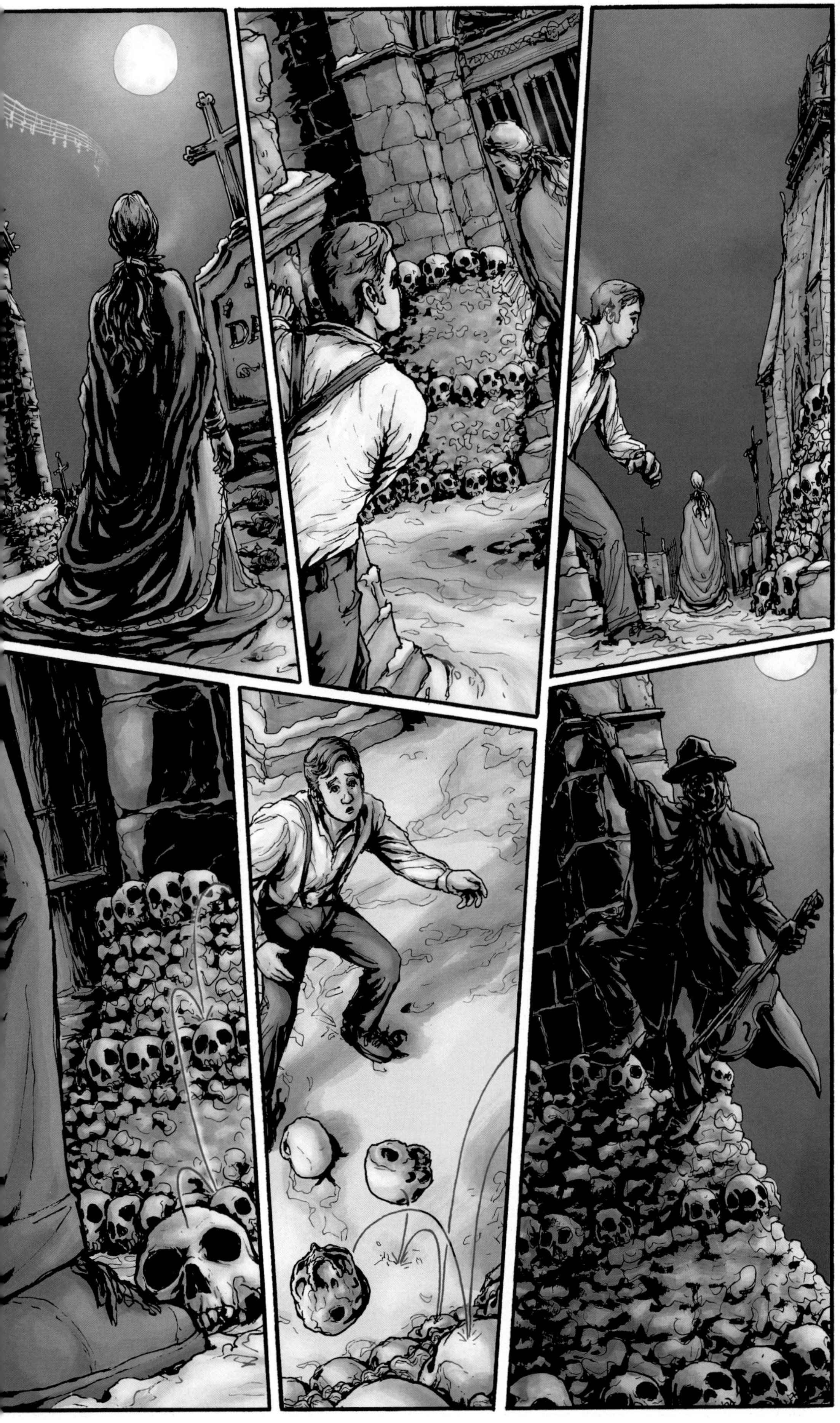

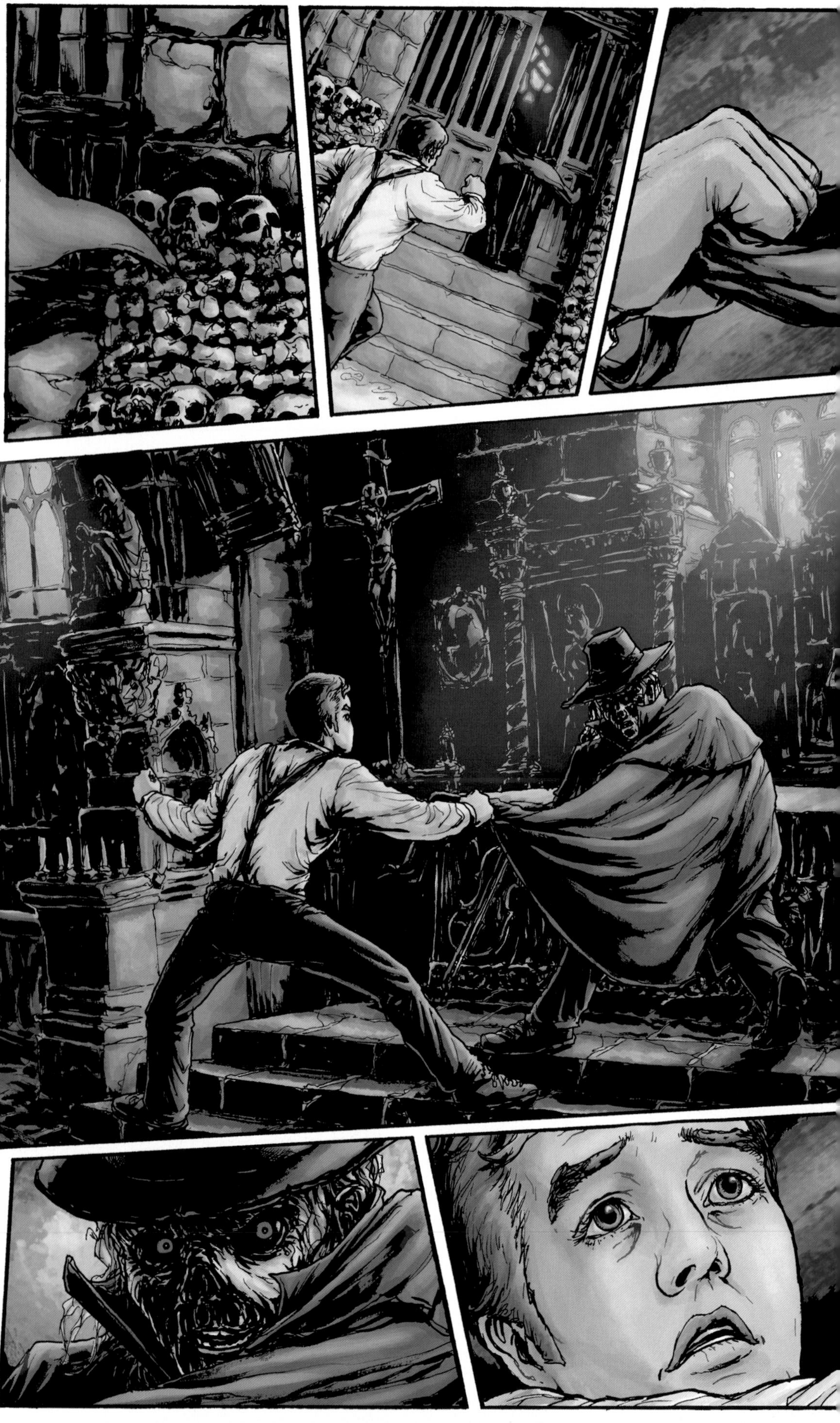

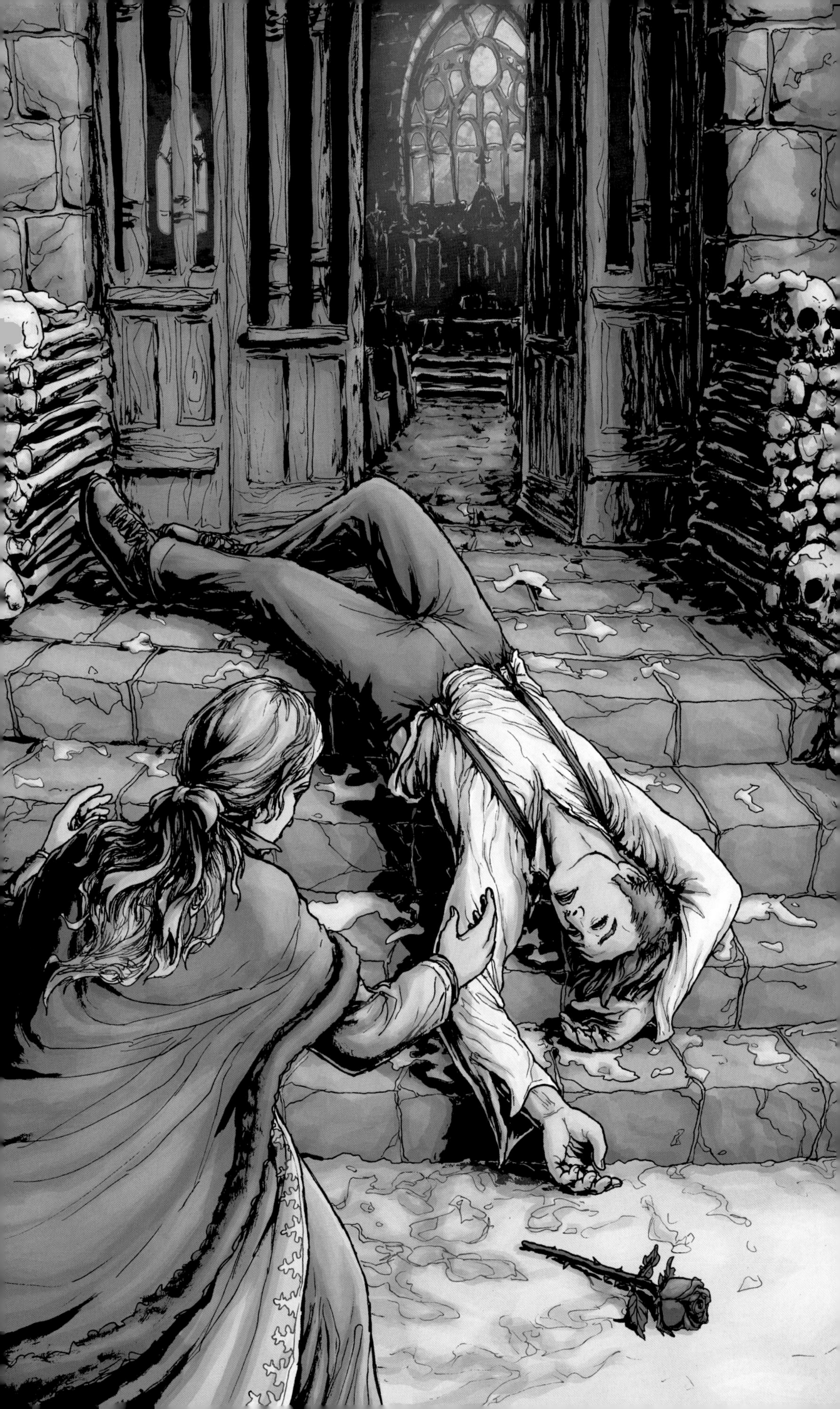

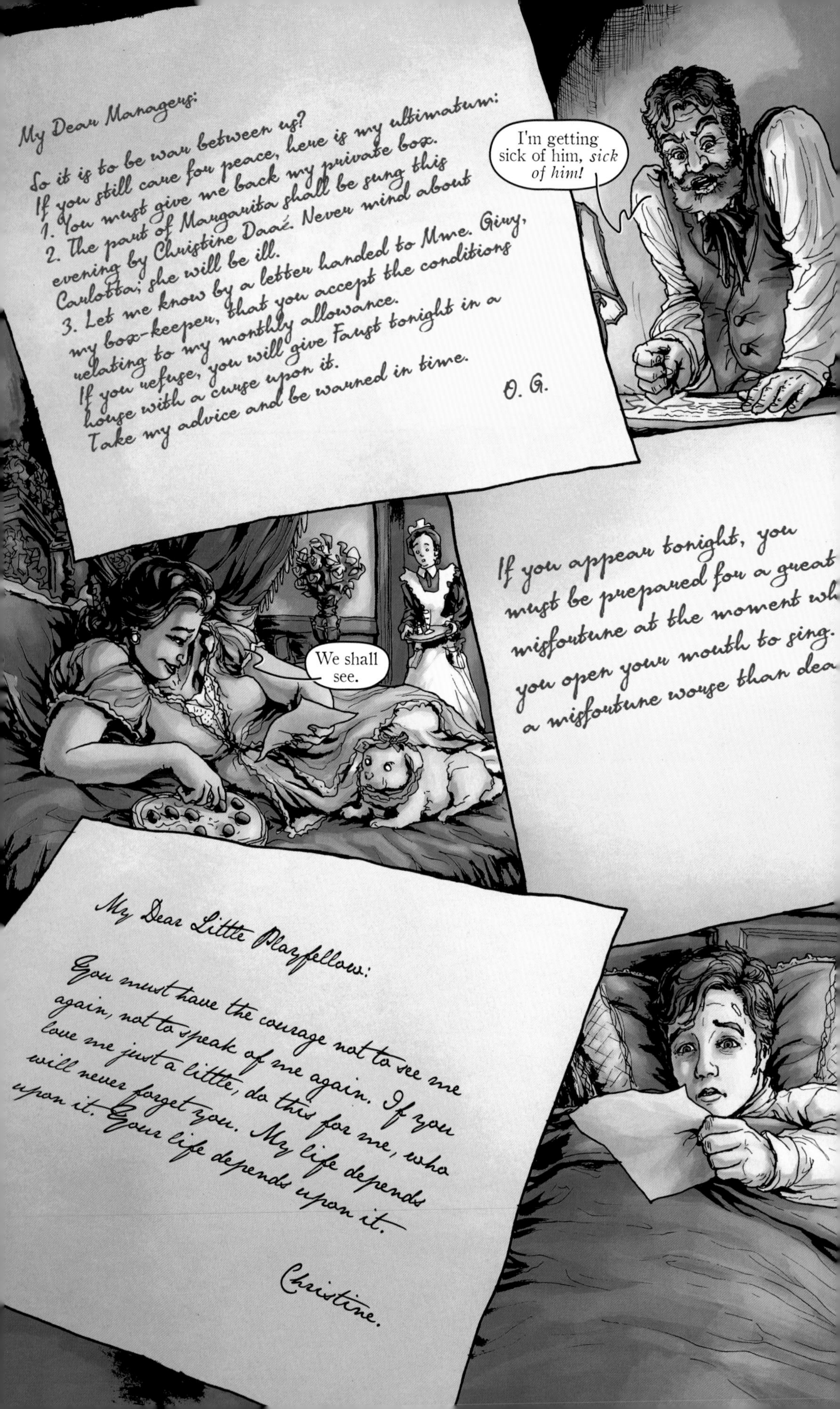
My Dear Managers:
So it is to be war between us?
If you still care for peace, here is my ultimatum:
1. You must give me back my private box.
2. The part of Margarita shall be sung this evening by Christine Daaé. Never mind about Carlotta; she will be ill.
3. Let me know by a letter handed to Mme. Giry, my box-keeper, that you accept the conditions relating to my monthly allowance.
If you refuse, you will give Faust tonight in a house with a curse upon it.
Take my advice and be warned in time.
O. G.
I'm getting sick of him, sick of him!
We shall see.
If you appear tonight, you must be prepared for a great misfortune at the moment wh
you open your mouth to sing.
a misfortune worse than dea
My Dear Little Playfellow:
You must have the courage not to see me again, not to speak of me again. If you love me just a little, do this for me, who will never forget you. My life depends upon it. Your life depends upon it.
Christine.

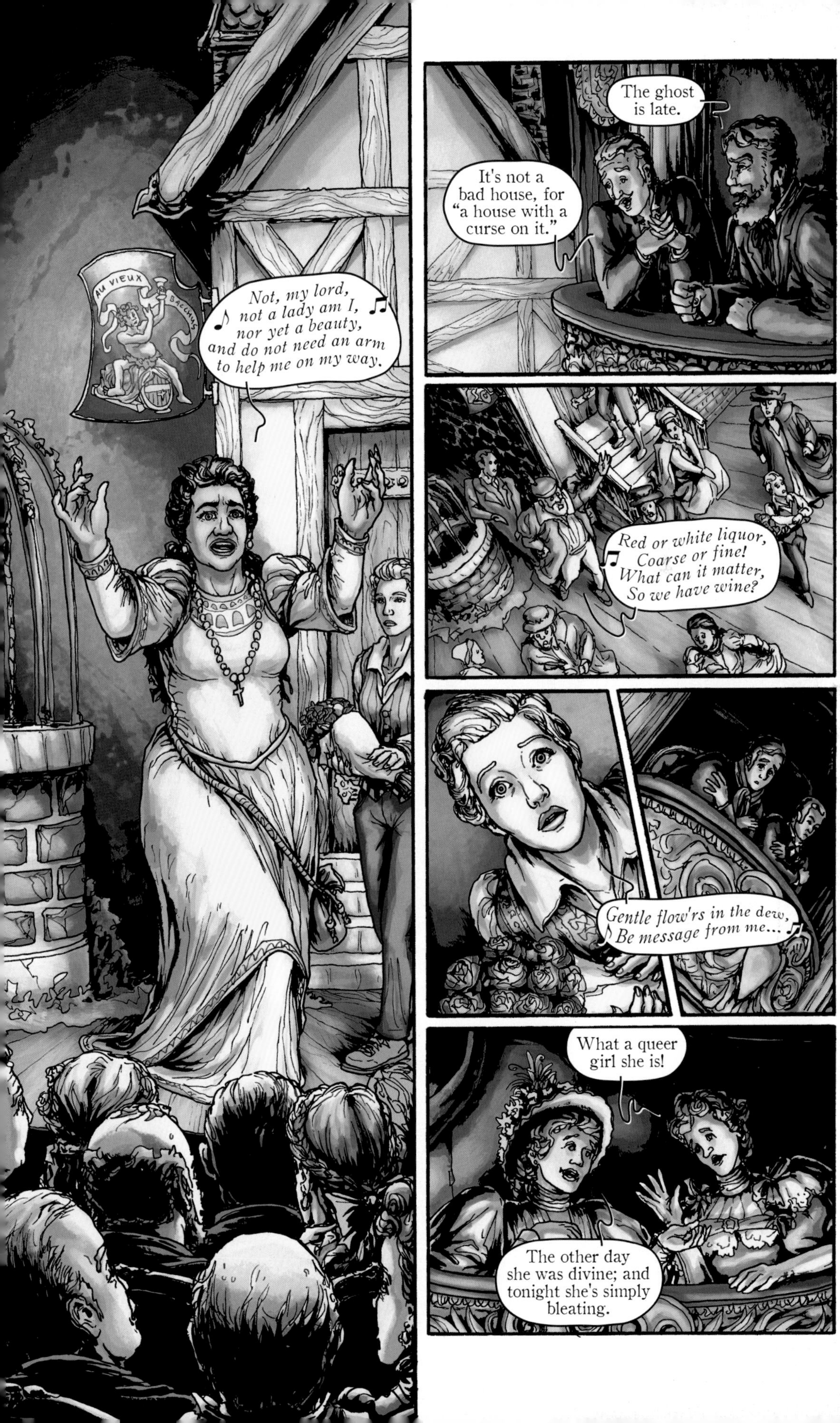
AU VIEUX BACCHUS
Not, my lord, not a lady am I, nor yet a beauty, and do not need an arm to help me on my way.
The ghost is late.
It's not a bad house, for "a house with a curse on it."
Red or white liquor, Coarse or fine! What can it matter, So we have wine?
Gentle flow'rs in the dew, Be message from me...
What a queer girl she is!
The other day she was divine; and tonight she's simply bleating.

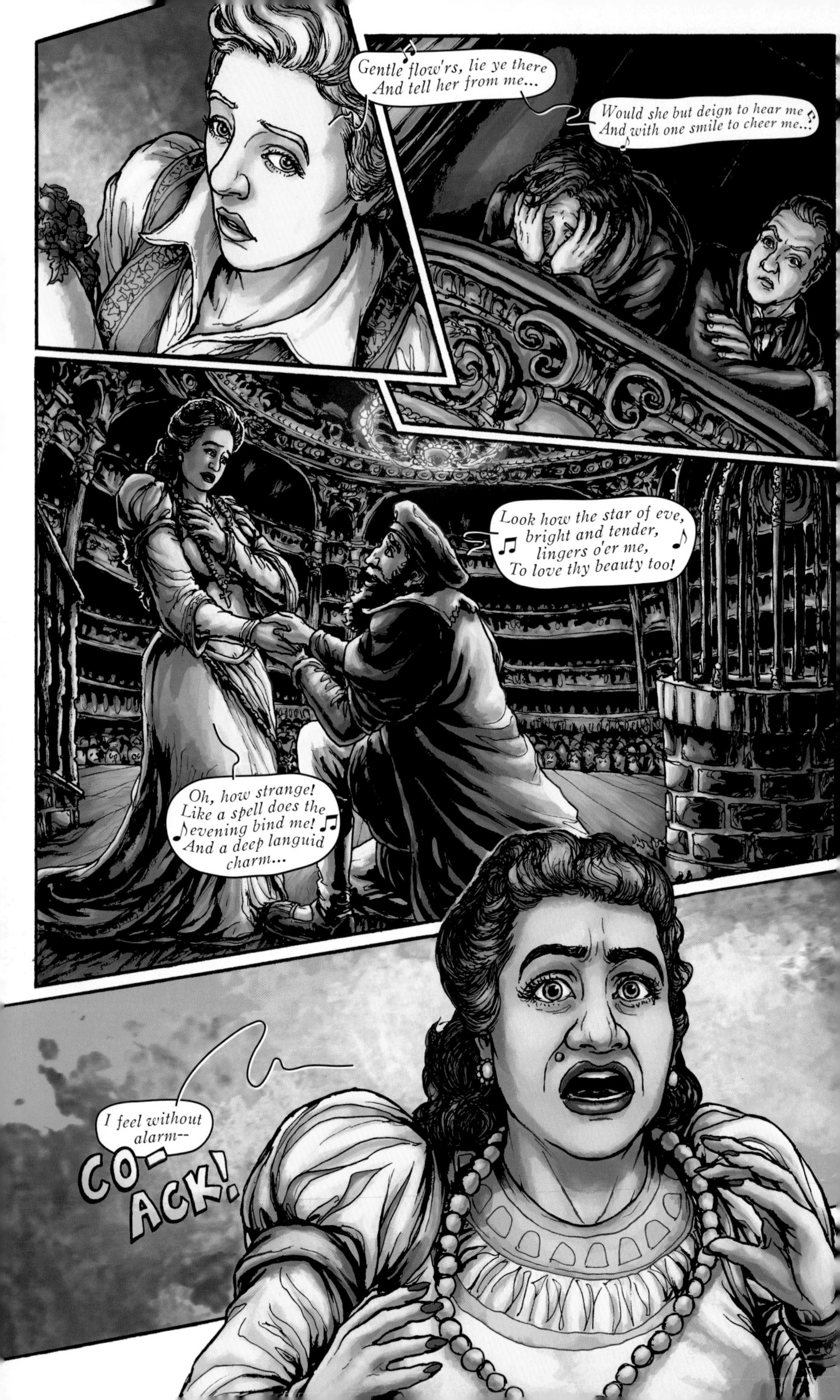
Gentle flow'rs, lie ye there
And tell her from me...
Would she but deign to hear me
And with one smile to cheer me...
Look how the star of eve, bright and tender, lingers o'er me, To love thy beauty too!
Oh, how strange! Like a spell does the evening bind me! And a deep languid charm...
I feel without alarm--
CO-ACK!

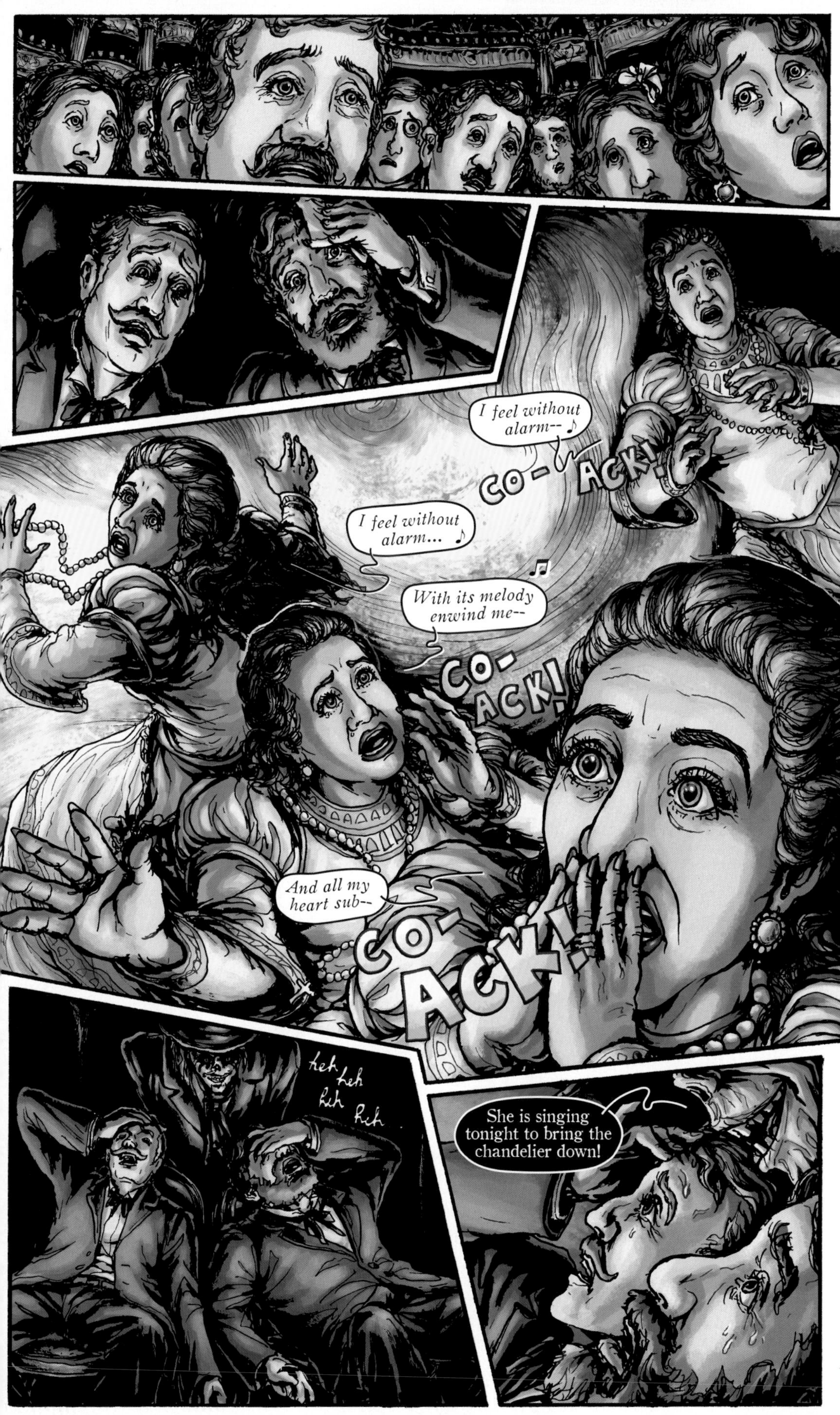
I feel without alarm-- ♪
CO-ACK!
I feel without alarm... ♪
With its melody enwind me--
CO-ACK!
And all my heart sub--
CO-ACK!
heh heh heh heh
She is singing tonight to bring the chandelier down!

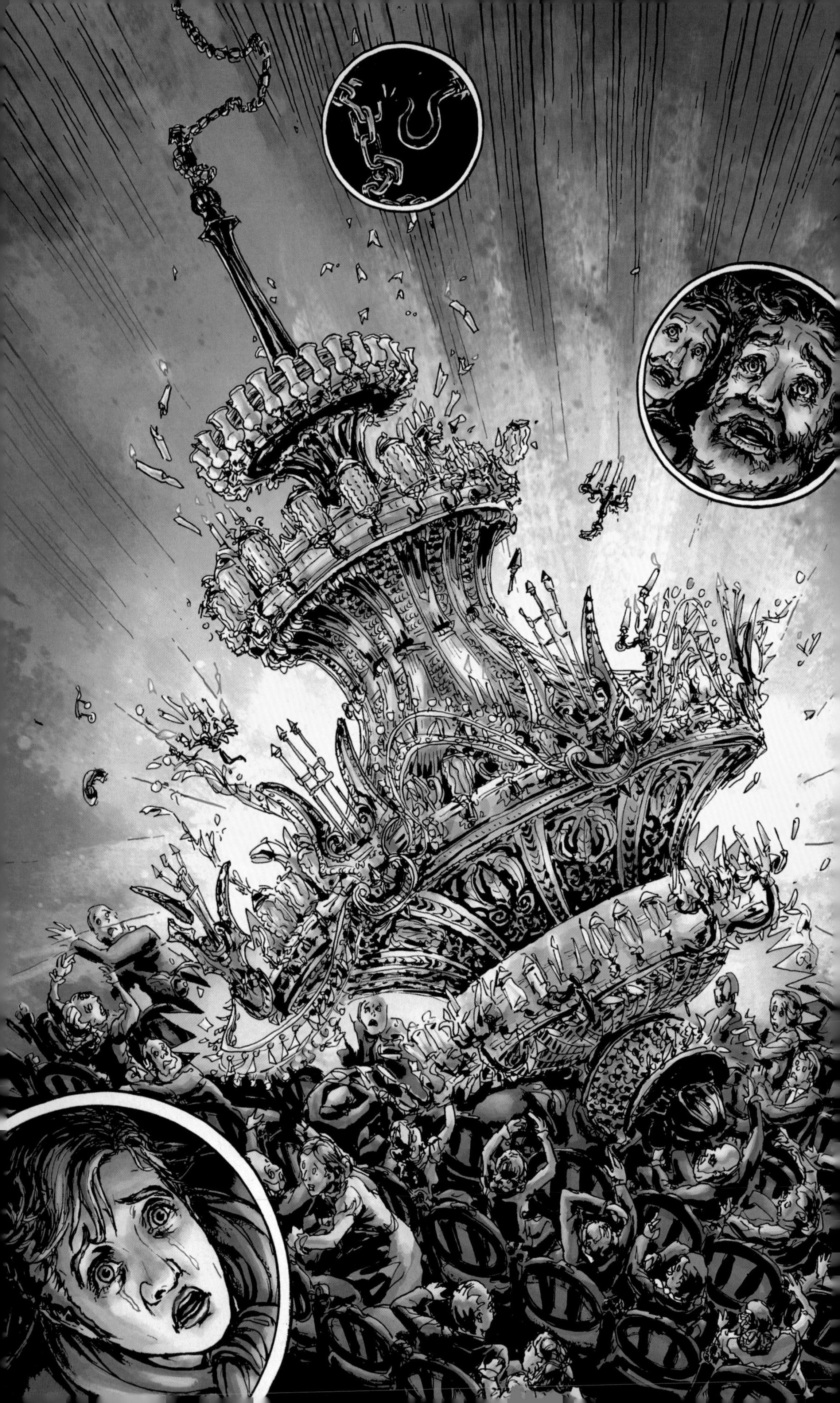

Chapter Three

After the tragic evening of the performance Christine Daaé disappeared.

A fortnight elapsed during which she was seen neither at the Opera nor outside. Raoul, of course, was the most astonished at the prima donna's absence. He wrote to her and received no reply. His grief increased at never seeing her name on the program.

One morning a passer-by picked up an unstamped envelope on the pavement by the Opera. It bore the words *"To be handed to M. le Vicomte Raoul de Chagny."*

Go to the masked ball at the Opera on the night after tomorrow. At twelve o'clock, be near the door that leads to the Rotunda. Don't mention this appointment to any one on earth. Wear a white domino and be carefully masked. Do not let yourself be recognized.

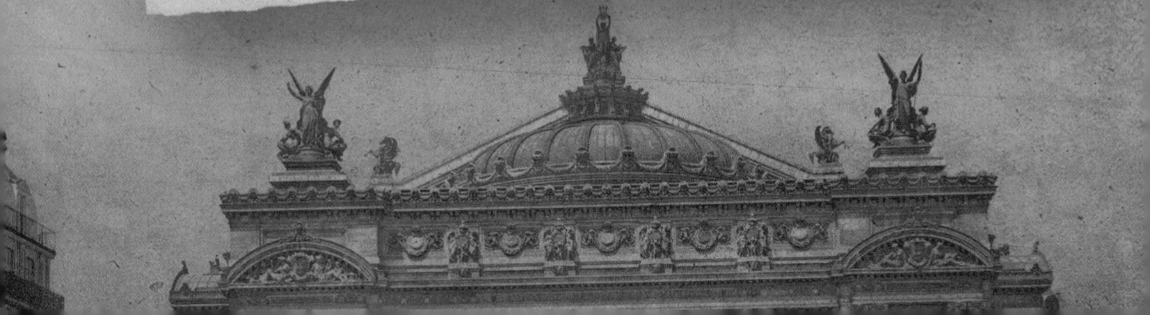

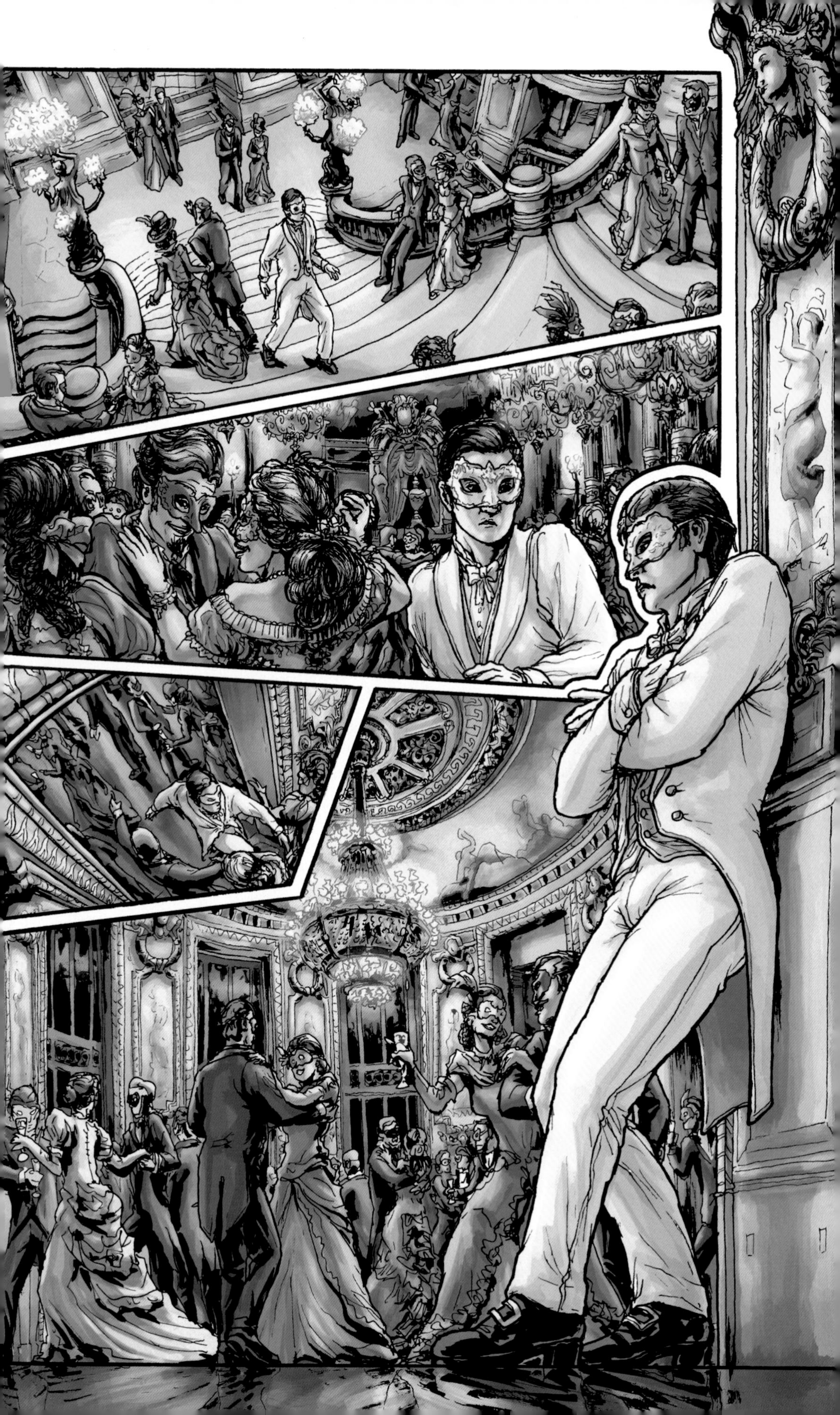

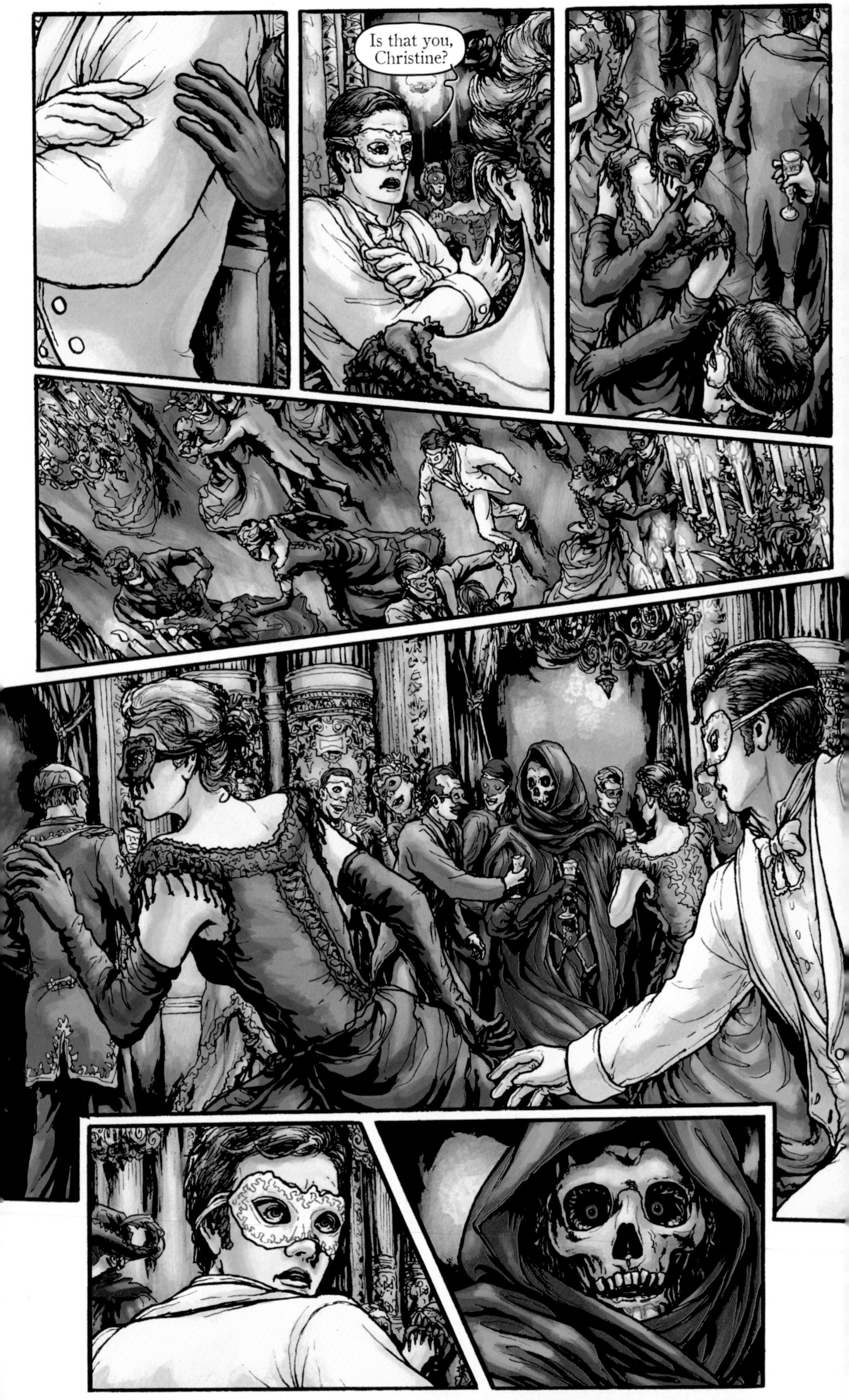
Is that you, Christine?

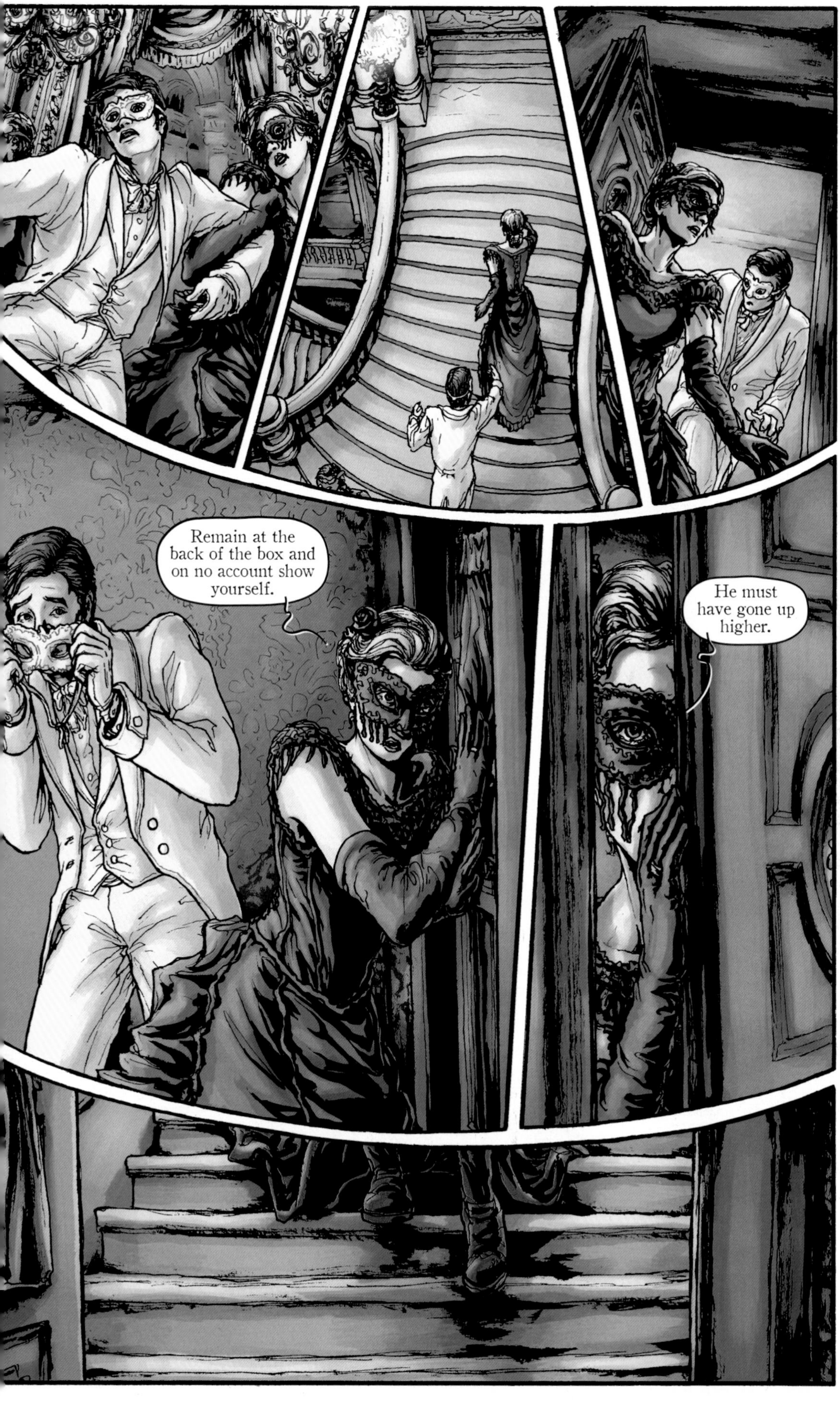
Remain at the back of the box and on no account show yourself.
He must have gone up higher.

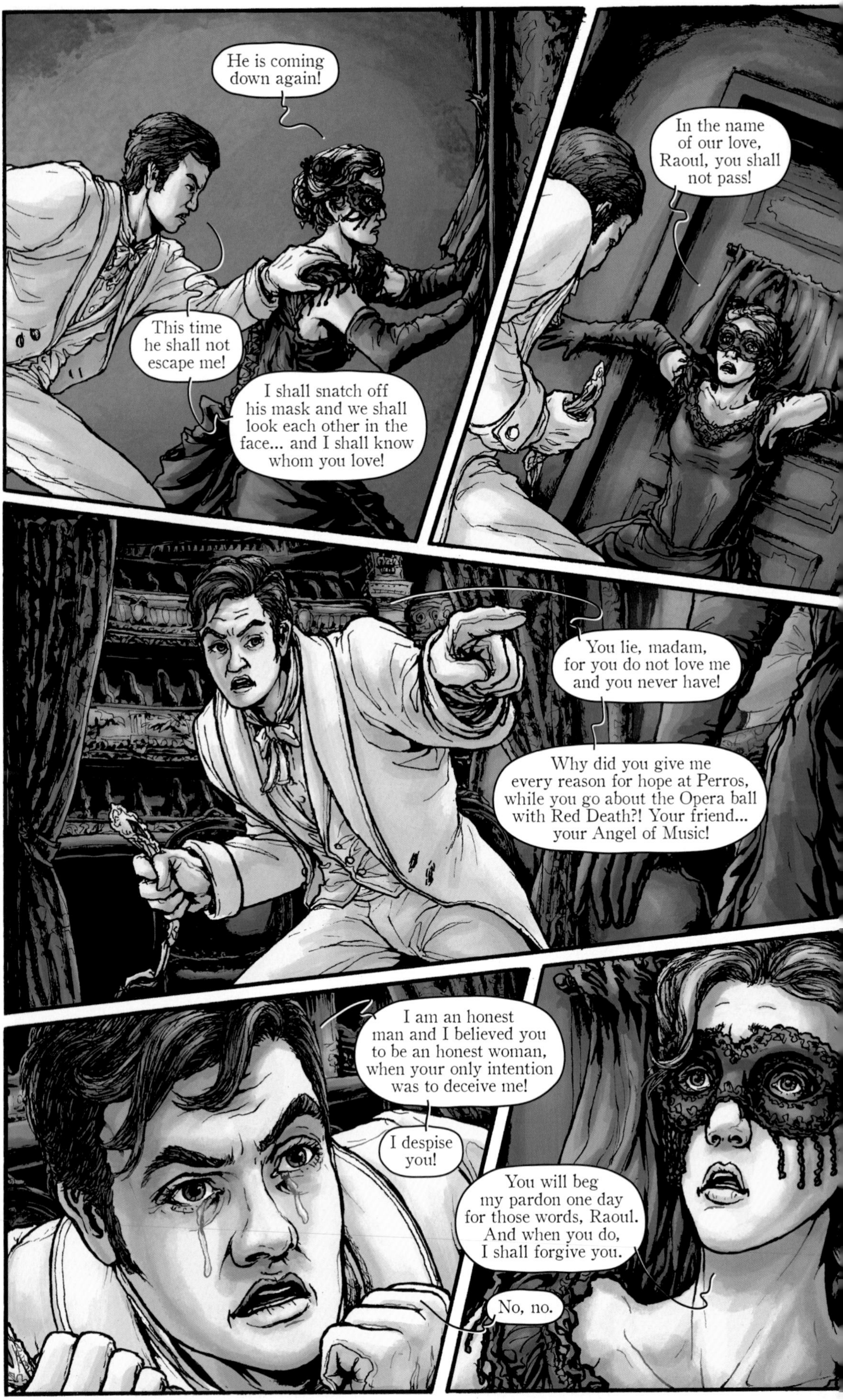
He is coming down again!
This time he shall not escape me!
I shall snatch off his mask and we shall look each other in the face... and I shall know whom you love!
In the name of our love, Raoul, you shall not pass!
You lie, madam, for you do not love me and you never have!
Why did you give me every reason for hope at Perros, while you go about the Opera ball with Red Death?! Your friend... your Angel of Music!
I am an honest man and I believed you to be an honest woman, when your only intention was to deceive me!
I despise you!
You will beg my pardon one day for those words, Raoul. And when you do, I shall forgive you.
No, no.

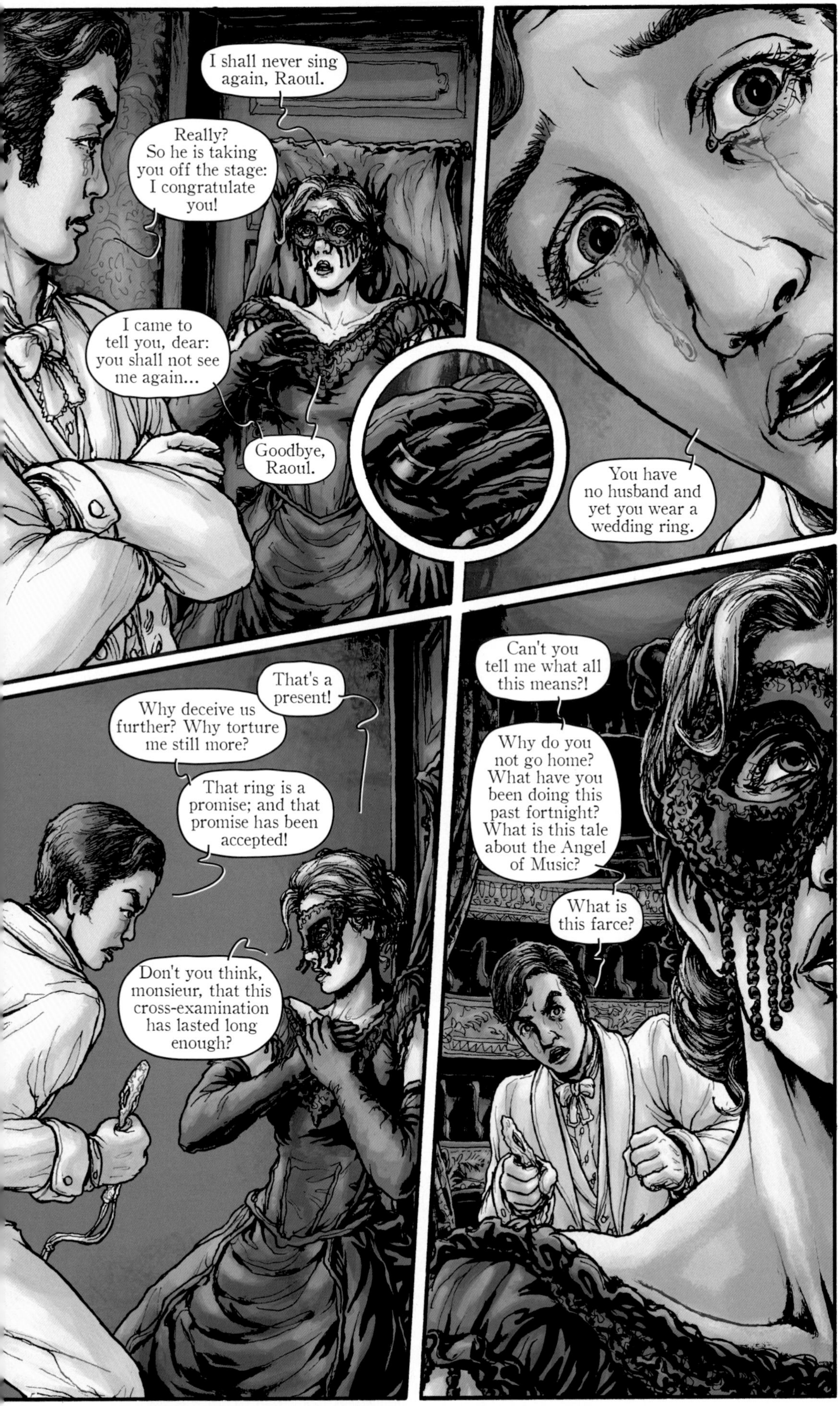
I shall never sing again, Raoul.
Really? So he is taking you off the stage: I congratulate you!
I came to tell you, dear: you shall not see me again...
Goodbye, Raoul.
You have no husband and yet you wear a wedding ring.
That's a present!
Why deceive us further? Why torture me still more?
That ring is a promise; and that promise has been accepted!
Don't you think, monsieur, that this cross-examination has lasted long enough?
Can't you tell me what all this means?!
Why do you not go home? What have you been doing this past fortnight? What is this tale about the Angel of Music?
What is this farce?

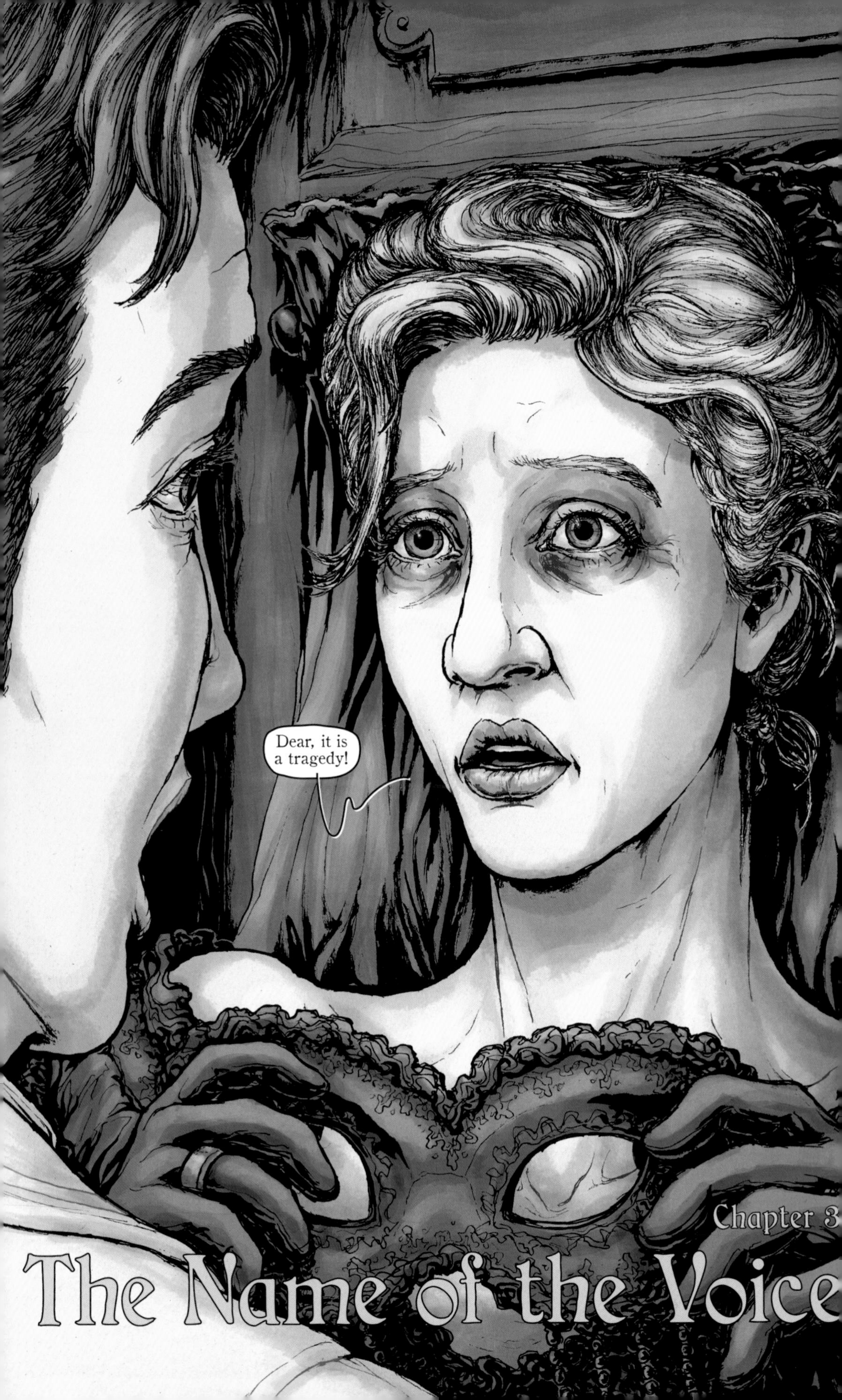
Dear, it is a tragedy!
Chapter 3
The Name of the Voice

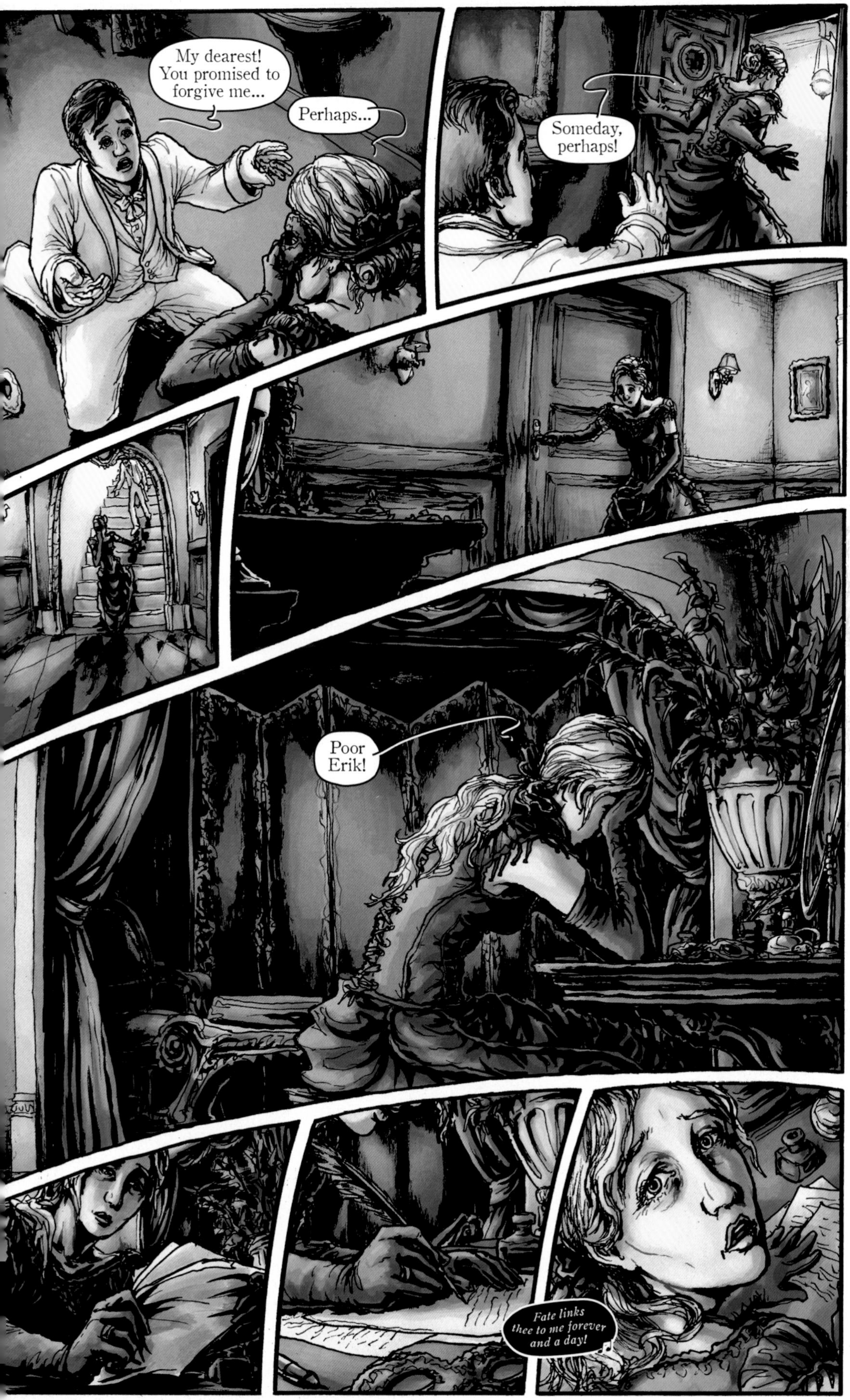
My dearest! You promised to forgive me...
Perhaps...
Someday, perhaps!
Poor Erik!
Fate links thee to me forever and a day!

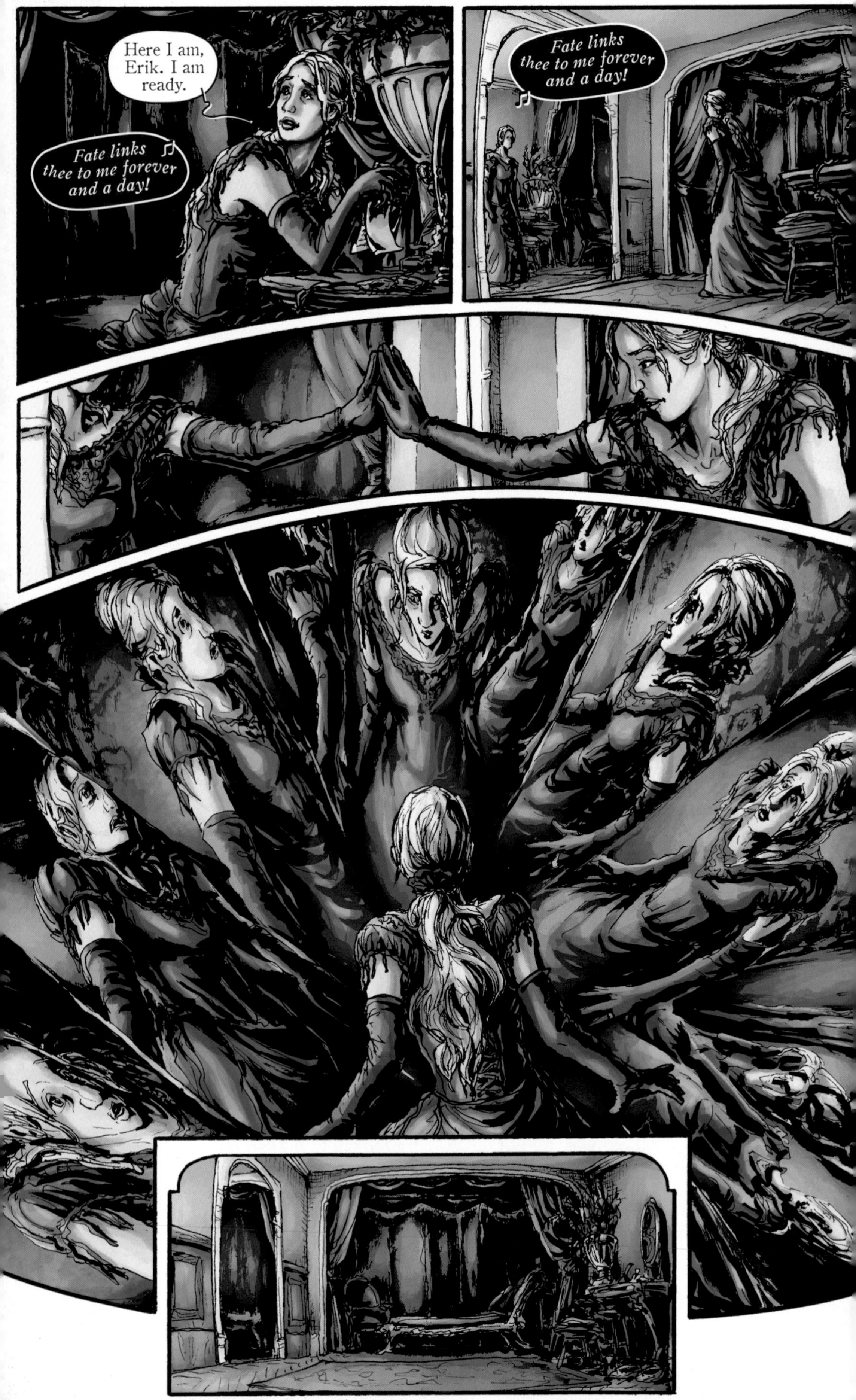
Here I am, Erik. I am ready.
Fate links thee to me forever and a day!
Fate links thee to me forever and a day!

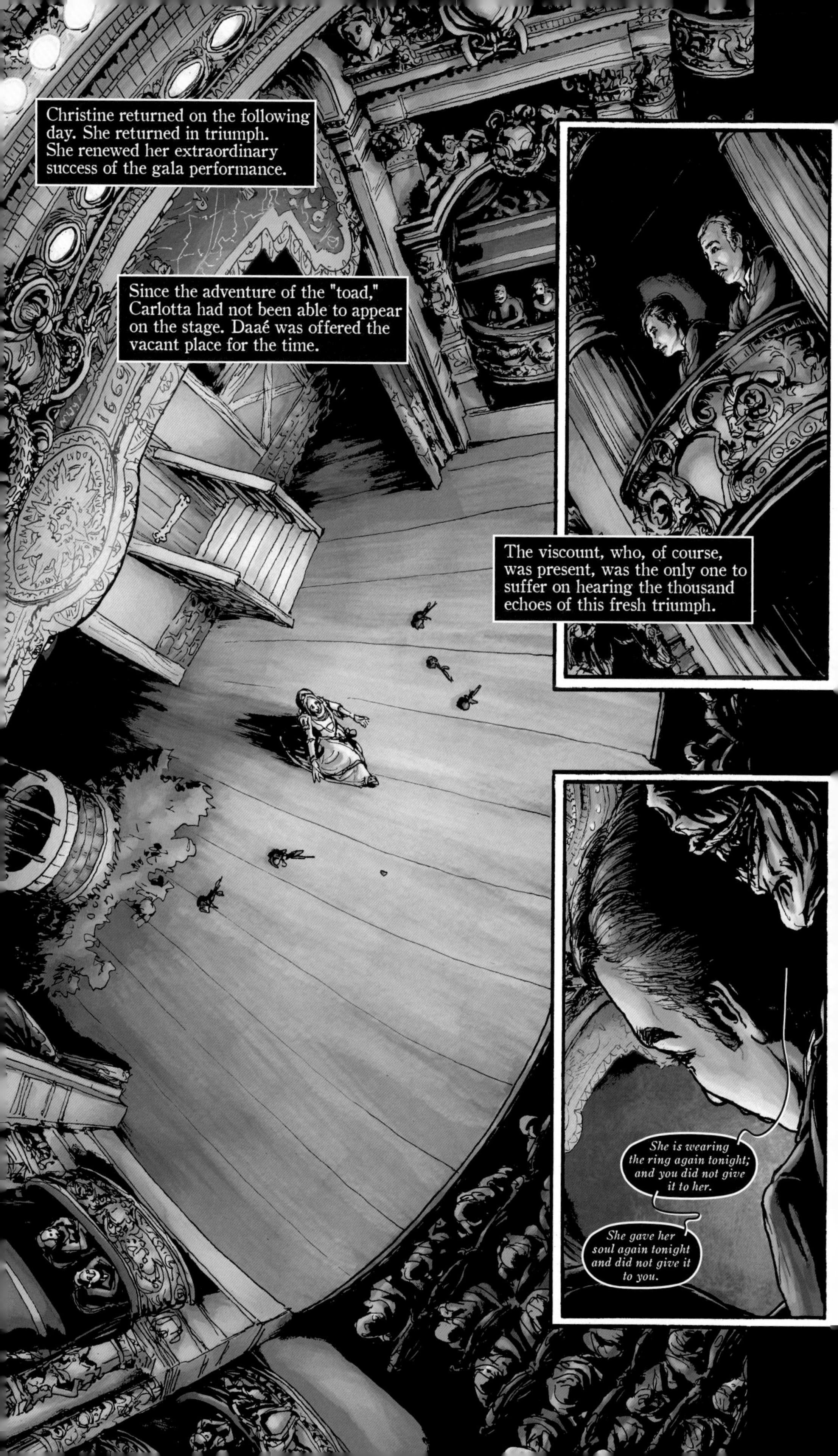
Christine returned on the following day. She returned in triumph. She renewed her extraordinary success of the gala performance.
Since the adventure of the "toad," Carlotta had not been able to appear on the stage. Daaé was offered the vacant place for the time.
The viscount, who, of course, was present, was the only one to suffer on hearing the thousand echoes of this fresh triumph.
She is wearing the ring again tonight; and you did not give it to her.
She gave her soul again tonight and did not give it to you.

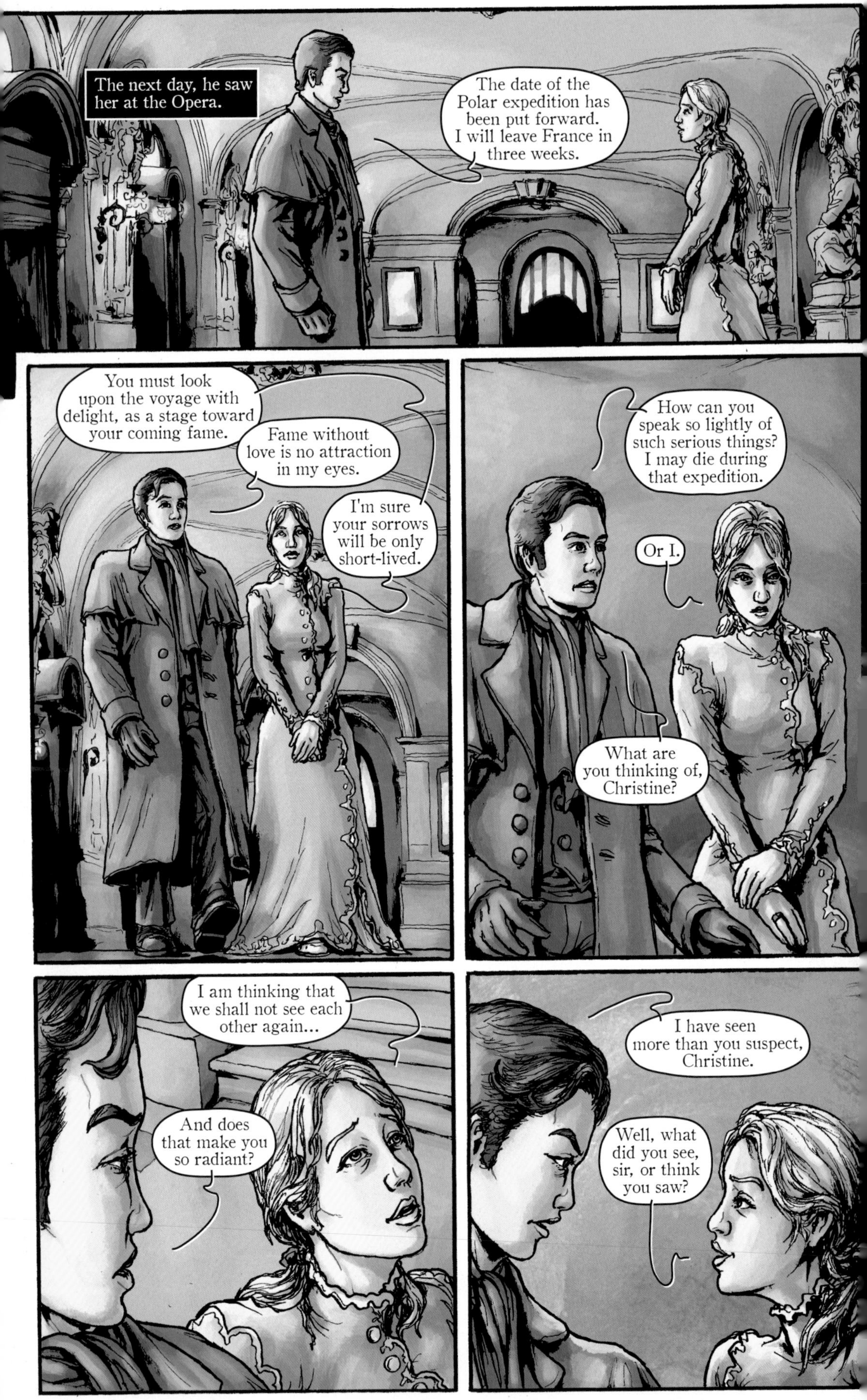
The next day, he saw her at the Opera.
The date of the Polar expedition has been put forward. I will leave France in three weeks.
You must look upon the voyage with delight, as a stage toward your coming fame.
Fame without love is no attraction in my eyes.
I'm sure your sorrows will be only short-lived.
How can you speak so lightly of such serious things? I may die during that expedition.
Or I.
What are you thinking of, Christine?
I am thinking that we shall not see each other again...
And does that make you so radiant?
I have seen more than you suspect, Christine.
Well, what did you see, sir, or think you saw?

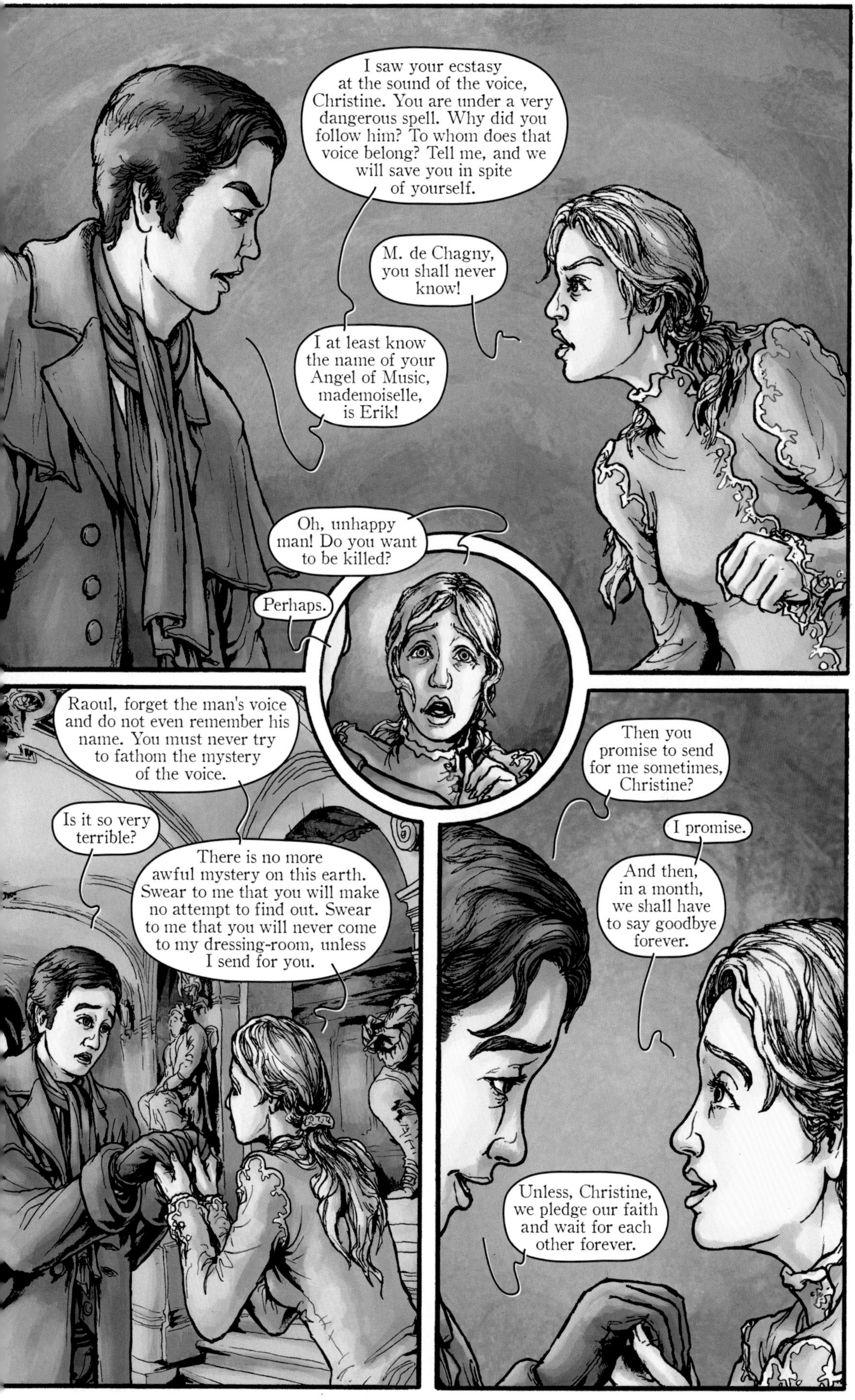
I saw your ecstasy at the sound of the voice, Christine. You are under a very dangerous spell. Why did you follow him? To whom does that voice belong? Tell me, and we will save you in spite of yourself.
M. de Chagny, you shall never know!
I at least know the name of your Angel of Music, mademoiselle, is Erik!
Oh, unhappy man! Do you want to be killed?
Perhaps.
Raoul, forget the man's voice and do not even remember his name. You must never try to fathom the mystery of the voice.
Is it so very terrible?
There is no more awful mystery on this earth. Swear to me that you will make no attempt to find out. Swear to me that you will never come to my dressing-room, unless I send for you.
Then you promise to send for me sometimes, Christine?
I promise.
And then, in a month, we shall have to say goodbye forever.
Unless, Christine, we pledge our faith and wait for each other forever.

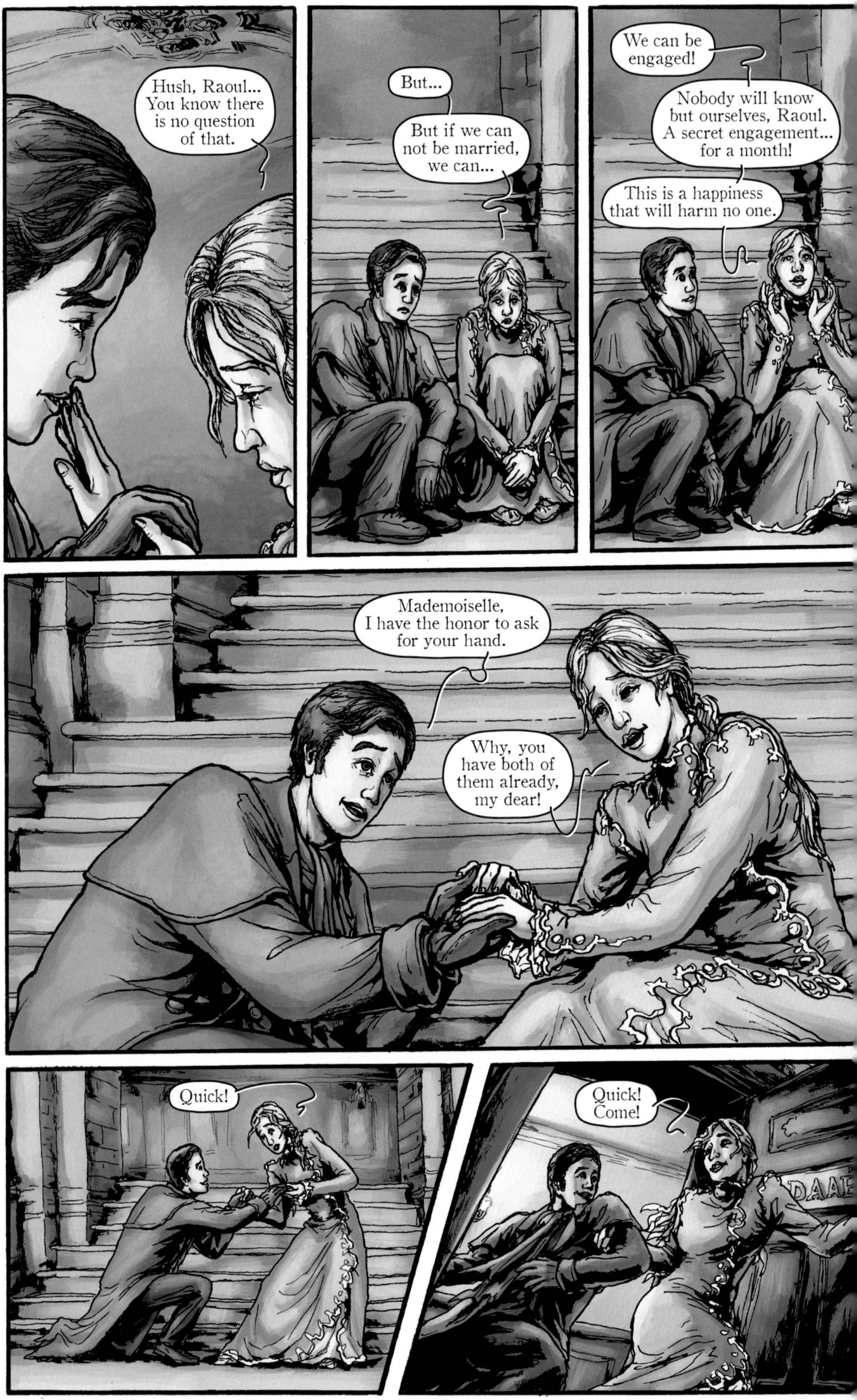
Hush, Raoul... You know there is no question of that.
But...
But if we can not be married, we can...
We can be engaged!
Nobody will know but ourselves, Raoul. A secret engagement... for a month!
This is a happiness that will harm no one.
Mademoiselle, I have the honor to ask for your hand.
Why, you have both of them already, my dear!
Quick!
Quick! Come!
DAAE

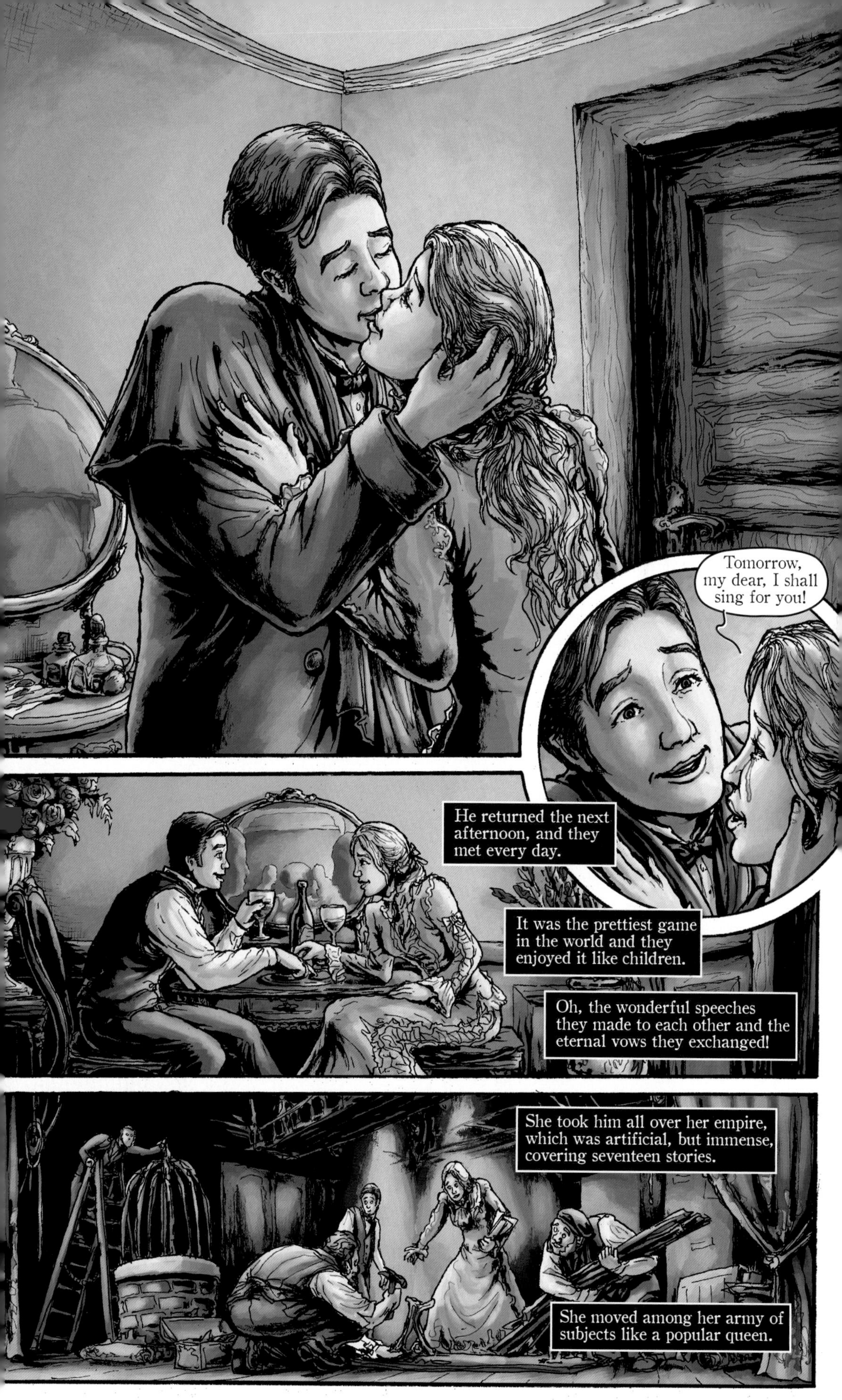
Tomorrow, my dear, I shall sing for you!
He returned the next afternoon, and they met every day.
It was the prettiest game in the world and they enjoyed it like children.
Oh, the wonderful speeches they made to each other and the eternal vows they exchanged!
She took him all over her empire, which was artificial, but immense, covering seventeen stories.
She moved among her army of subjects like a popular queen.

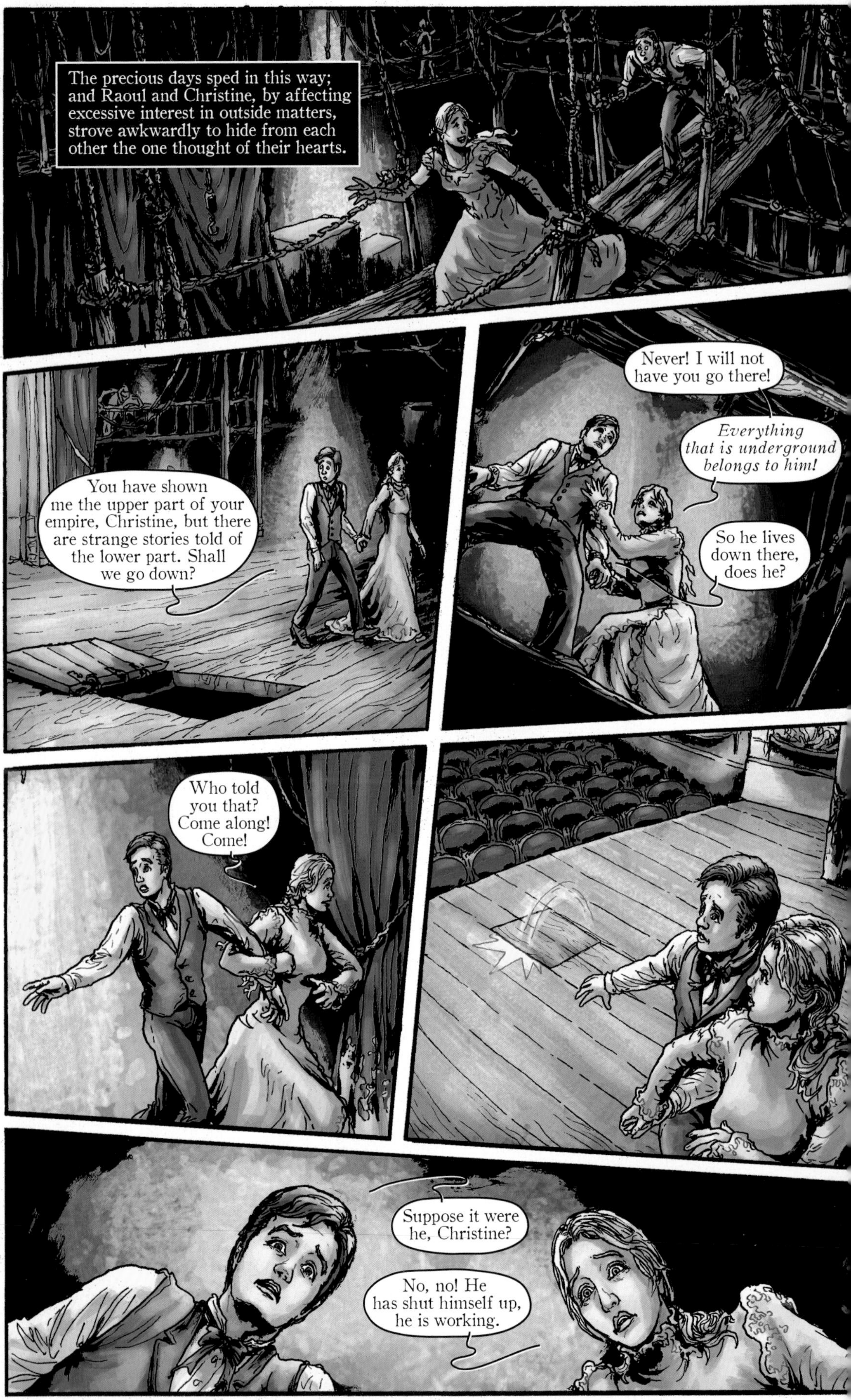

The precious days sped in this way; and Raoul and Christine, by affecting excessive interest in outside matters, strove awkwardly to hide from each other the one thought of their hearts.
You have shown me the upper part of your empire, Christine, but there are strange stories told of the lower part. Shall we go down?
Never! I will not have you go there!
Everything that is underground belongs to him!
So he lives down there, does he?
Who told you that? Come along! Come!
Suppose it were he, Christine?
No, no! He has shut himself up, he is working.

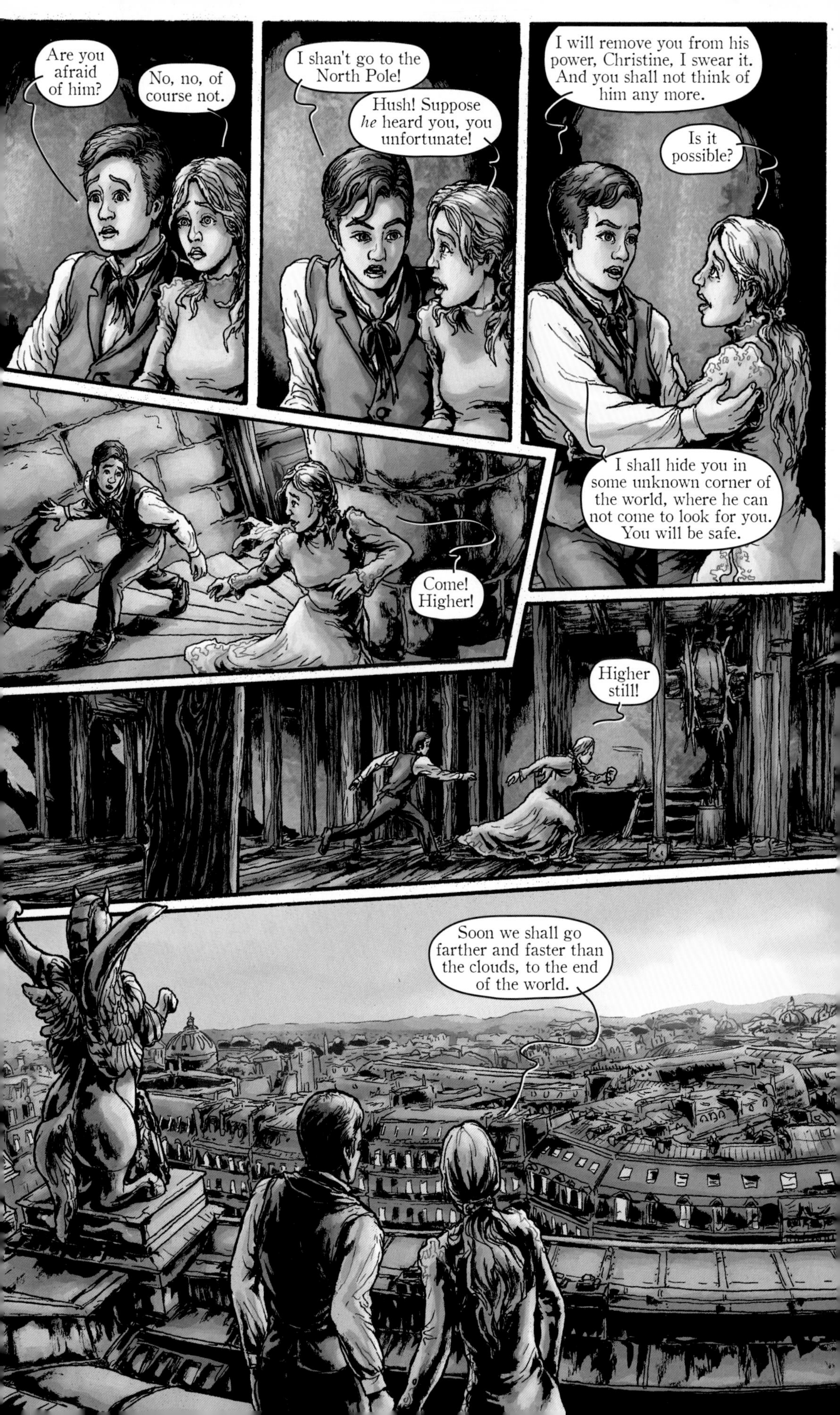
Are you afraid of him?
No, no, of course not.
I shan't go to the North Pole!
Hush! Suppose *he* heard you, you unfortunate!
I will remove you from his power, Christine, I swear it. And you shall not think of him any more.
Is it possible?
I shall hide you in some unknown corner of the world, where he can not come to look for you. You will be safe.
Come! Higher!
Higher still!
Soon we shall go farther and faster than the clouds, to the end of the world.

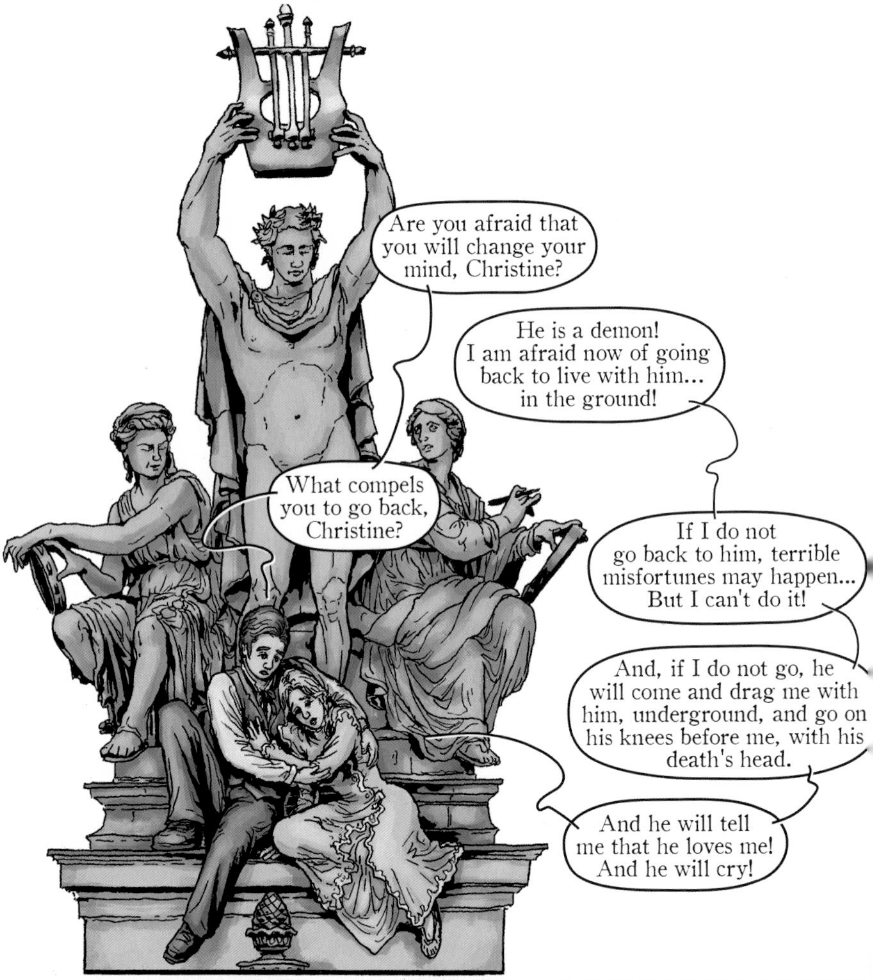
Are you afraid that you will change your mind, Christine?
He is a demon! I am afraid now of going back to live with him... in the ground!
What compels you to go back, Christine?
If I do not go back to him, terrible misfortunes may happen... But I can't do it!
And, if I do not go, he will come and drag me with him, underground, and go on his knees before me, with his death's head.
And he will tell me that he loves me! And he will cry!

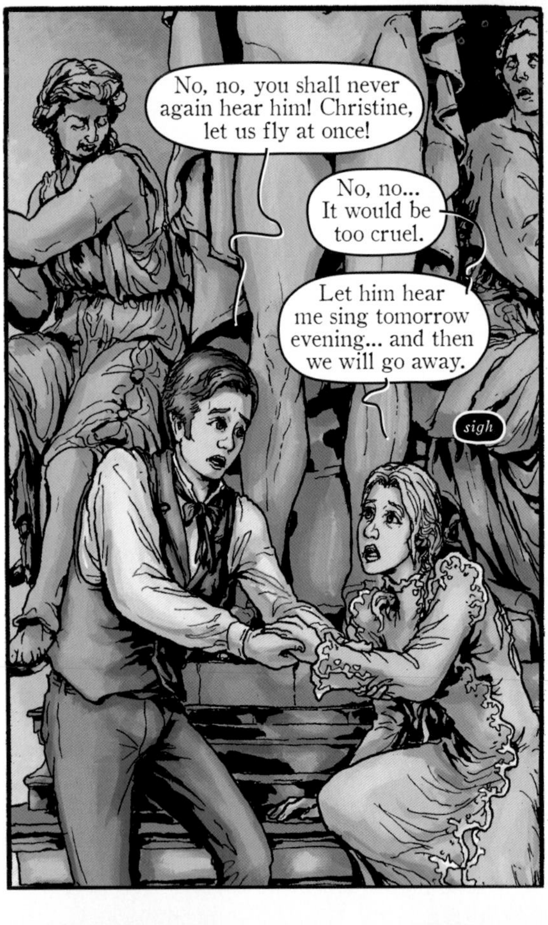
No, no, you shall never again hear him! Christine, let us fly at once!
No, no... It would be too cruel.
Let him hear me sing tomorrow evening... and then we will go away.
sigh

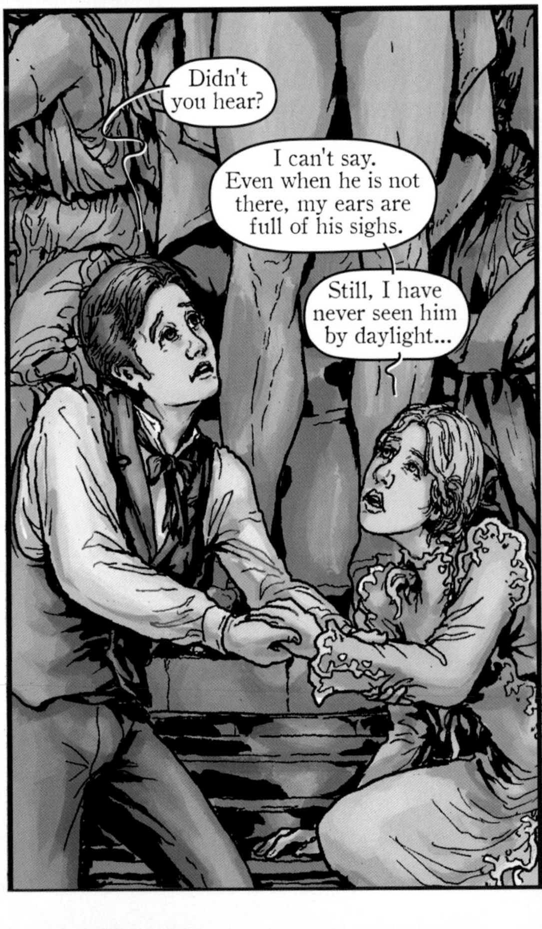
Didn't you hear?
I can't say. Even when he is not there, my ears are full of his sighs.
Still, I have never seen him by daylight...

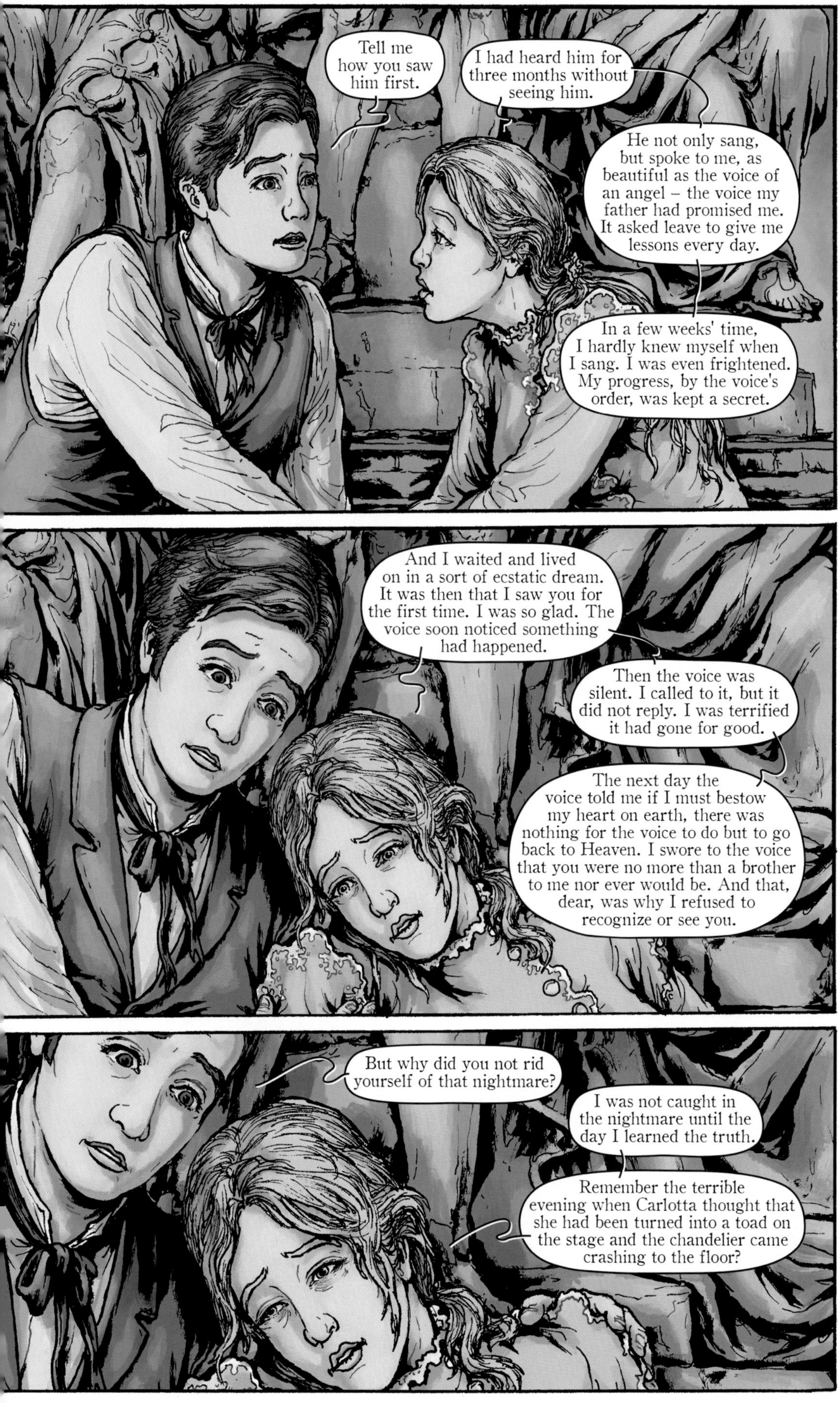
Tell me how you saw him first.
I had heard him for three months without seeing him.
He not only sang, but spoke to me, as beautiful as the voice of an angel – the voice my father had promised me. It asked leave to give me lessons every day.
In a few weeks' time, I hardly knew myself when I sang. I was even frightened. My progress, by the voice's order, was kept a secret.
And I waited and lived on in a sort of ecstatic dream. It was then that I saw you for the first time. I was so glad. The voice soon noticed something had happened.
Then the voice was silent. I called to it, but it did not reply. I was terrified it had gone for good.
The next day the voice told me if I must bestow my heart on earth, there was nothing for the voice to do but to go back to Heaven. I swore to the voice that you were no more than a brother to me nor ever would be. And that, dear, was why I refused to recognize or see you.
But why did you not rid yourself of that nightmare?
I was not caught in the nightmare until the day I learned the truth.
Remember the terrible evening when Carlotta thought that she had been turned into a toad on the stage and the chandelier came crashing to the floor?

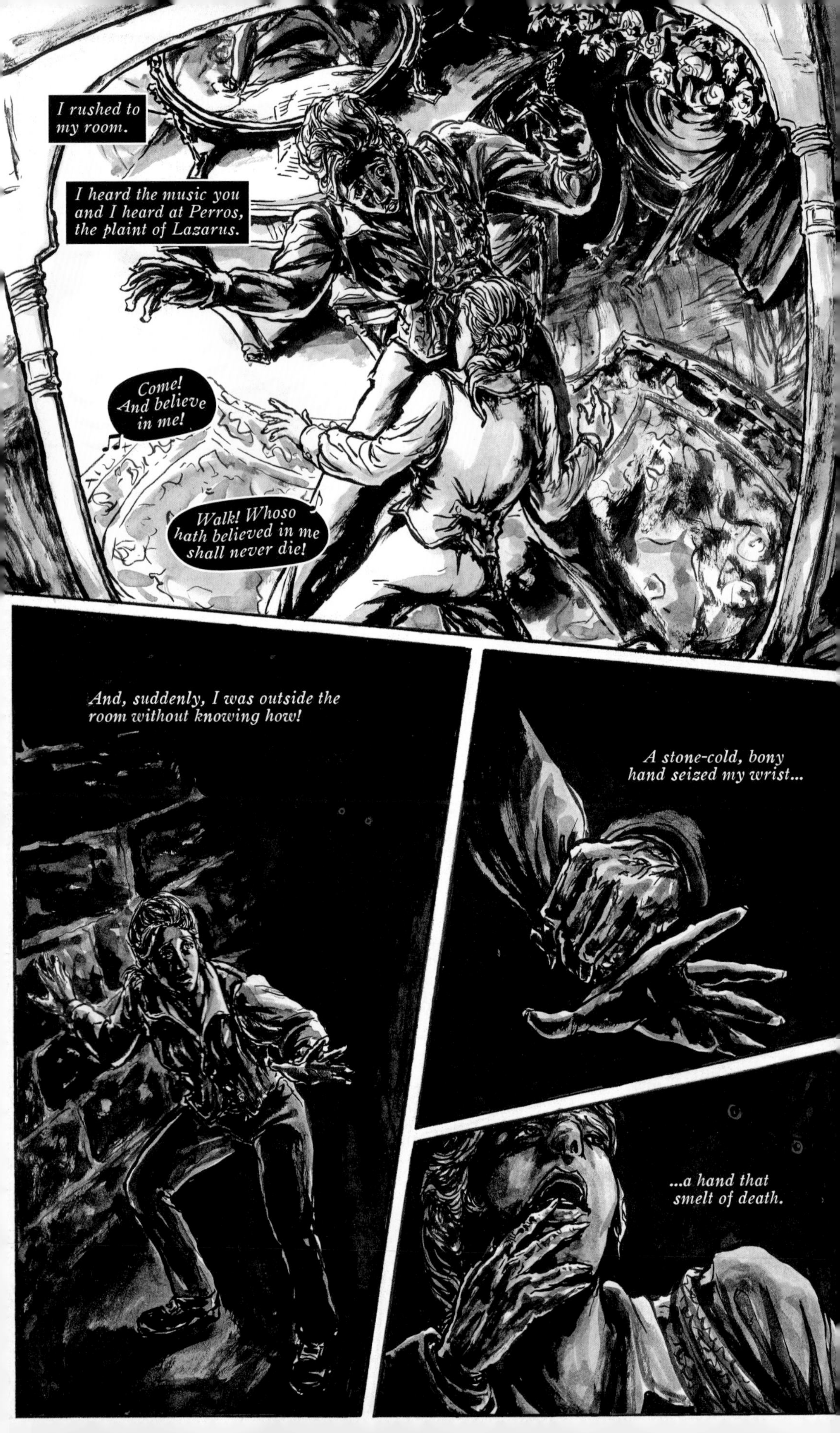
I rushed to my room.
I heard the music you and I heard at Perros, the plaint of Lazarus.
Come! And believe in me!
Walk! Whoso hath believed in me shall never die!
And, suddenly, I was outside the room without knowing how!
A stone-cold, bony hand seized my wrist...
...a hand that smelt of death.

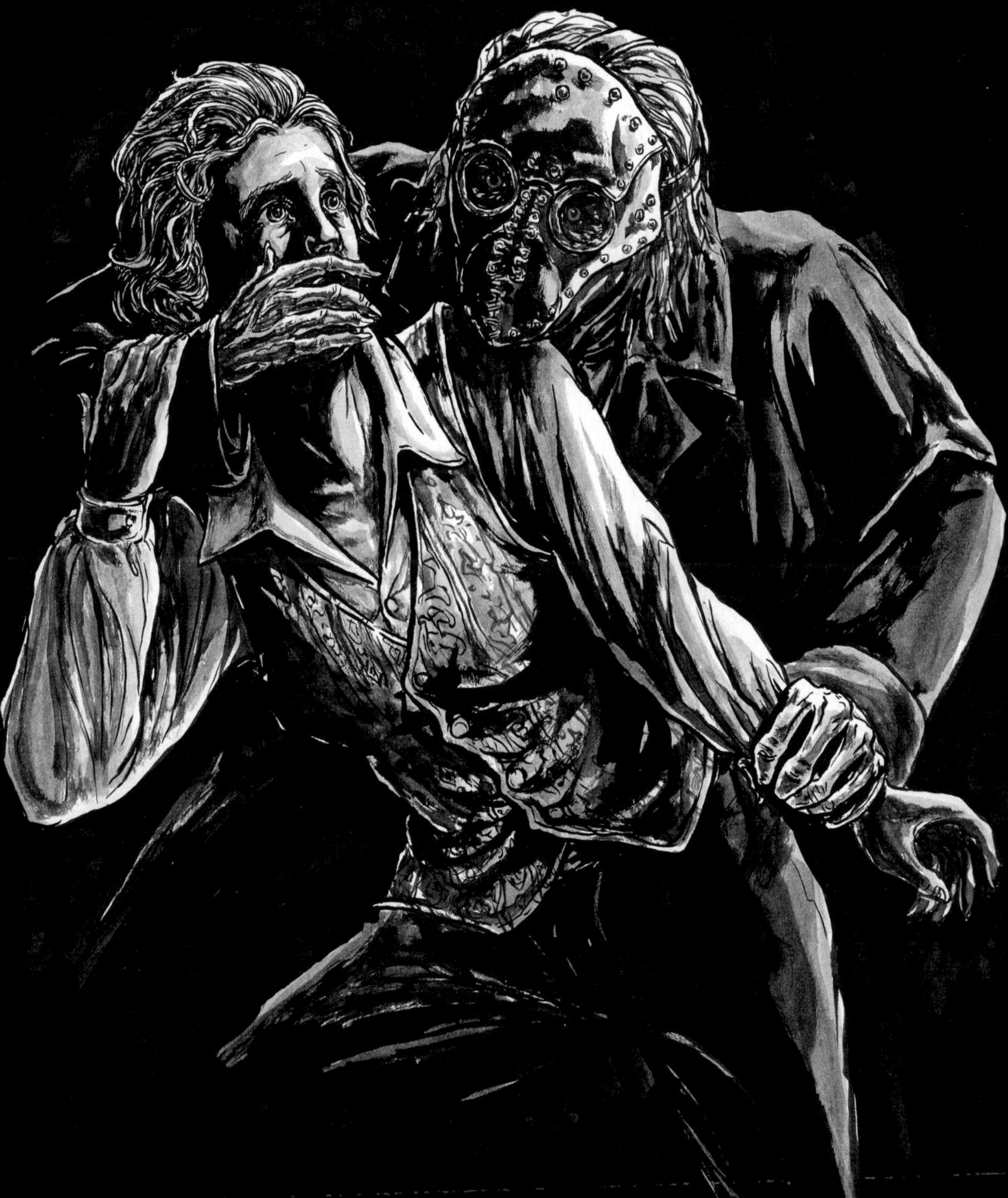

Then I fainted away.

Chapter Four

*When I opened my eyes, we were still
surrounded by darkness.*

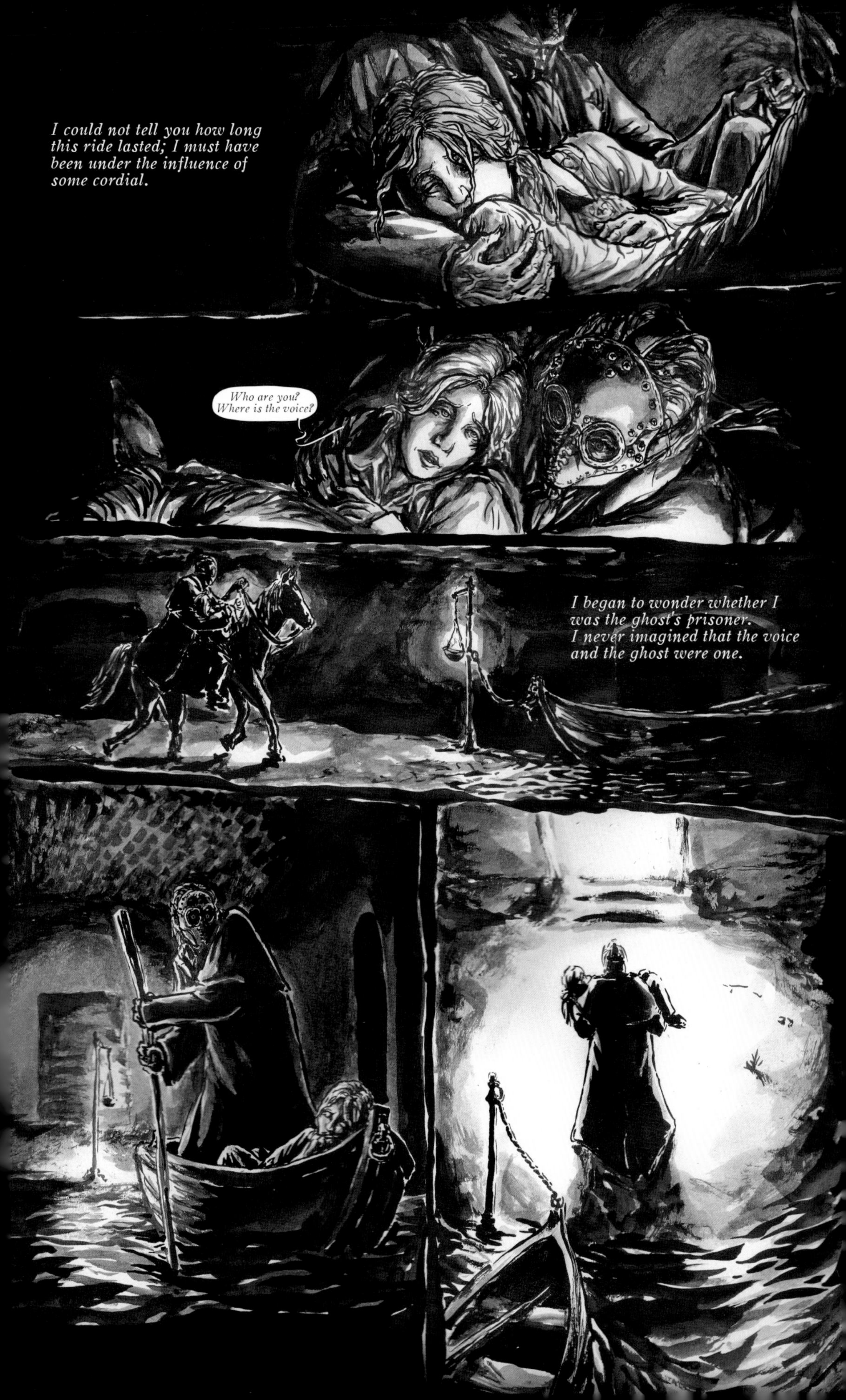
I could not tell you how long this ride lasted; I must have been under the influence of some cordial.
Who are you? Where is the voice?
I began to wonder whether I was the ghost's prisoner. I never imagined that the voice and the ghost were one.

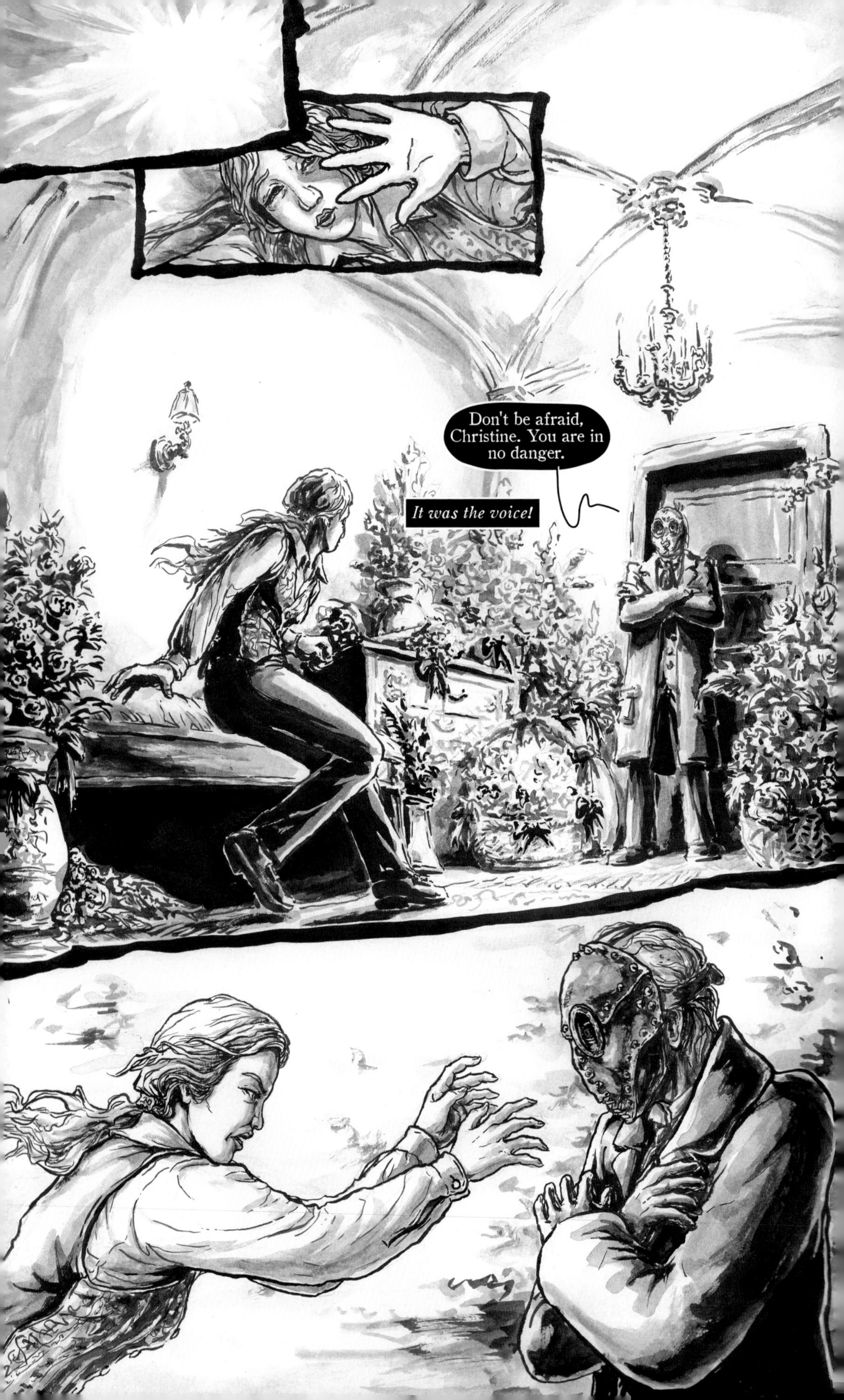
Don't be afraid, Christine. You are in no danger.
It was the voice!

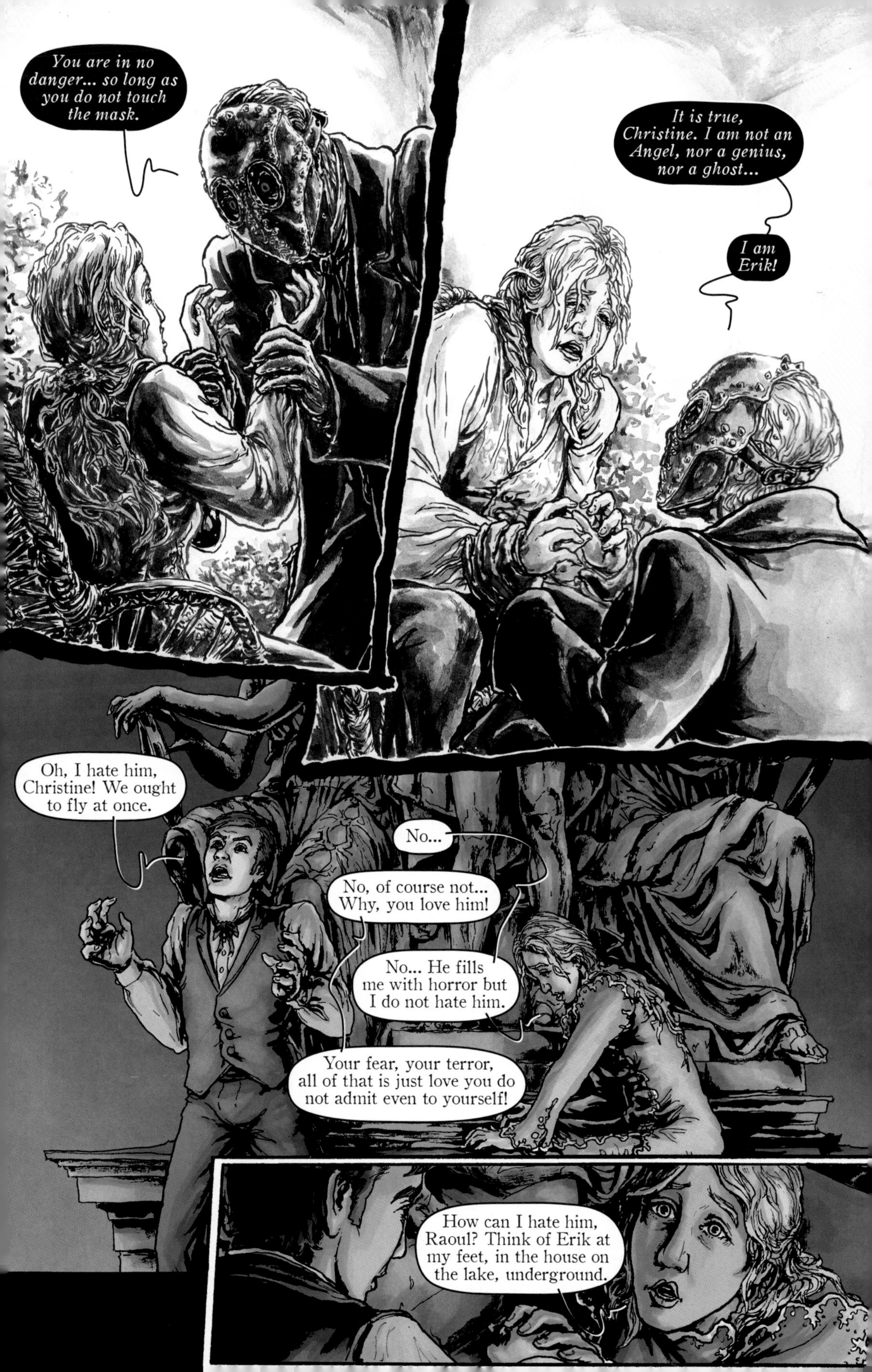
You are in no danger... so long as you do not touch the mask.
It is true, Christine. I am not an Angel, nor a genius, nor a ghost...
I am Erik!
Oh, I hate him, Christine! We ought to fly at once.
No...
No, of course not... Why, you love him!
No... He fills me with horror but I do not hate him.
Your fear, your terror, all of that is just love you do not admit even to yourself!
How can I hate him, Raoul? Think of Erik at my feet, in the house on the lake, underground.

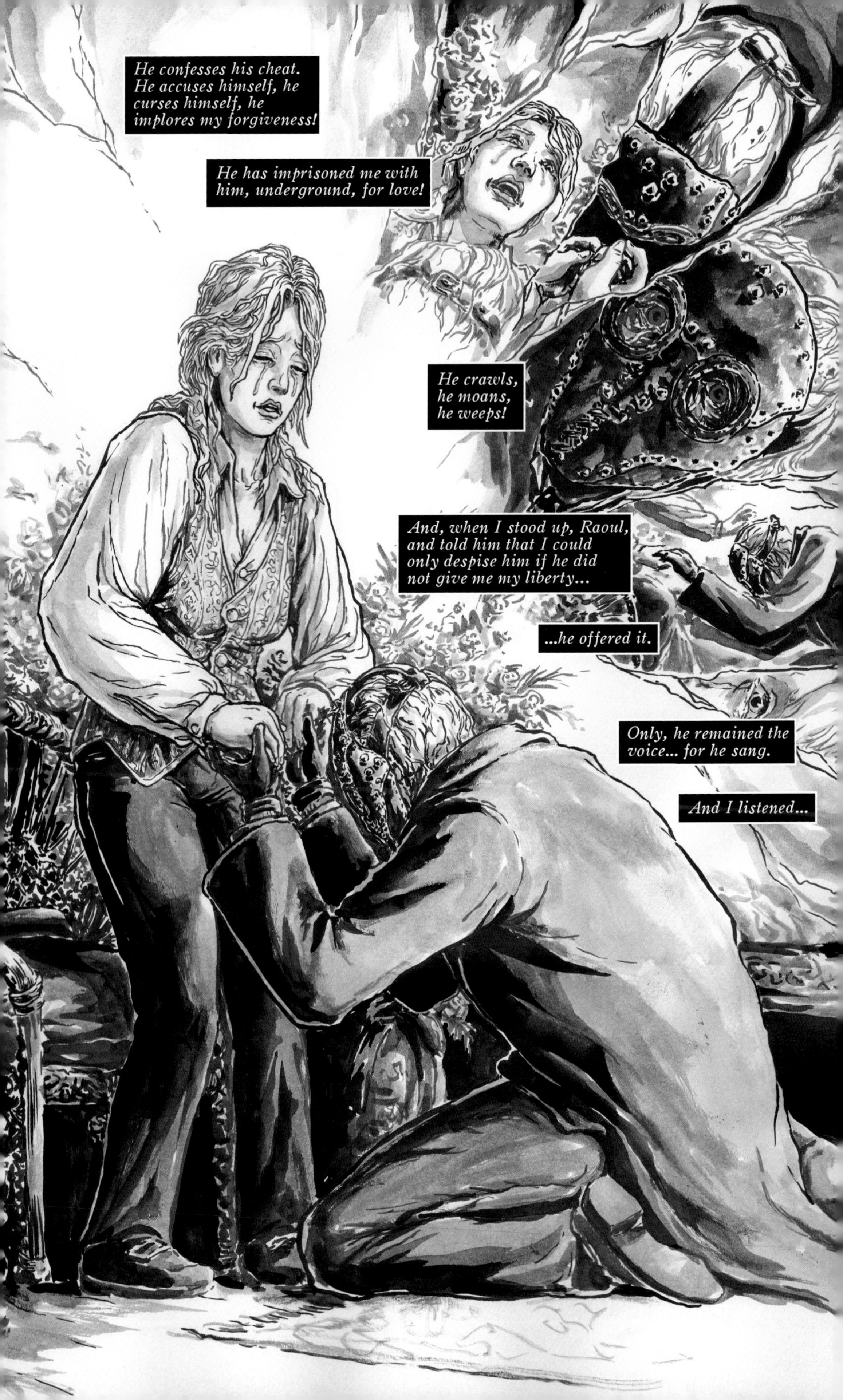

He confesses his cheat. He accuses himself, he curses himself, he implores my forgiveness!
He has imprisoned me with him, underground, for love!
He crawls, he moans, he weeps!
And, when I stood up, Raoul, and told him that I could only despise him if he did not give me my liberty...
...he offered it.
Only, he remained the voice... for he sang.
And I listened...

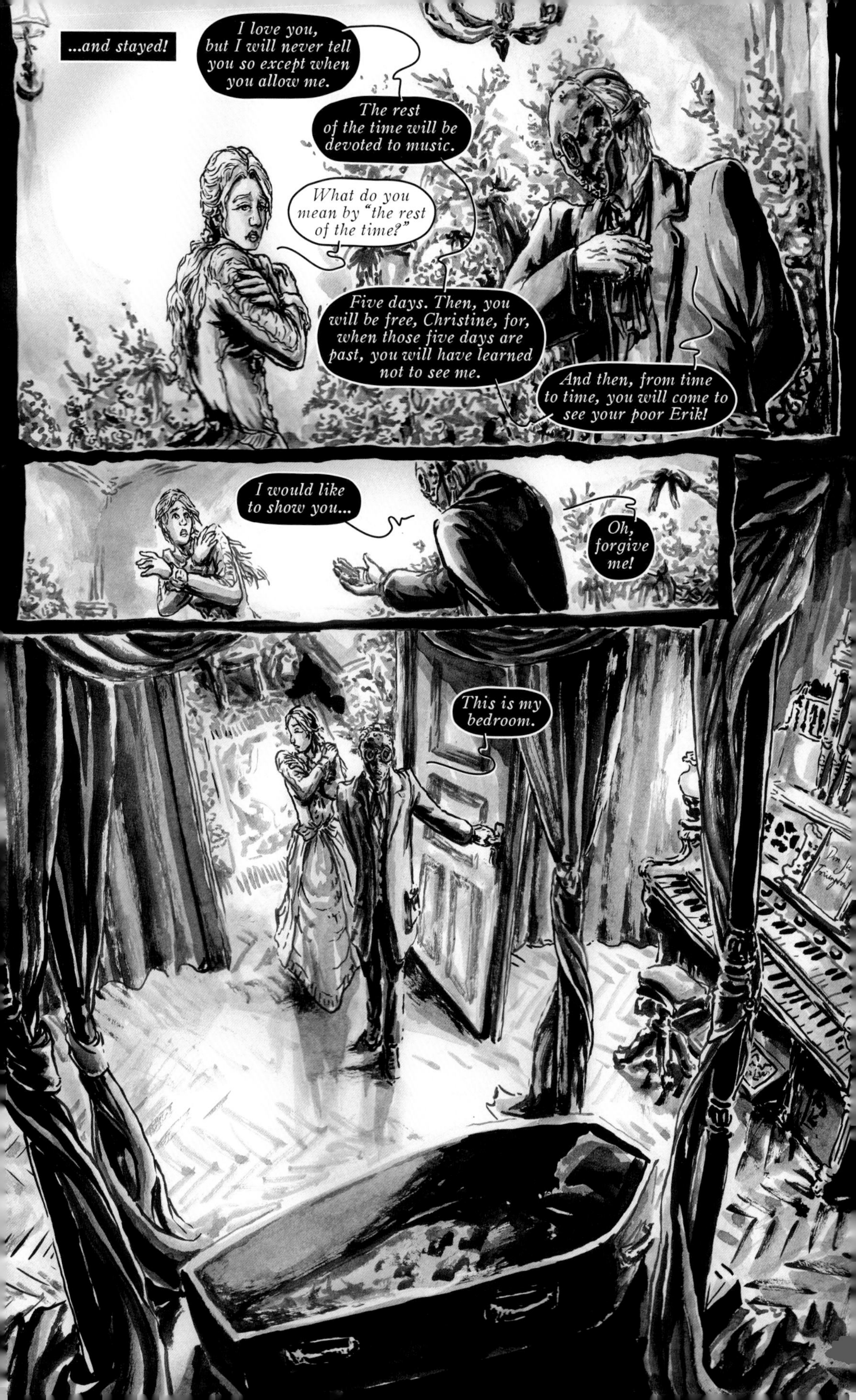
...and stayed!
I love you, but I will never tell you so except when you allow me.
The rest of the time will be devoted to music.
What do you mean by "the rest of the time?"
Five days. Then, you will be free, Christine, for, when those five days are past, you will have learned not to see me.
And then, from time to time, you will come to see your poor Erik!
I would like to show you...
Oh, forgive me!
This is my bedroom.

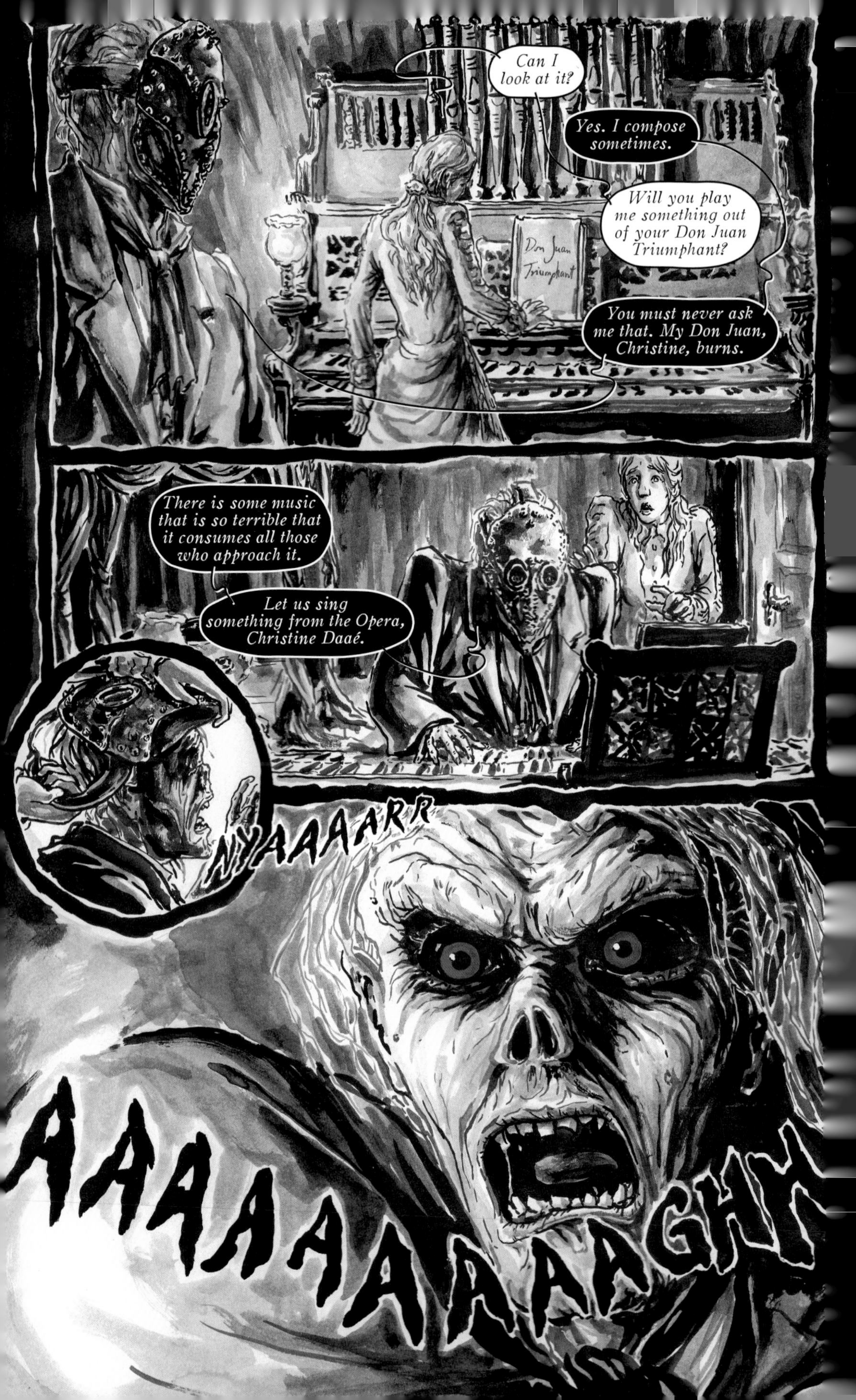
Can I look at it?
Yes. I compose sometimes.
Will you play me something out of your Don Juan Triumphant?
Don Juan Triumphant
You must never ask me that. My Don Juan, Christine, burns.
There is some music that is so terrible that it consumes all those who approach it.
Let us sing something from the Opera, Christine Daaé.
NYAAAAARR
AAAAAAAAAGHH

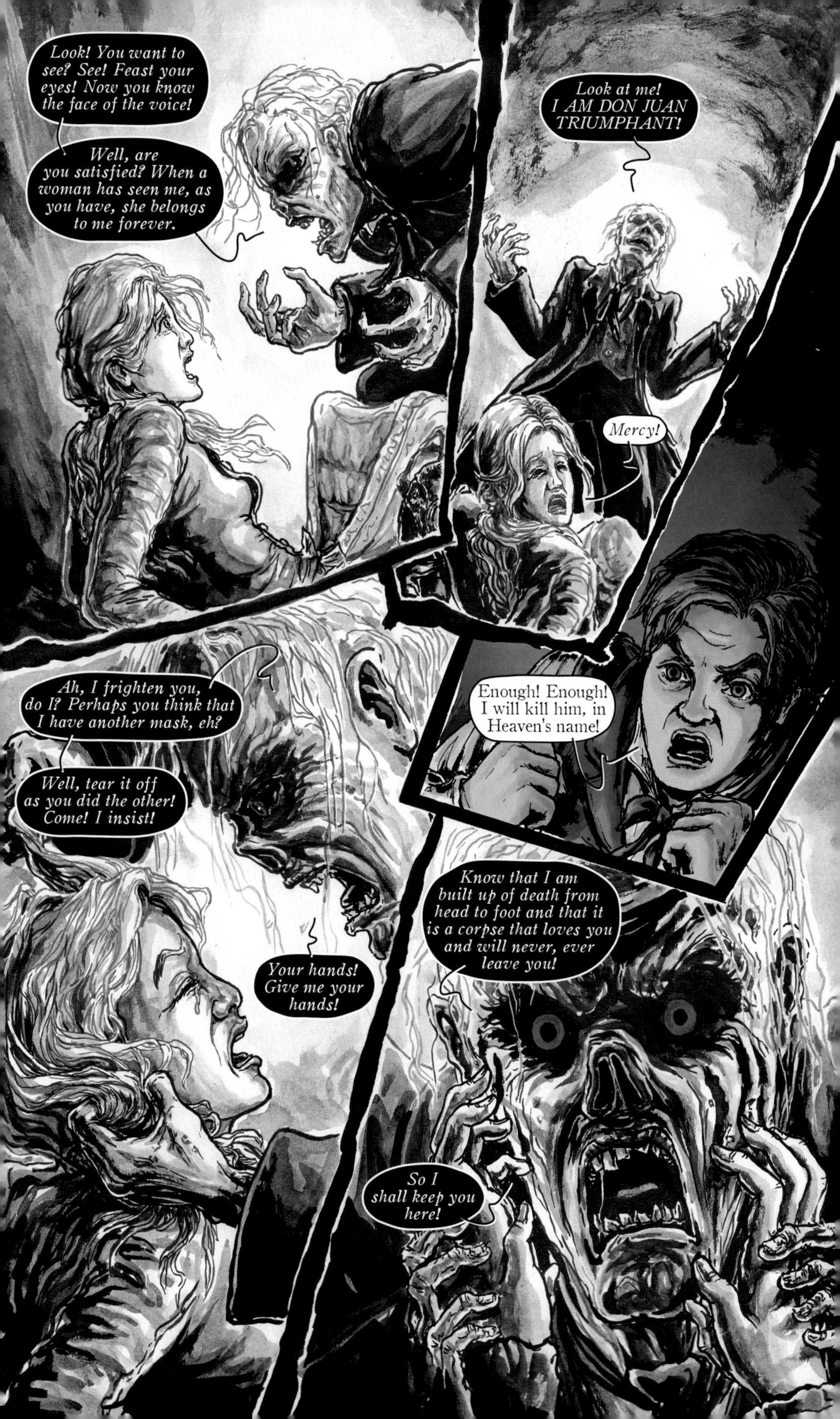

Look! You want to see? See! Feast your eyes! Now you know the face of the voice!
Well, are you satisfied? When a woman has seen me, as you have, she belongs to me forever.
Look at me! I AM DON JUAN TRIUMPHANT!
Mercy!
Ah, I frighten you, do I? Perhaps you think that I have another mask, eh?
Well, tear it off as you did the other! Come! I insist!
Your hands! Give me your hands!
Enough! Enough! I will kill him, in Heaven's name!
Know that I am built up of death from head to foot and that it is a corpse that loves you and will never, ever leave you!
So I shall keep you here!

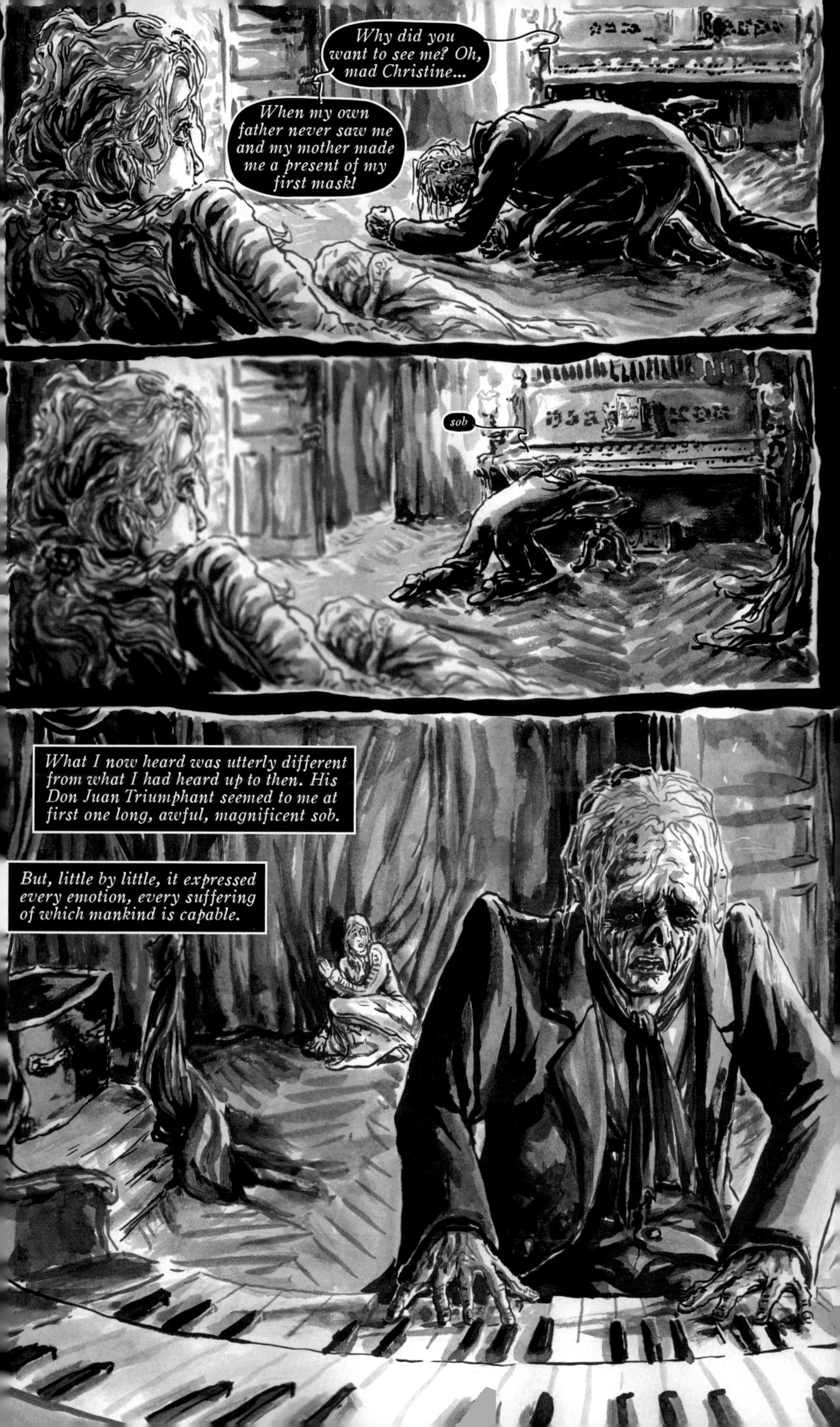
Why did you want to see me? Oh, mad Christine...
When my own father never saw me and my mother made me a present of my first mask!
sob
What I now heard was utterly different from what I had heard up to then. His Don Juan Triumphant seemed to me at first one long, awful, magnificent sob.
But, little by little, it expressed every emotion, every suffering of which mankind is capable.

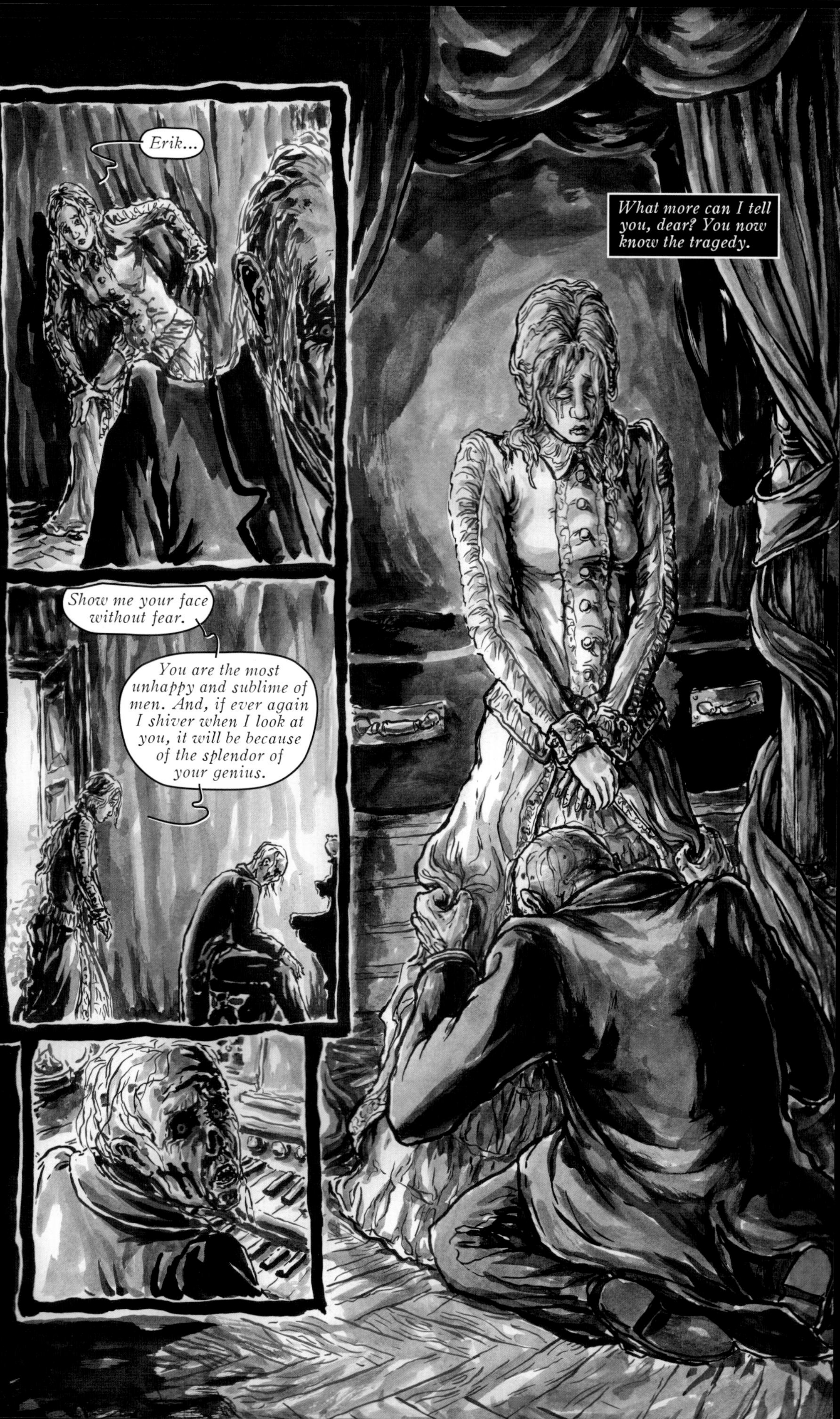
Erik...
Show me your face without fear.
You are the most unhappy and sublime of men. And, if ever again I shiver when I look at you, it will be because of the splendor of your genius.
What more can I tell you, dear? You now know the tragedy.

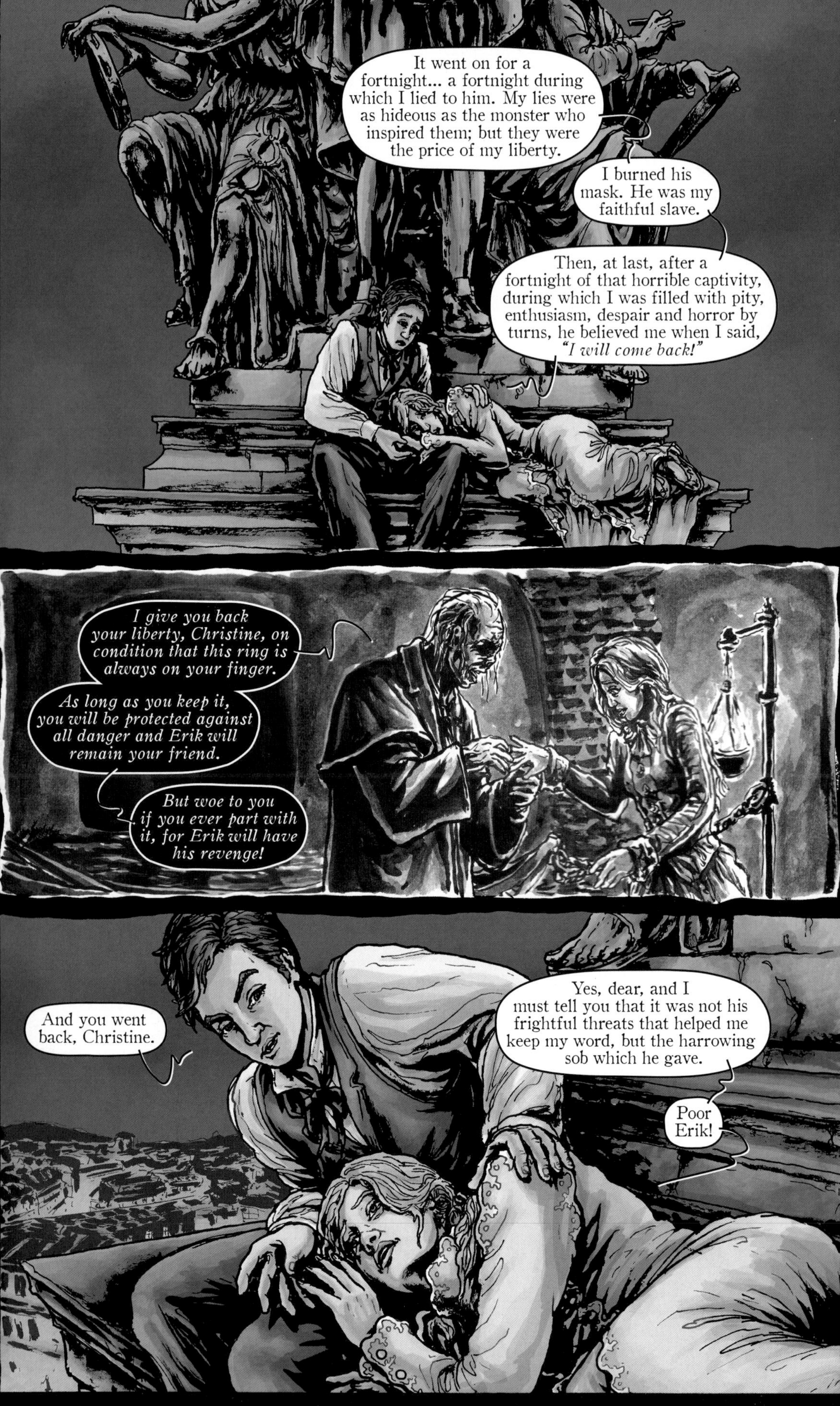
It went on for a fortnight... a fortnight during which I lied to him. My lies were as hideous as the monster who inspired them; but they were the price of my liberty.
I burned his mask. He was my faithful slave.
Then, at last, after a fortnight of that horrible captivity, during which I was filled with pity, enthusiasm, despair and horror by turns, he believed me when I said, *"I will come back!"*
I give you back your liberty, Christine, on condition that this ring is always on your finger.
As long as you keep it, you will be protected against all danger and Erik will remain your friend.
But woe to you if you ever part with it, for Erik will have his revenge!
And you went back, Christine.
Yes, dear, and I must tell you that it was not his frightful threats that helped me keep my word, but the harrowing sob which he gave.
Poor Erik!

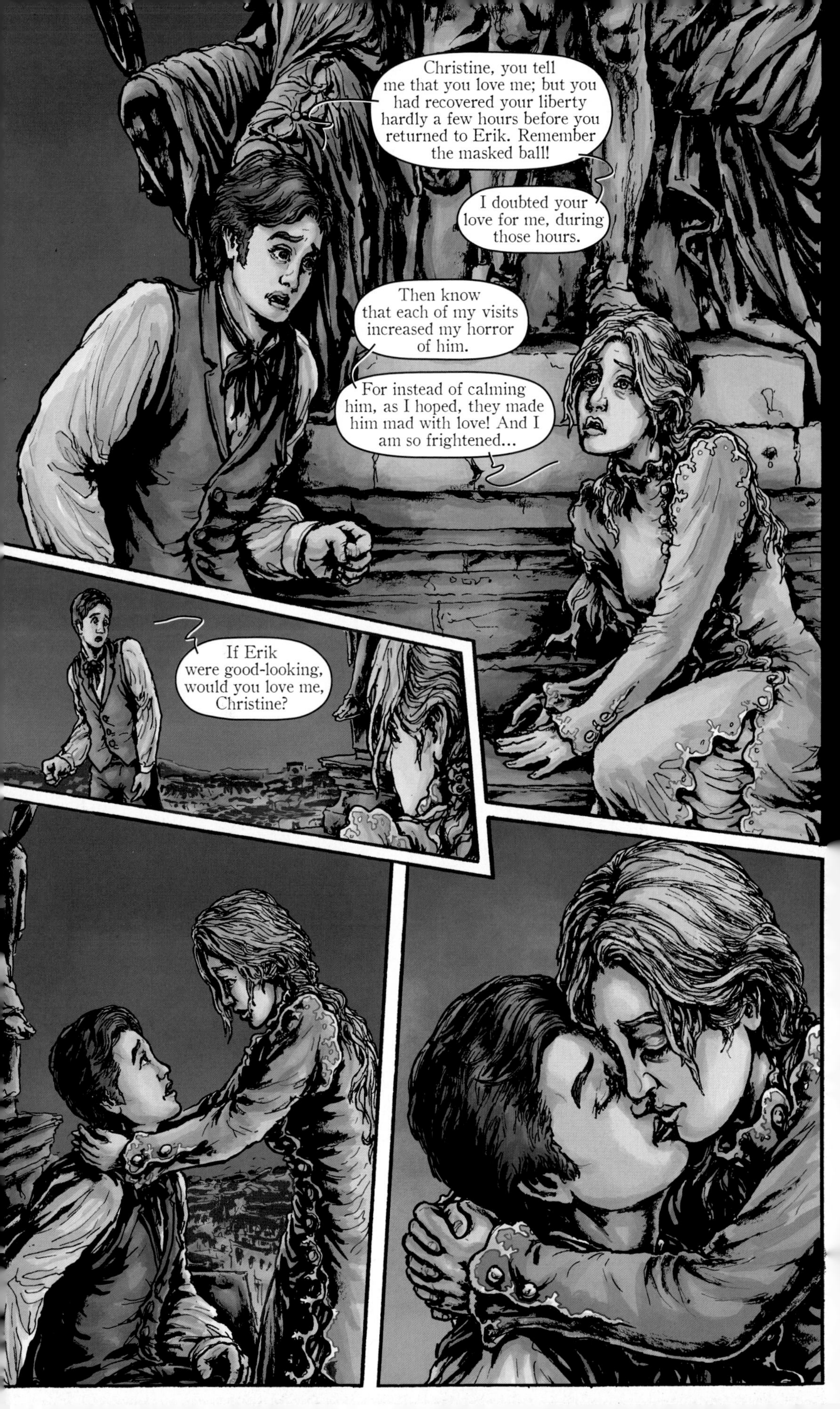
Christine, you tell me that you love me; but you had recovered your liberty hardly a few hours before you returned to Erik. Remember the masked ball!
I doubted your love for me, during those hours.
Then know that each of my visits increased my horror of him.
For instead of calming him, as I hoped, they made him mad with love! And I am so frightened...
If Erik were good-looking, would you love me, Christine?

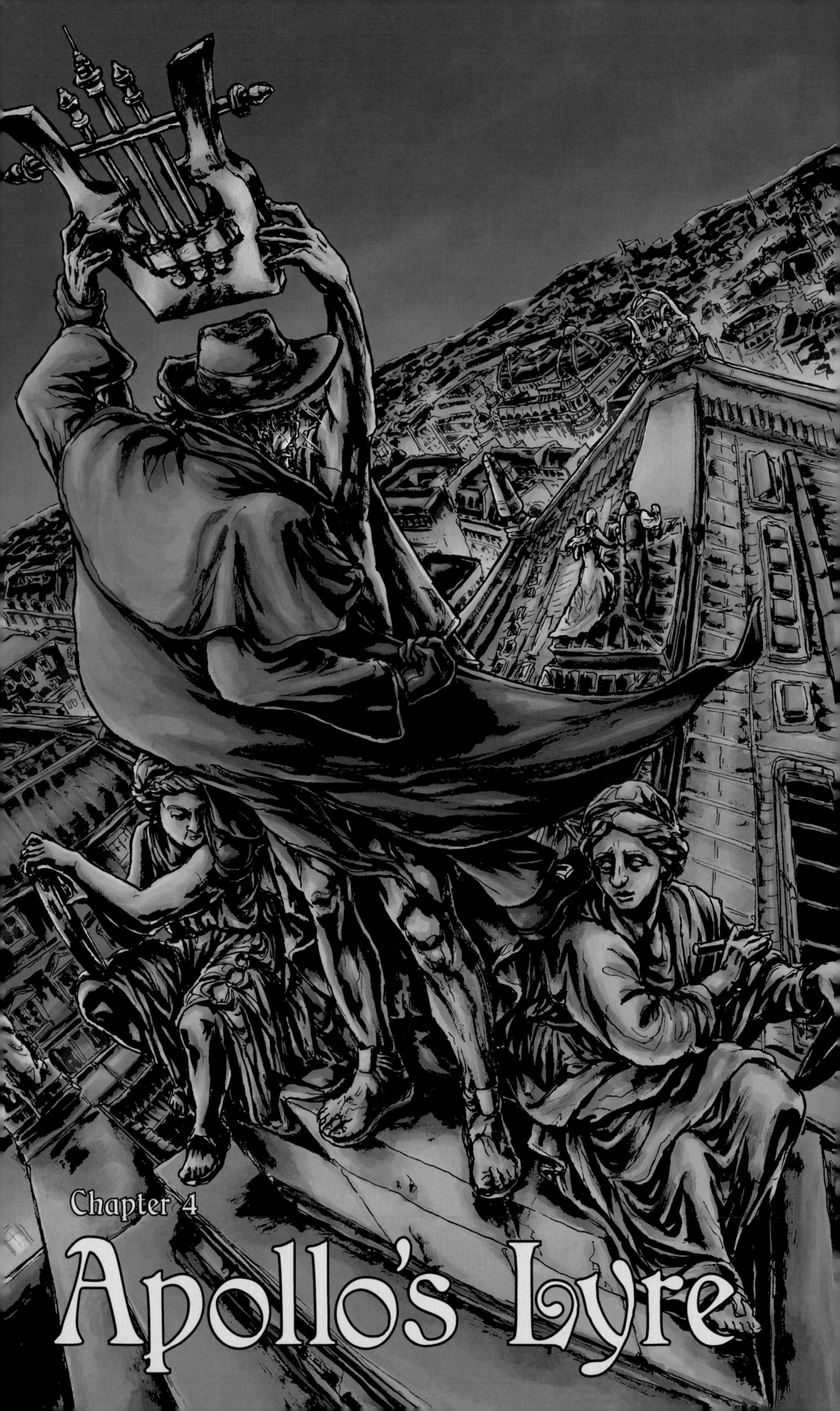

Chapter 4

Apollo's Lyre

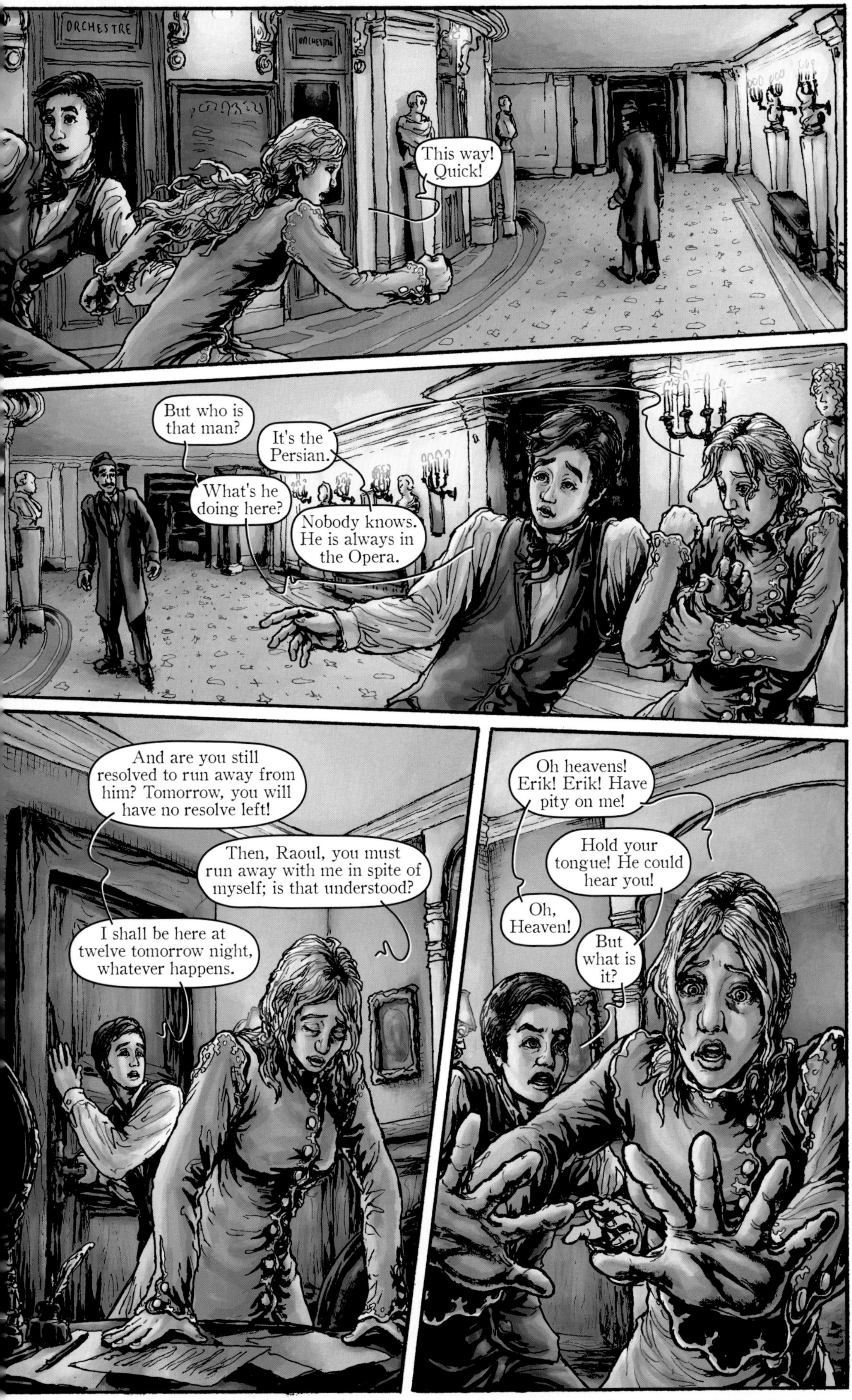
ORCHESTRE
ORCHESTRE
This way! Quick!
But who is that man?
It's the Persian.
What's he doing here?
Nobody knows. He is always in the Opera.
And are you still resolved to run away from him? Tomorrow, you will have no resolve left!
Then, Raoul, you must run away with me in spite of myself; is that understood?
I shall be here at twelve tomorrow night, whatever happens.
Oh heavens! Erik! Erik! Have pity on me!
Hold your tongue! He could hear you!
Oh, Heaven!
But what is it?

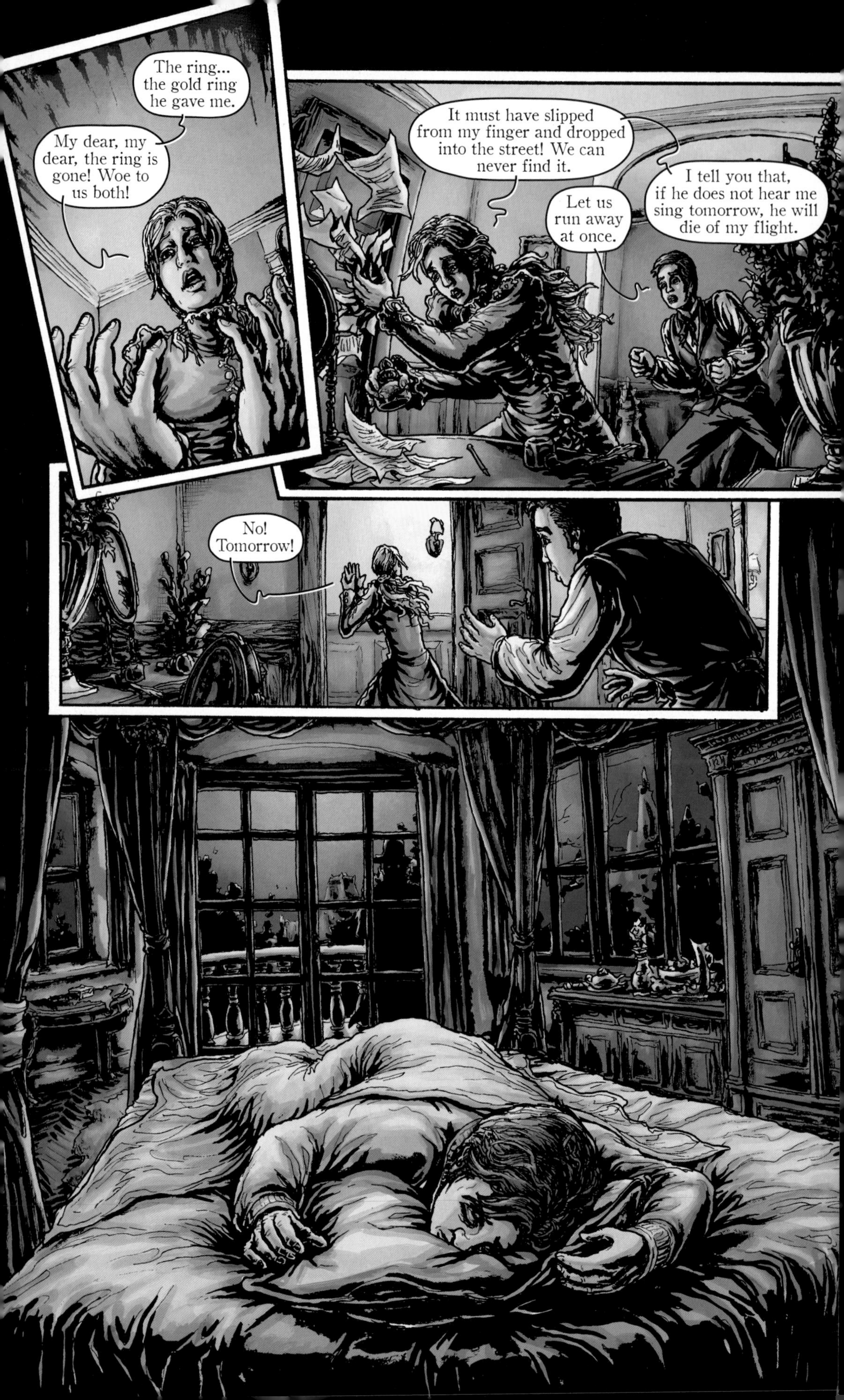
The ring... the gold ring he gave me.
My dear, my dear, the ring is gone! Woe to us both!
It must have slipped from my finger and dropped into the street! We can never find it.
Let us run away at once.
I tell you that, if he does not hear me sing tomorrow, he will die of my flight.
No! Tomorrow!

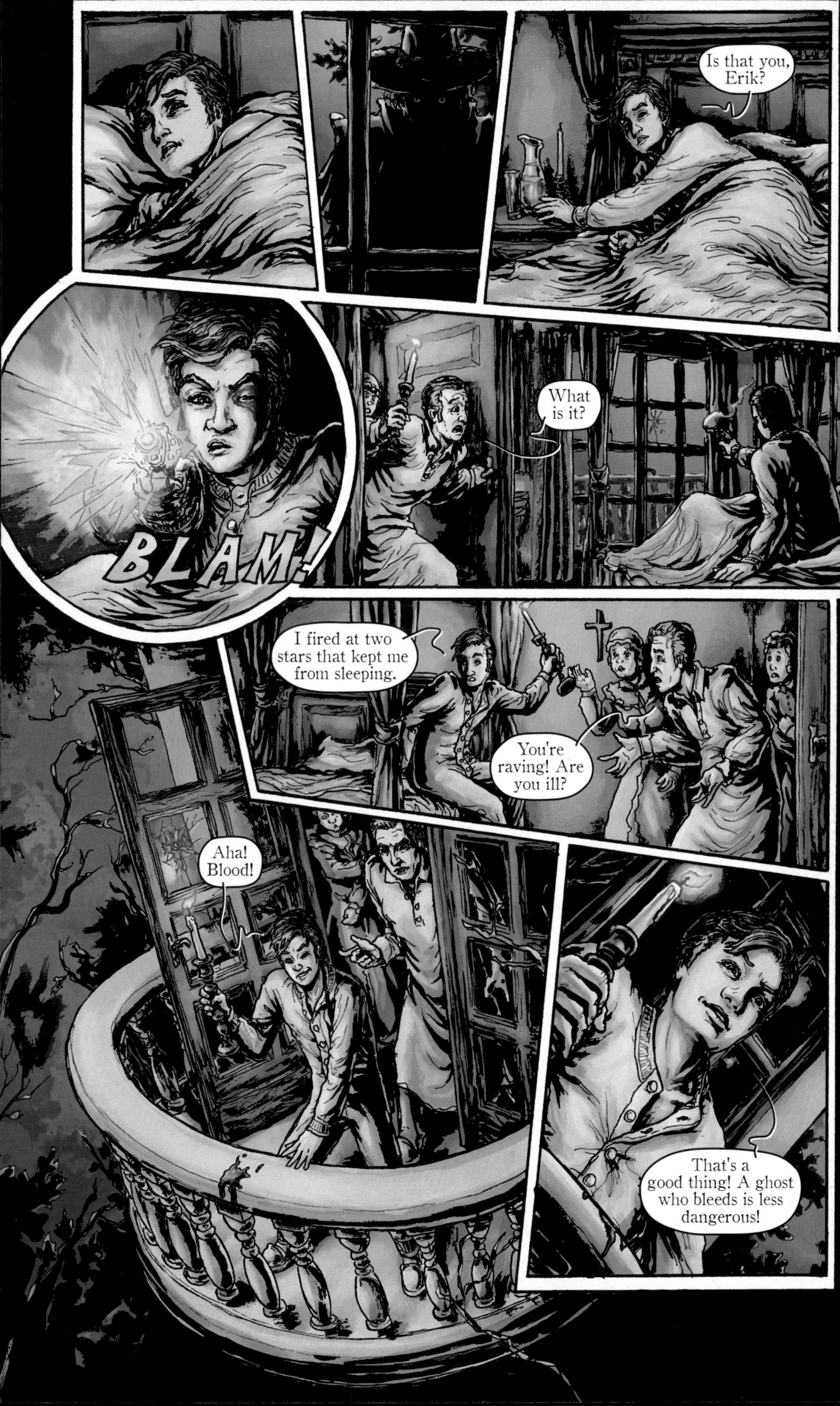
Is that you, Erik?
BLAM!
What is it?
I fired at two stars that kept me from sleeping.
You're raving! Are you ill?
Aha! Blood!
That's a good thing! A ghost who bleeds is less dangerous!

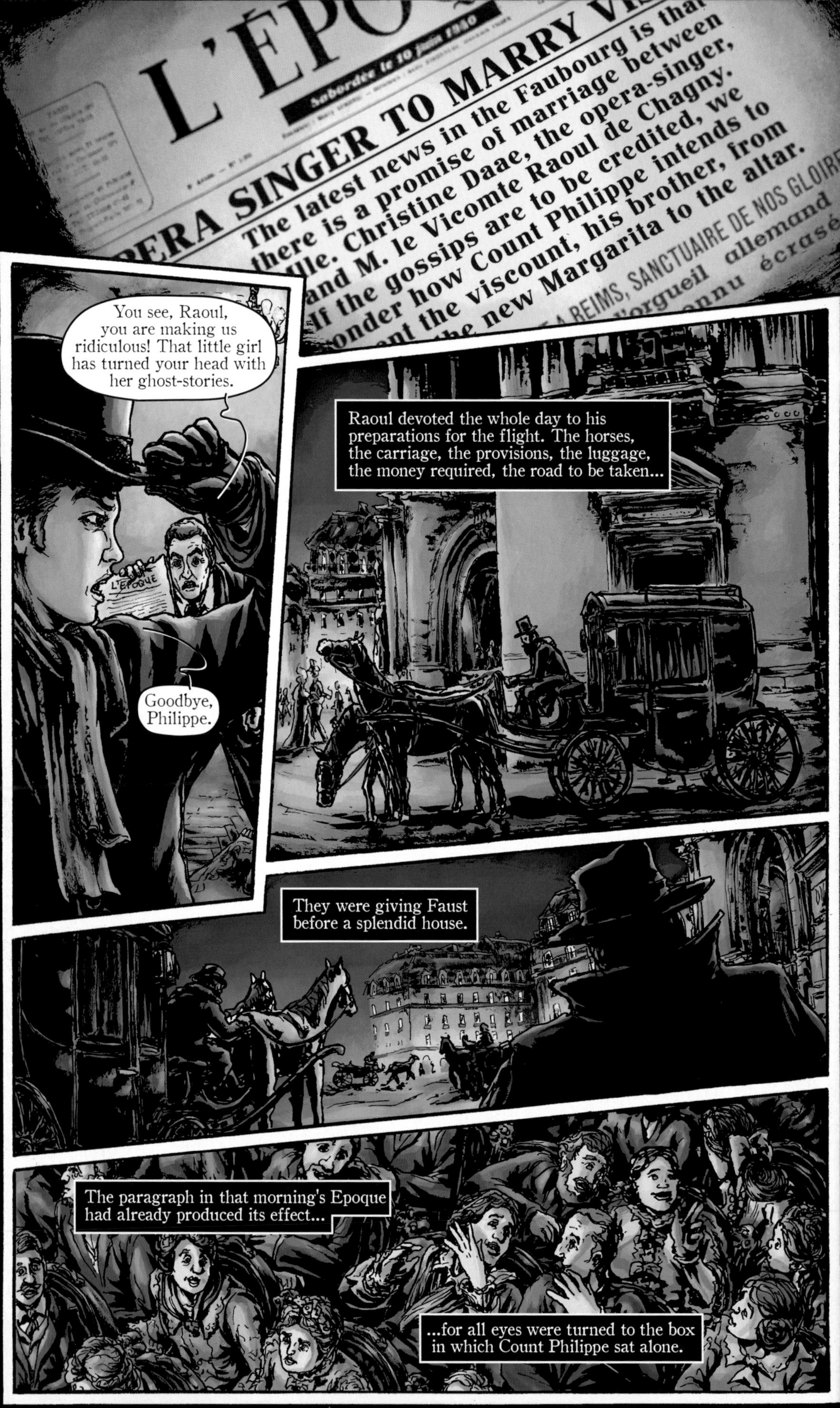
L'ÉPO
PERA SINGER TO MARRY VI
The latest news in the Faubourg is that
there is a promise of marriage between
Mlle. Christine Daae, the opera-singer,
and M. le Vicomte Raoul de Chagny.
If the gossips are to be credited, we
wonder how Count Philippe intends to
the viscount, his brother, from
the new Margarita to the altar.
À REIMS, SANCTUAIRE DE NOS GLOIRES
You see, Raoul, you are making us ridiculous! That little girl has turned your head with her ghost-stories.
L'EPOQUE
Goodbye, Philippe.
Raoul devoted the whole day to his preparations for the flight. The horses, the carriage, the provisions, the luggage, the money required, the road to be taken...
They were giving Faust before a splendid house.
The paragraph in that morning's Epoque had already produced its effect...
...for all eyes were turned to the box in which Count Philippe sat alone.

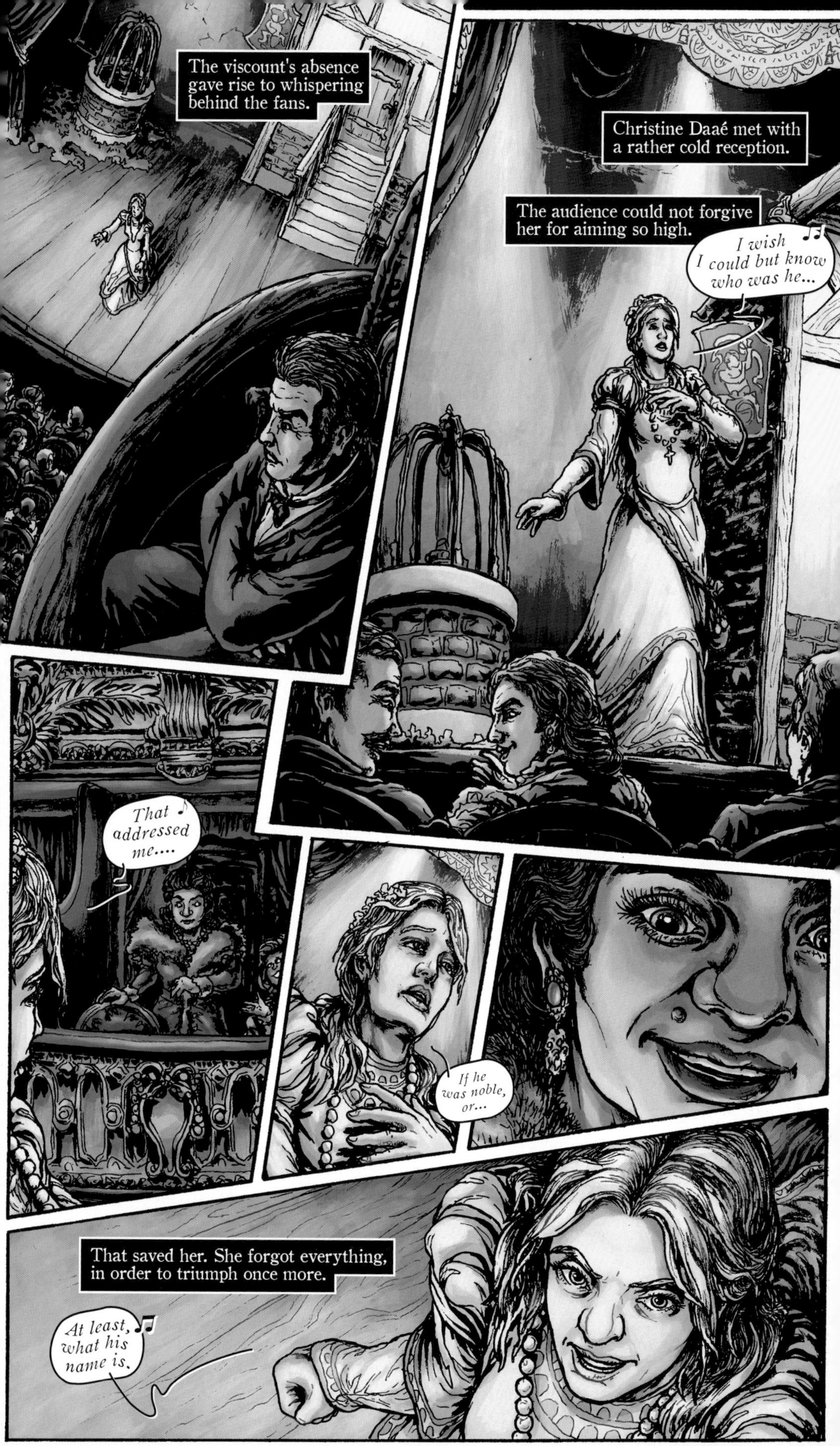
The viscount's absence gave rise to whispering behind the fans.
Christine Daaé met with a rather cold reception.
The audience could not forgive her for aiming so high.
I wish I could but know who was he...
That addressed me....
If he was noble, or...
That saved her. She forgot everything, in order to triumph once more.
At least, what his name is.

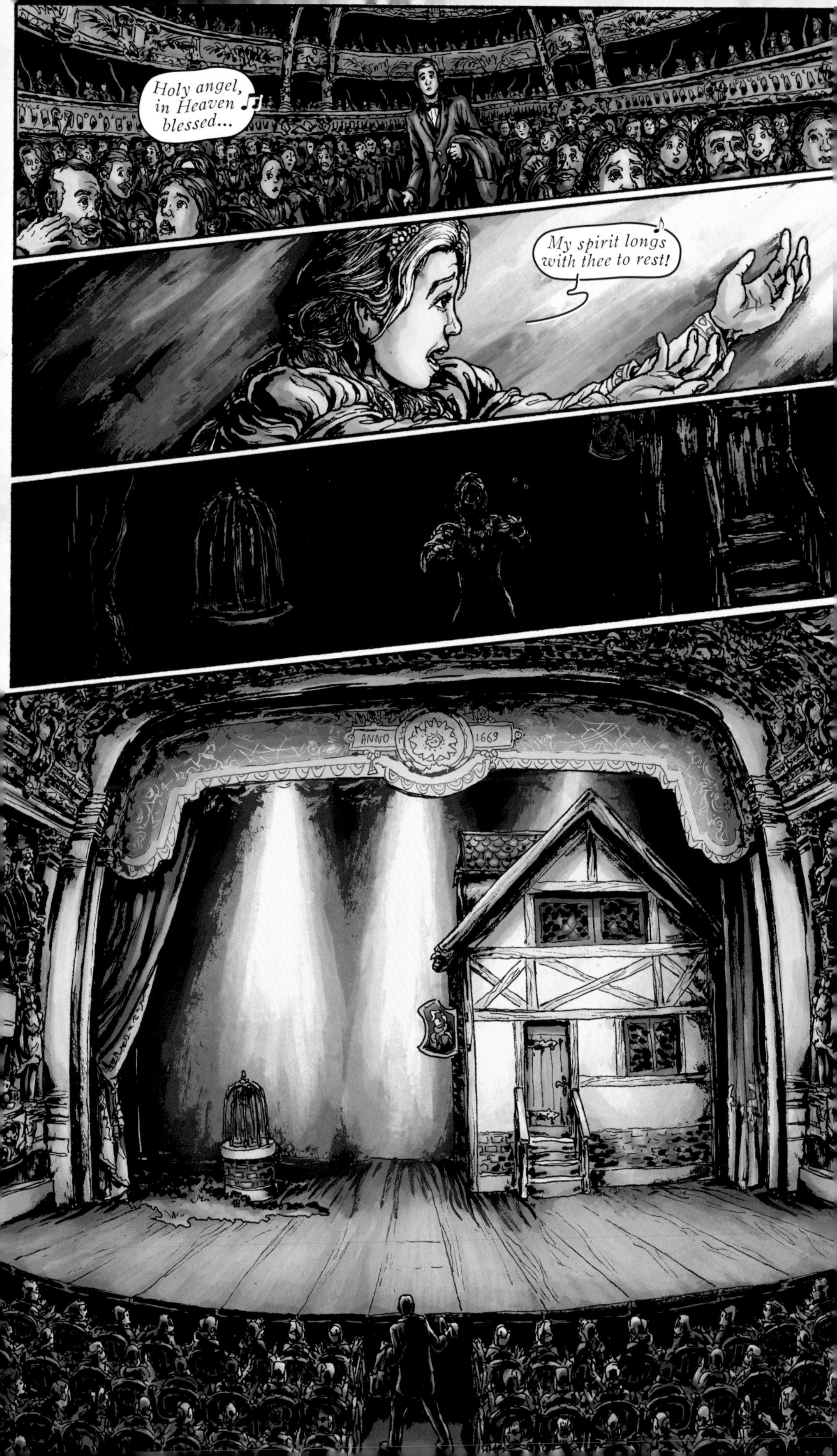
Holy angel, in Heaven blessed...
My spirit longs with thee to rest!
ANNO 1669

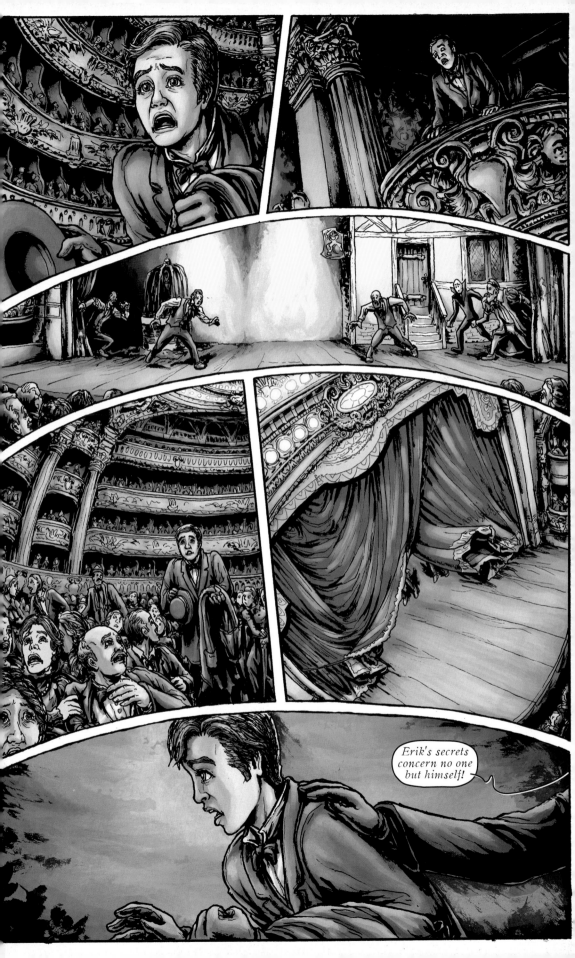

Erik's secrets concern no one but himself!

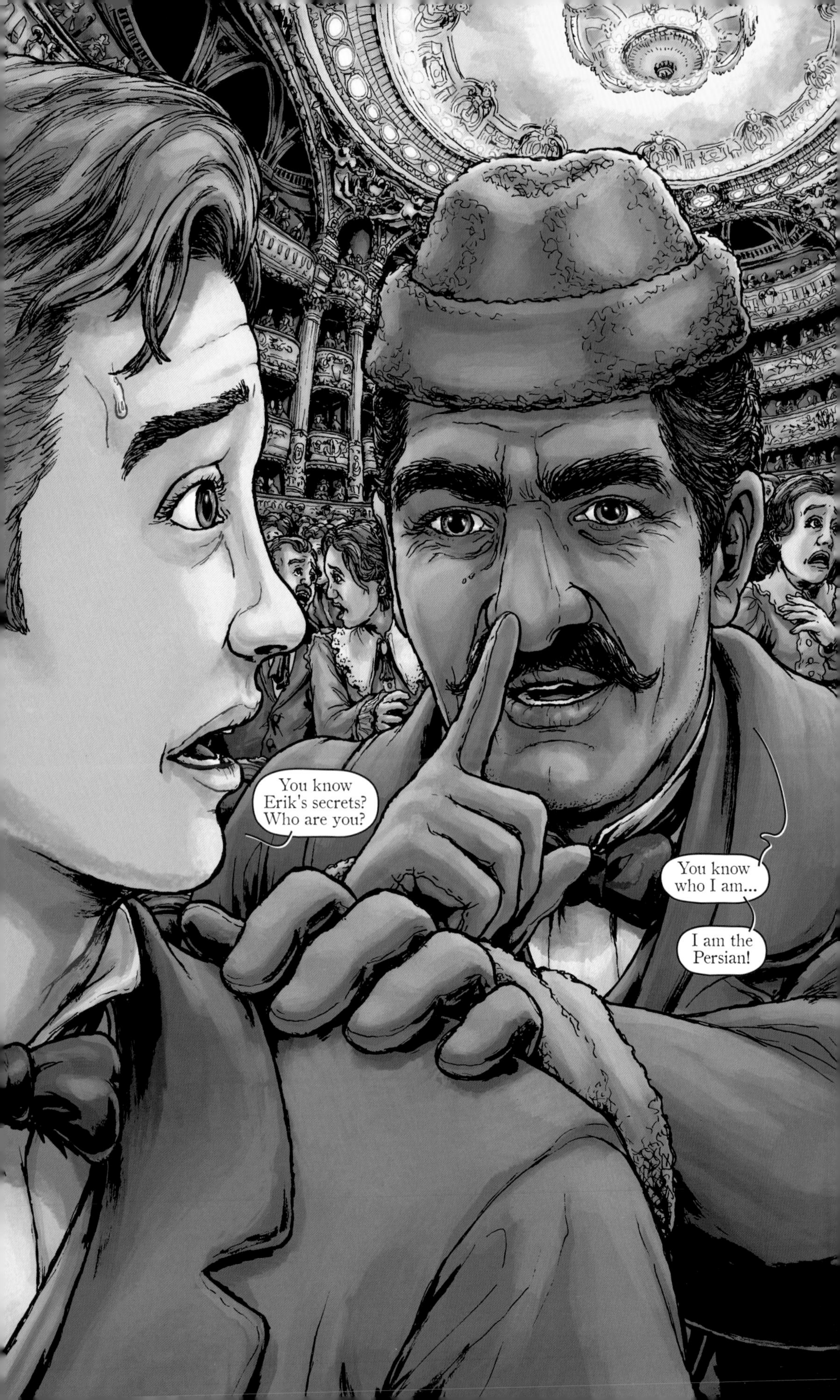
You know Erik's secrets? Who are you?
You know who I am...
I am the Persian!

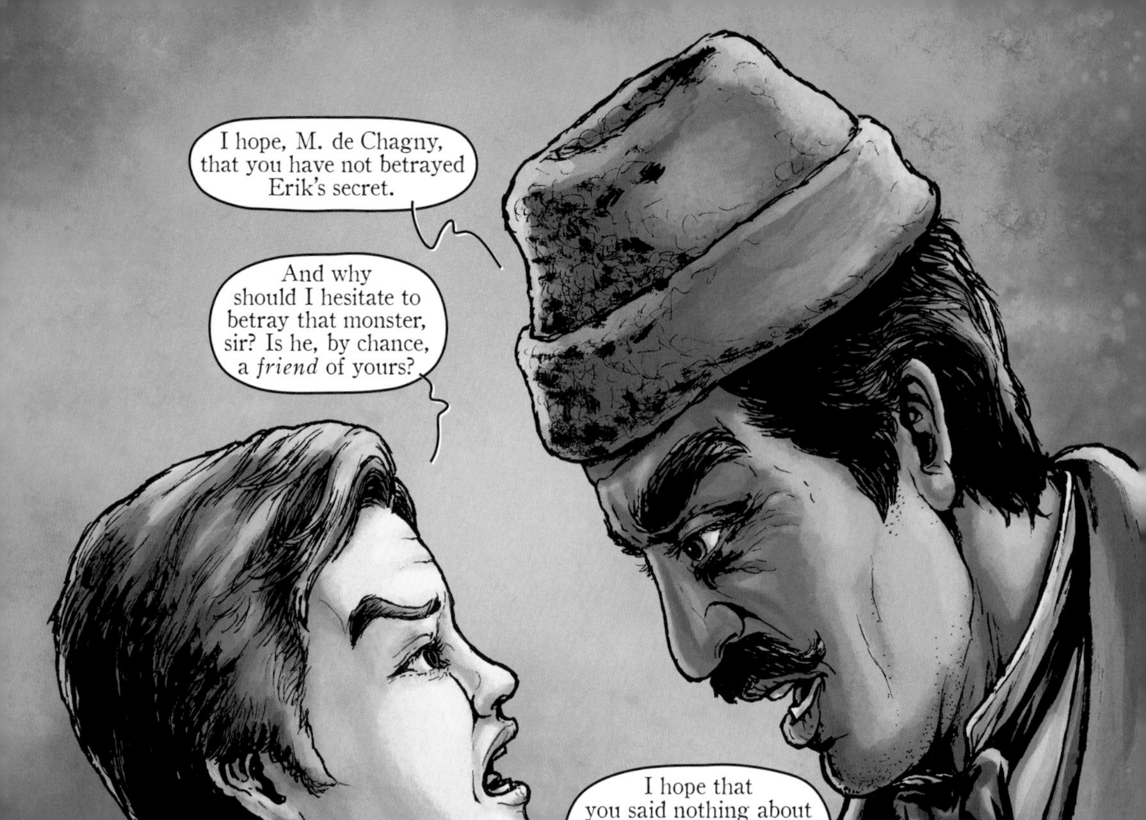
I hope, M. de Chagny, that you have not betrayed Erik's secret.
And why should I hesitate to betray that monster, sir? Is he, by chance, a *friend* of yours?
I hope that you said nothing about Erik, sir, because Erik's secret is also *Christine Daaé's*.

Chapter 5

The Scorpion & the Grasshopper

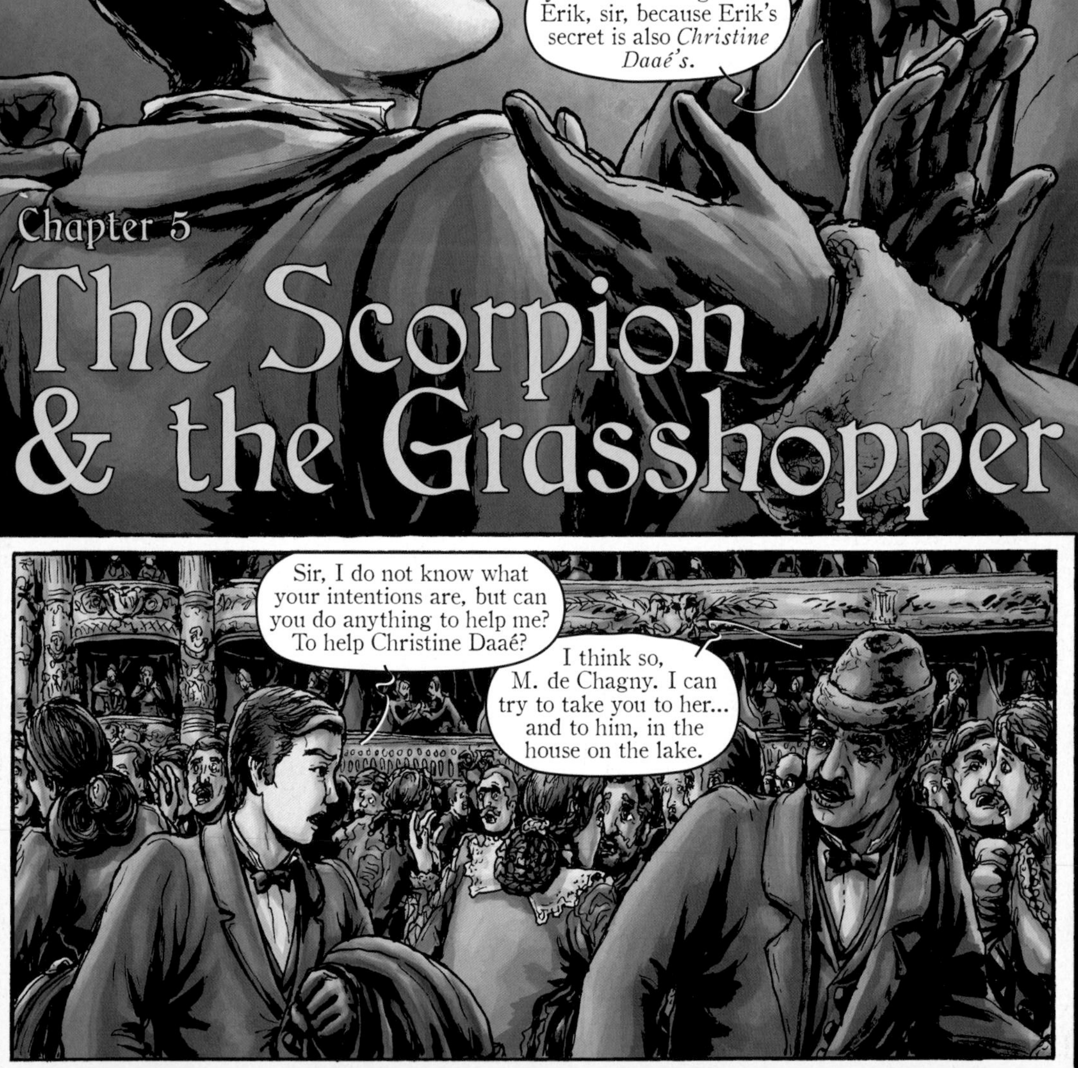
Sir, I do not know what your intentions are, but can you do anything to help me? To help Christine Daaé?
I think so, M. de Chagny. I can try to take you to her... and to him, in the house on the lake.

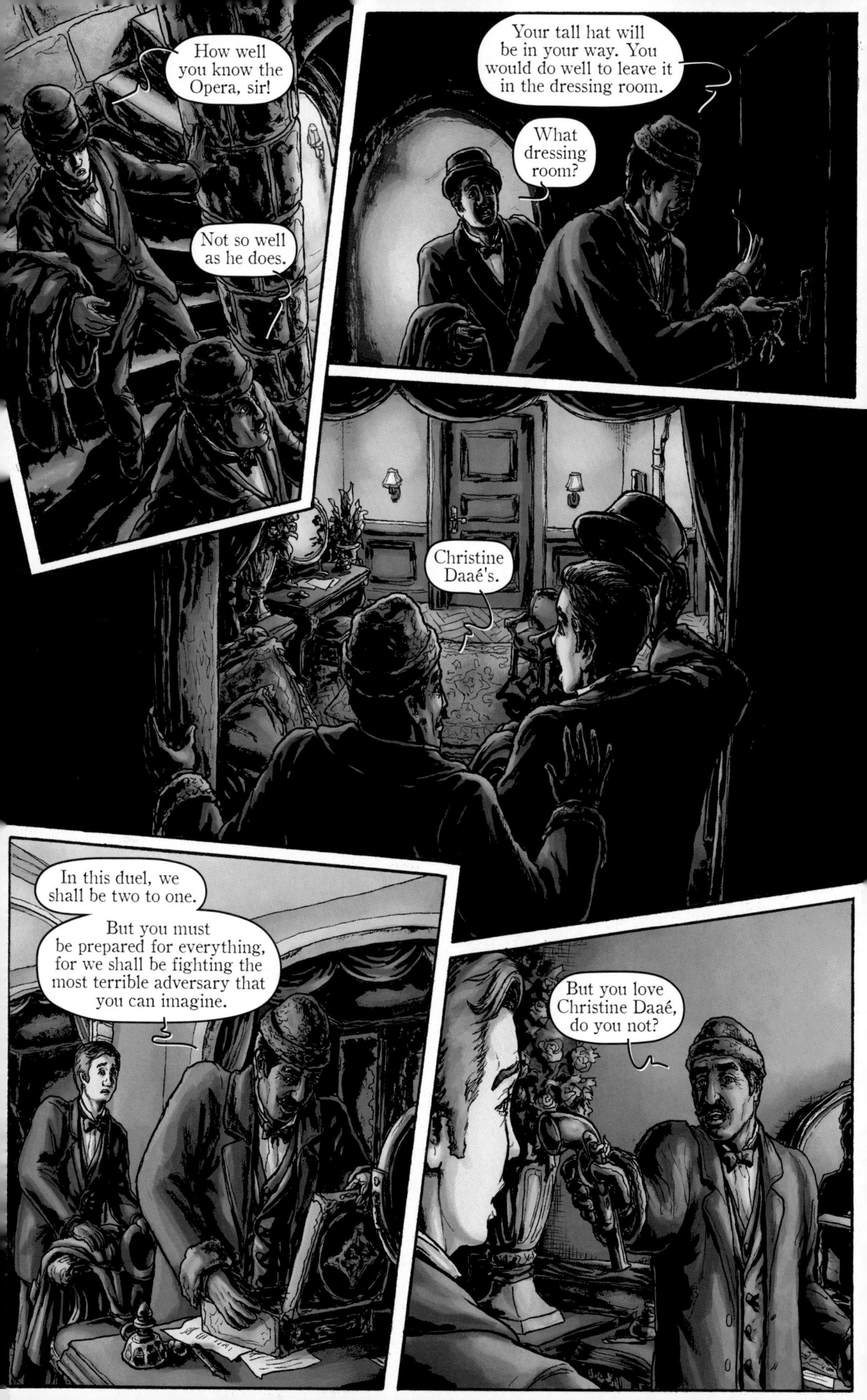
How well you know the Opera, sir!
Not so well as he does.
Your tall hat will be in your way. You would do well to leave it in the dressing room.
What dressing room?
Christine Daaé's.
In this duel, we shall be two to one.
But you must be prepared for everything, for we shall be fighting the most terrible adversary that you can imagine.
But you love Christine Daaé, do you not?

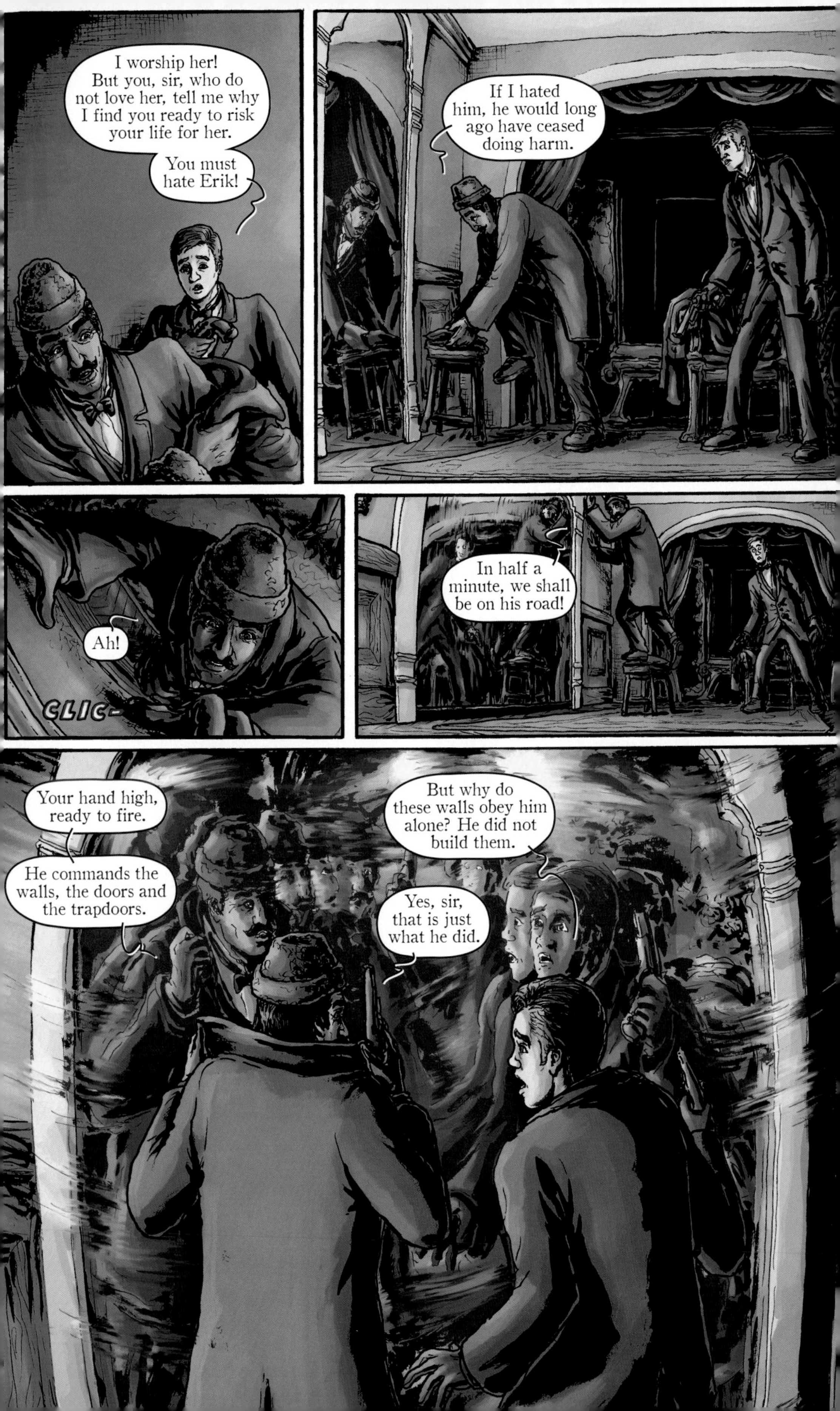
I worship her! But you, sir, who do not love her, tell me why I find you ready to risk your life for her.
You must hate Erik!
If I hated him, he would long ago have ceased doing harm.
Ah!
CLIC-
In half a minute, we shall be on his road!
Your hand high, ready to fire.
He commands the walls, the doors and the trapdoors.
But why do these walls obey him alone? He did not build them.
Yes, sir, that is just what he did.

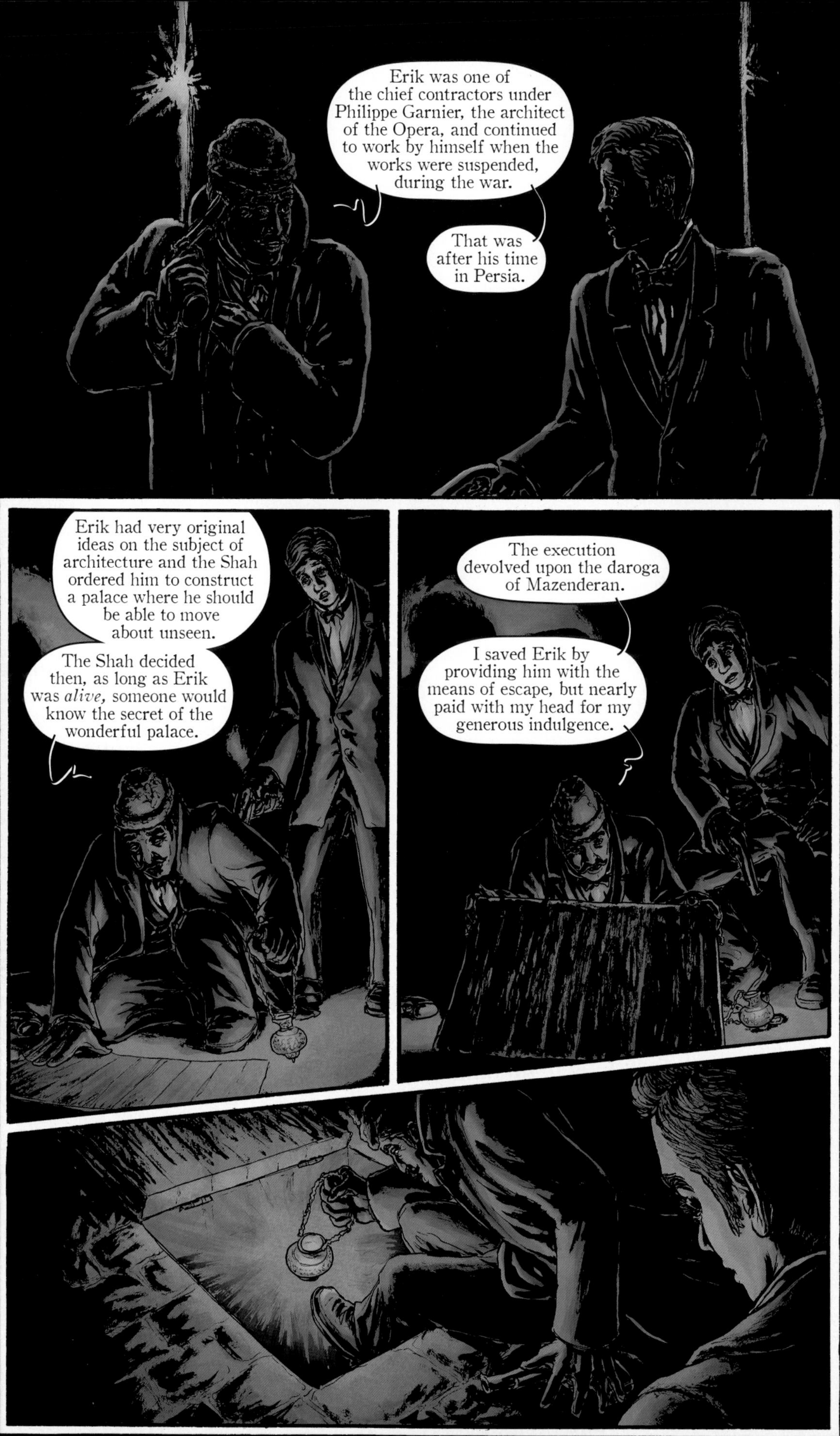
Erik was one of the chief contractors under Philippe Garnier, the architect of the Opera, and continued to work by himself when the works were suspended, during the war.
That was after his time in Persia.
Erik had very original ideas on the subject of architecture and the Shah ordered him to construct a palace where he should be able to move about unseen.
The Shah decided then, as long as Erik was *alive,* someone would know the secret of the wonderful palace.
The execution devolved upon the daroga of Mazenderan.
I saved Erik by providing him with the means of escape, but nearly paid with my head for my generous indulgence.

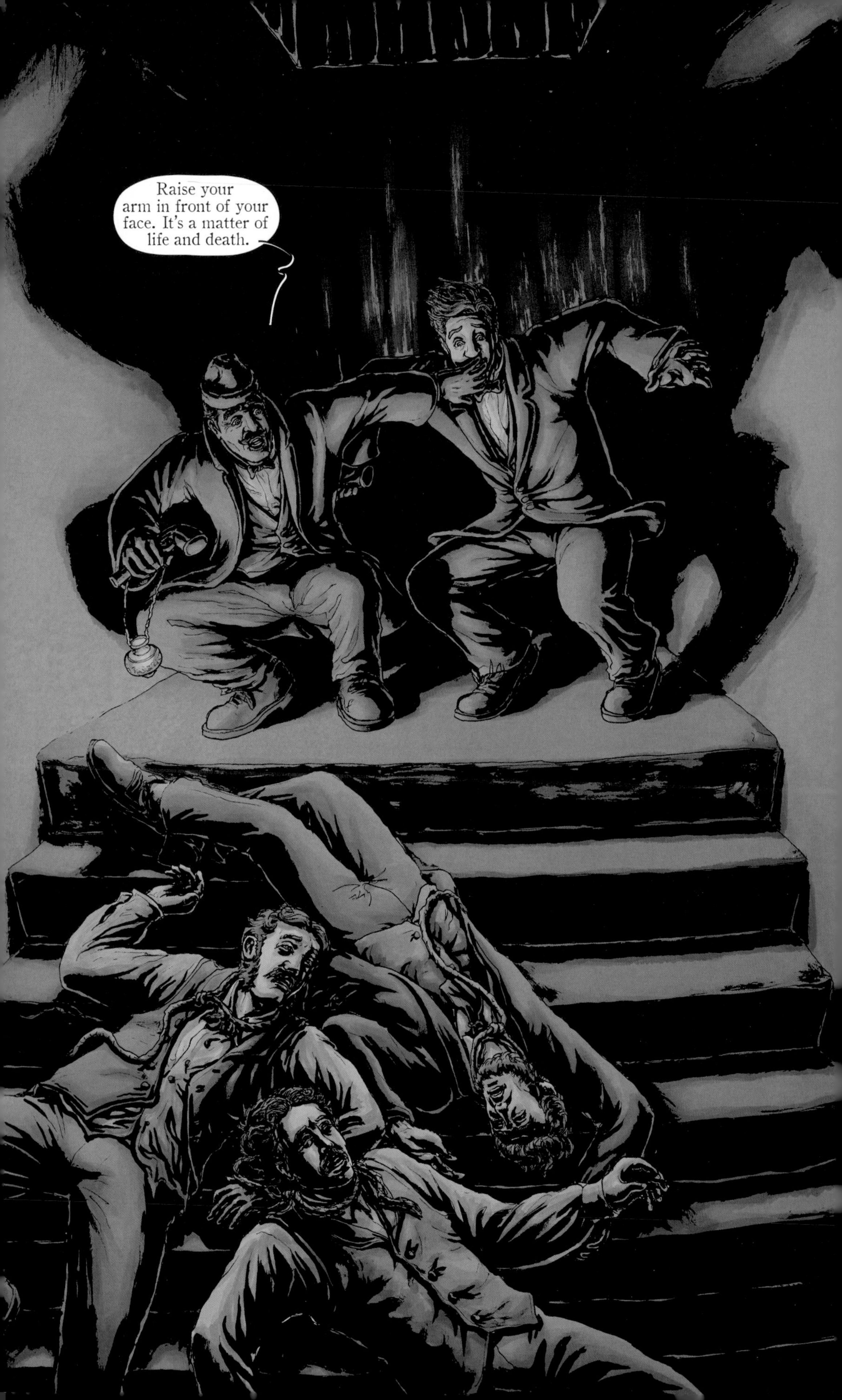
Raise your arm in front of your face. It's a matter of life and death.

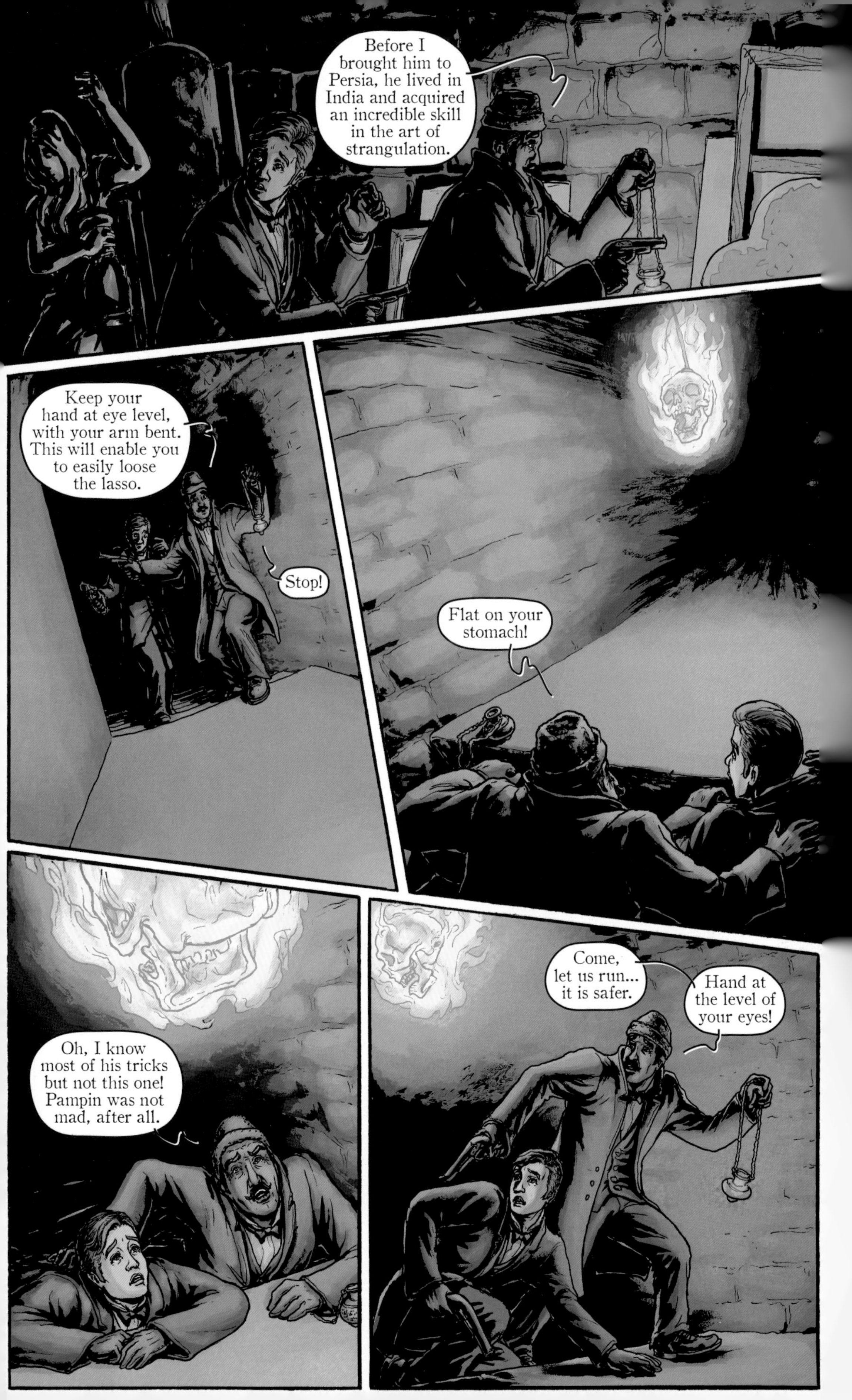
Before I brought him to Persia, he lived in India and acquired an incredible skill in the art of strangulation.
Keep your hand at eye level, with your arm bent. This will enable you to easily loose the lasso.
Stop!
Flat on your stomach!
Oh, I know most of his tricks but not this one! Pampin was not mad, after all.
Come, let us run... it is safer.
Hand at the level of your eyes!

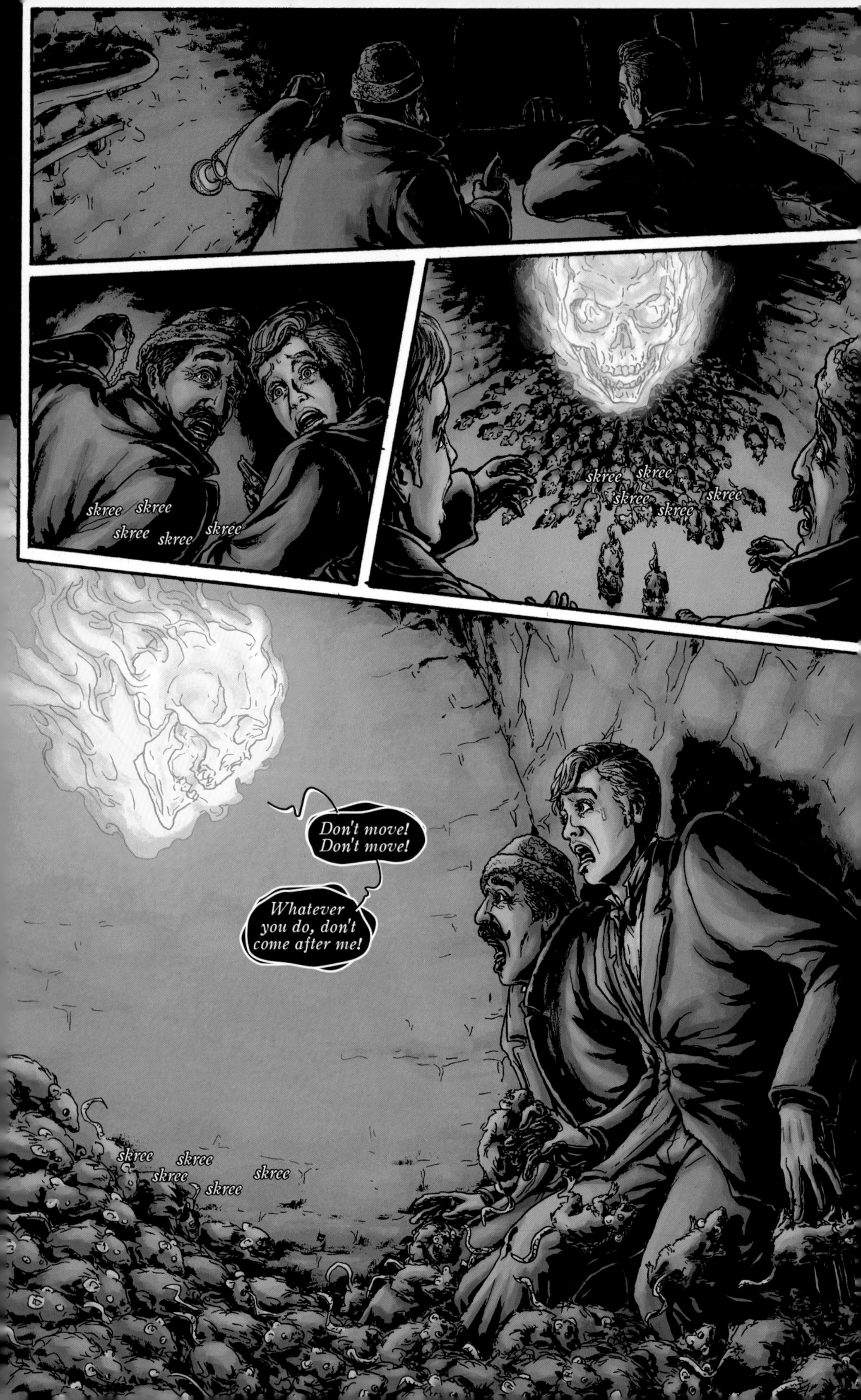
skree skree
skree skree skree
skree skree
skree skree
skree skree
Don't move! Don't move!
Whatever you do, don't come after me!
skree skree
skree skree
skree

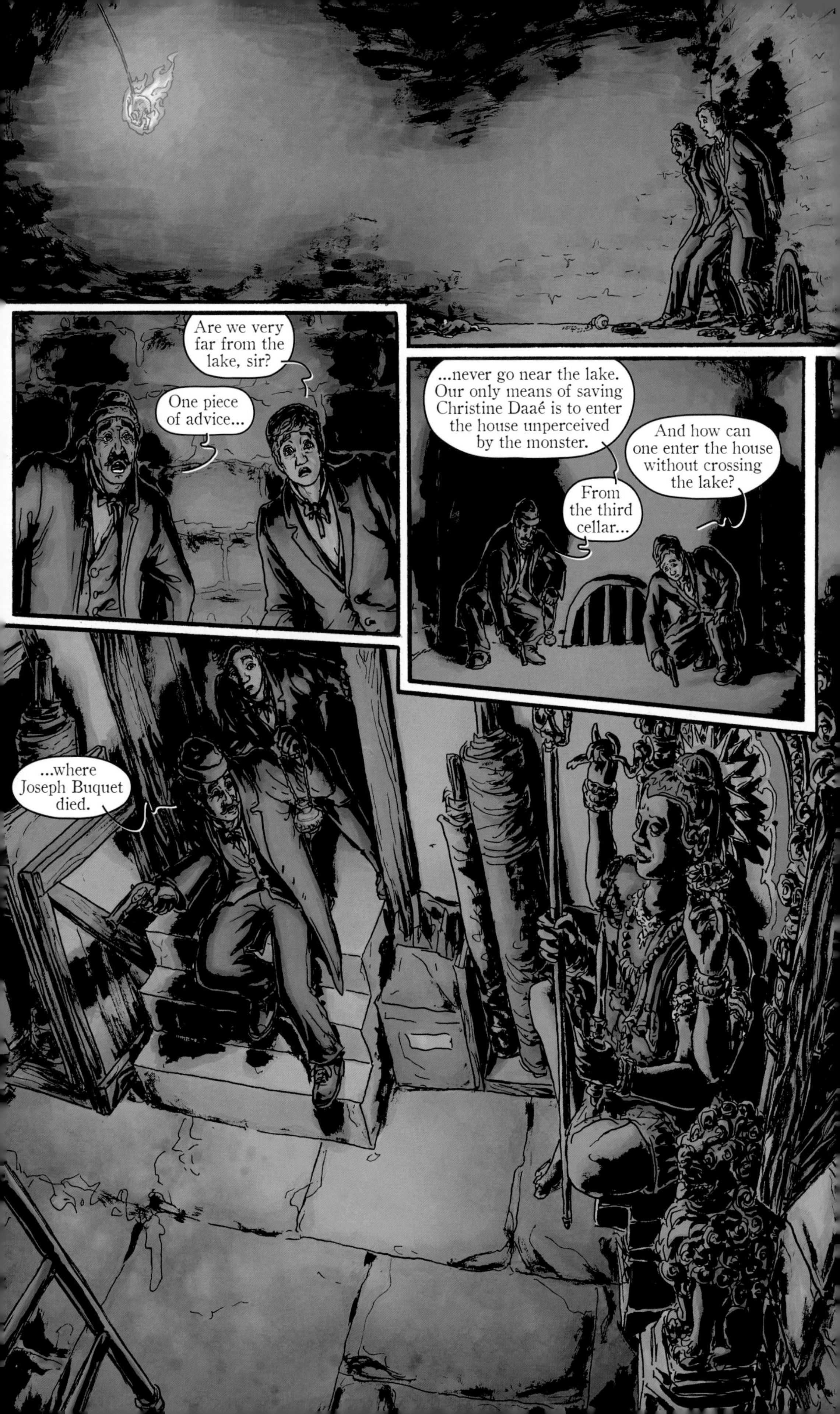
Are we very far from the lake, sir?
One piece of advice...
...never go near the lake. Our only means of saving Christine Daaé is to enter the house unperceived by the monster.
And how can one enter the house without crossing the lake?
From the third cellar...
...where Joseph Buquet died.

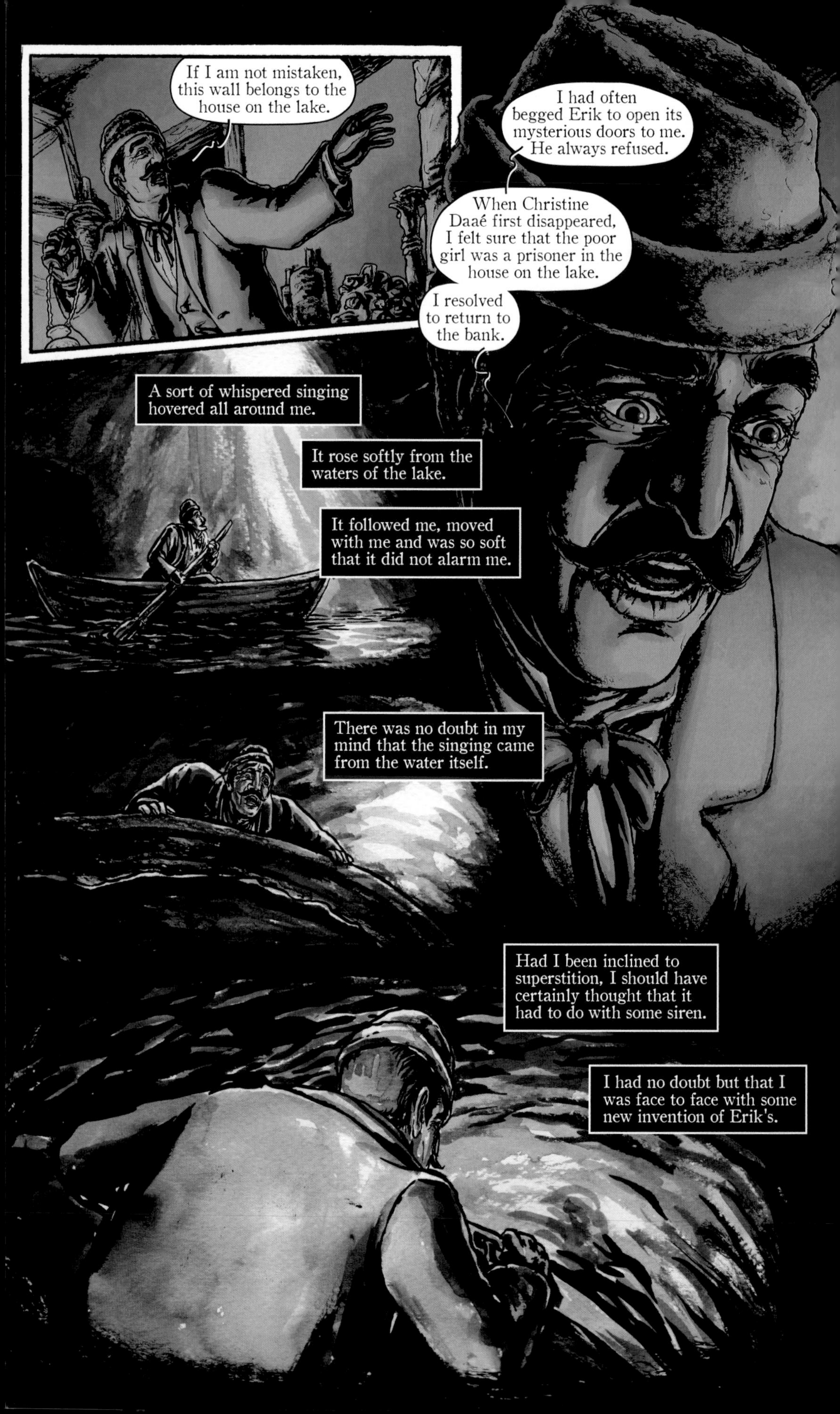
If I am not mistaken, this wall belongs to the house on the lake.
I had often begged Erik to open its mysterious doors to me. He always refused.
When Christine Daaé first disappeared, I felt sure that the poor girl was a prisoner in the house on the lake.
I resolved to return to the bank.
A sort of whispered singing hovered all around me.
It rose softly from the waters of the lake.
It followed me, moved with me and was so soft that it did not alarm me.
There was no doubt in my mind that the singing came from the water itself.
Had I been inclined to superstition, I should have certainly thought that it had to do with some siren.
I had no doubt but that I was face to face with some new invention of Erik's.

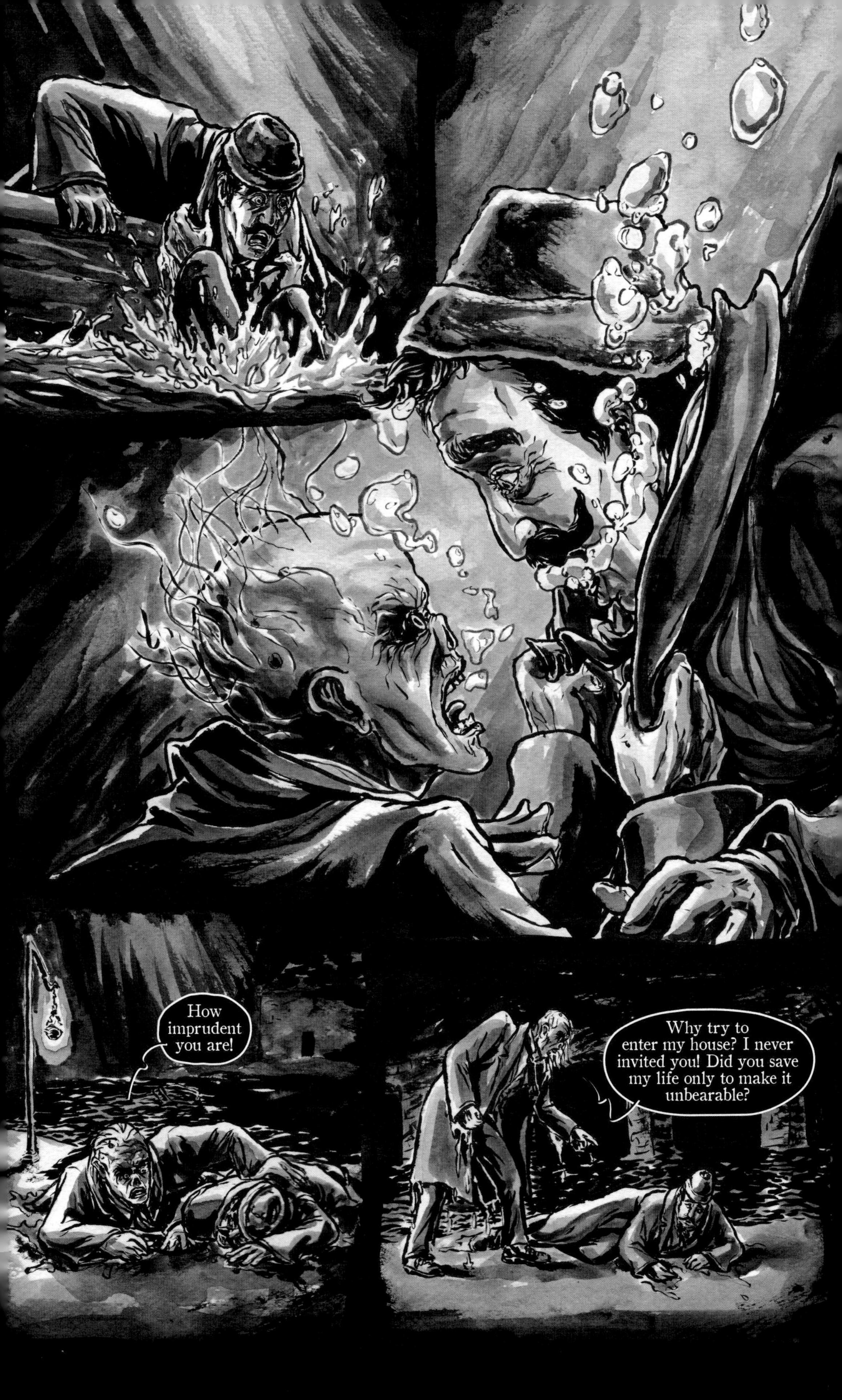
How imprudent you are!
Why try to enter my house? I never invited you! Did you save my life only to make it unbearable?

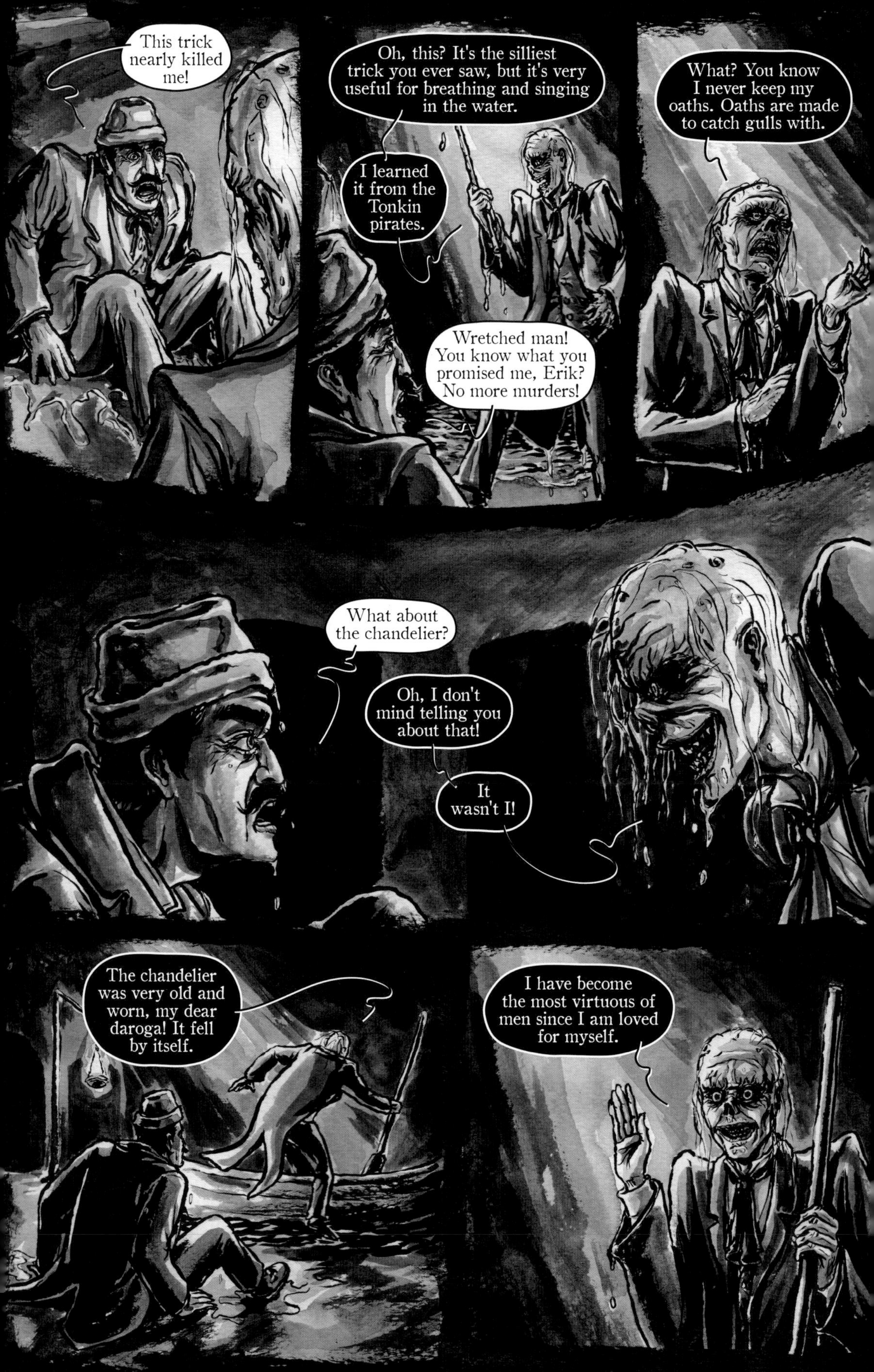
This trick nearly killed me!
Oh, this? It's the silliest trick you ever saw, but it's very useful for breathing and singing in the water.
I learned it from the Tonkin pirates.
Wretched man! You know what you promised me, Erik? No more murders!
What? You know I never keep my oaths. Oaths are made to catch gulls with.
What about the chandelier?
Oh, I don't mind telling you about that!
It wasn't I!
The chandelier was very old and worn, my dear daroga! It fell by itself.
I have become the most virtuous of men since I am loved for myself.

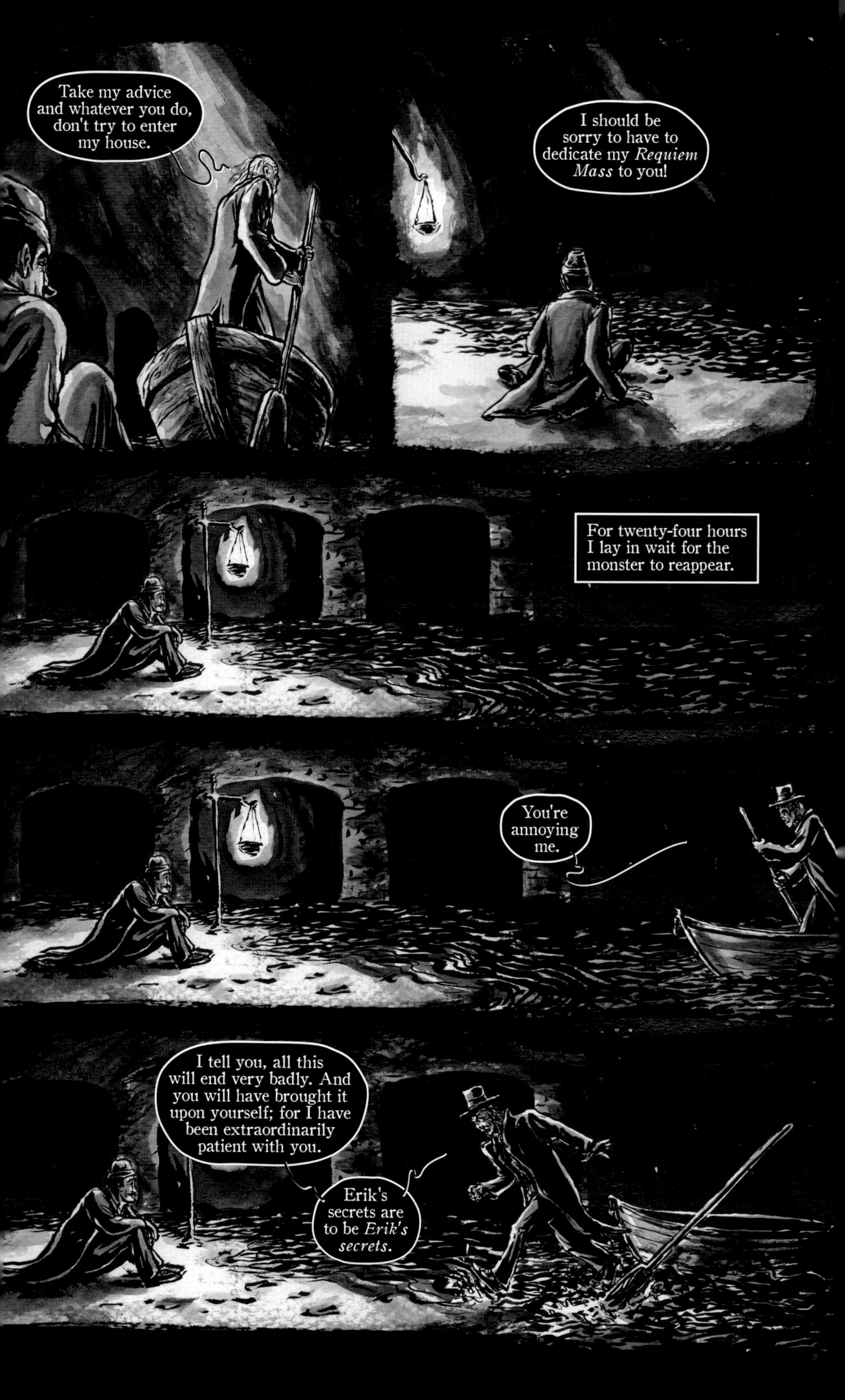
Take my advice and whatever you do, don't try to enter my house.
I should be sorry to have to dedicate my *Requiem Mass* to you!
For twenty-four hours I lay in wait for the monster to reappear.
You're annoying me.
I tell you, all this will end very badly. And you will have brought it upon yourself; for I have been extraordinarily patient with you.
Erik's secrets are to be *Erik's secrets*.

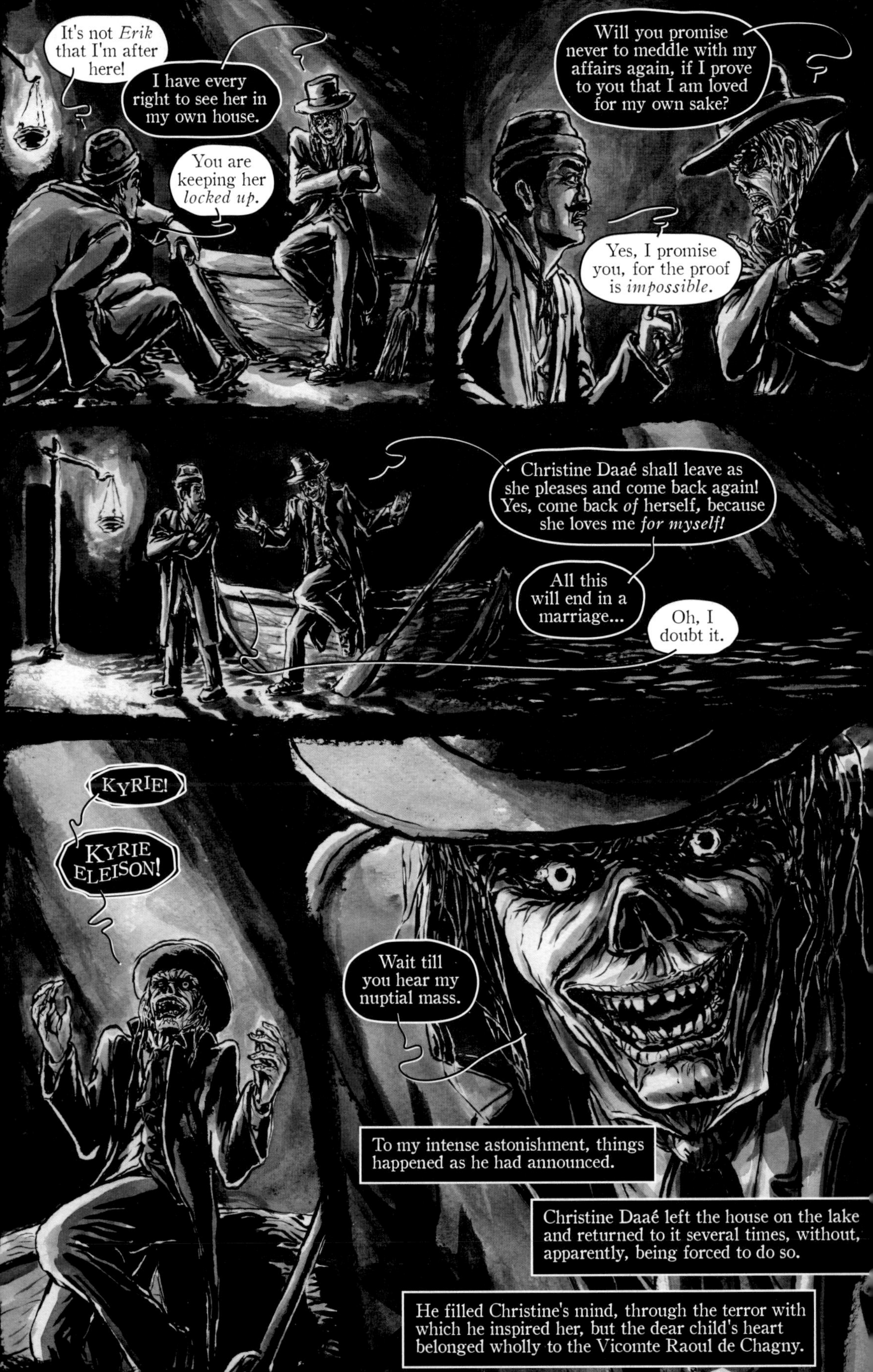

It's not *Erik* that I'm after here!
I have every right to see her in my own house.
You are keeping her *locked up.*
Will you promise never to meddle with my affairs again, if I prove to you that I am loved for my own sake?
Yes, I promise you, for the proof is *impossible.*
Christine Daaé shall leave as she pleases and come back again! Yes, come back *of* herself, because she loves me *for myself!*
All this will end in a marriage...
Oh, I doubt it.
KYRIE!
KYRIE ELEISON!
Wait till you hear my nuptial mass.
To my intense astonishment, things happened as he had announced.
Christine Daaé left the house on the lake and returned to it several times, without, apparently, being forced to do so.
He filled Christine's mind, through the terror with which he inspired her, but the dear child's heart belonged wholly to the Vicomte Raoul de Chagny.

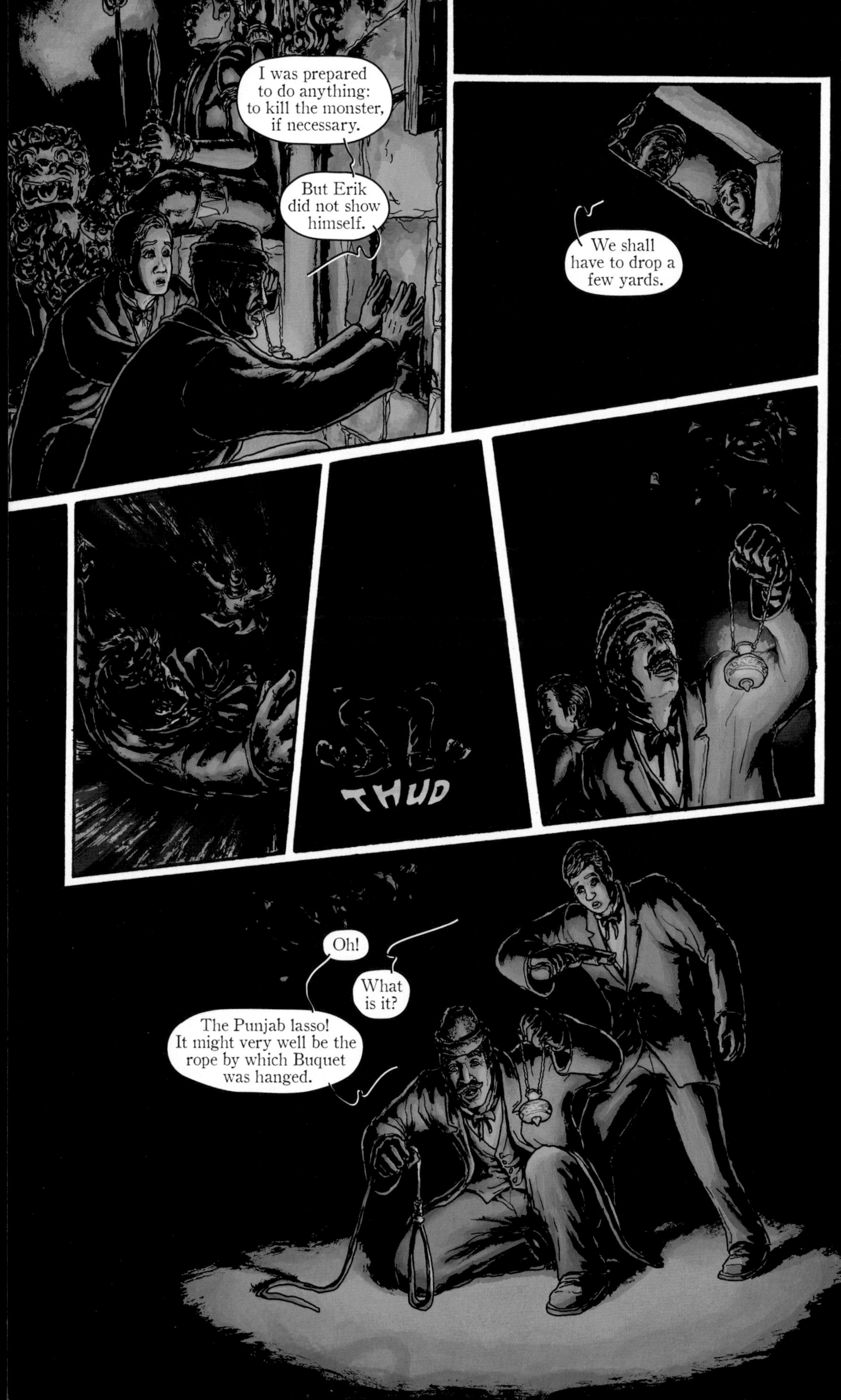
I was prepared to do anything: to kill the monster, if necessary.
But Erik did not show himself.
We shall have to drop a few yards.
THUD
Oh!
What is it?
The Punjab lasso! It might very well be the rope by which Buquet was hanged.

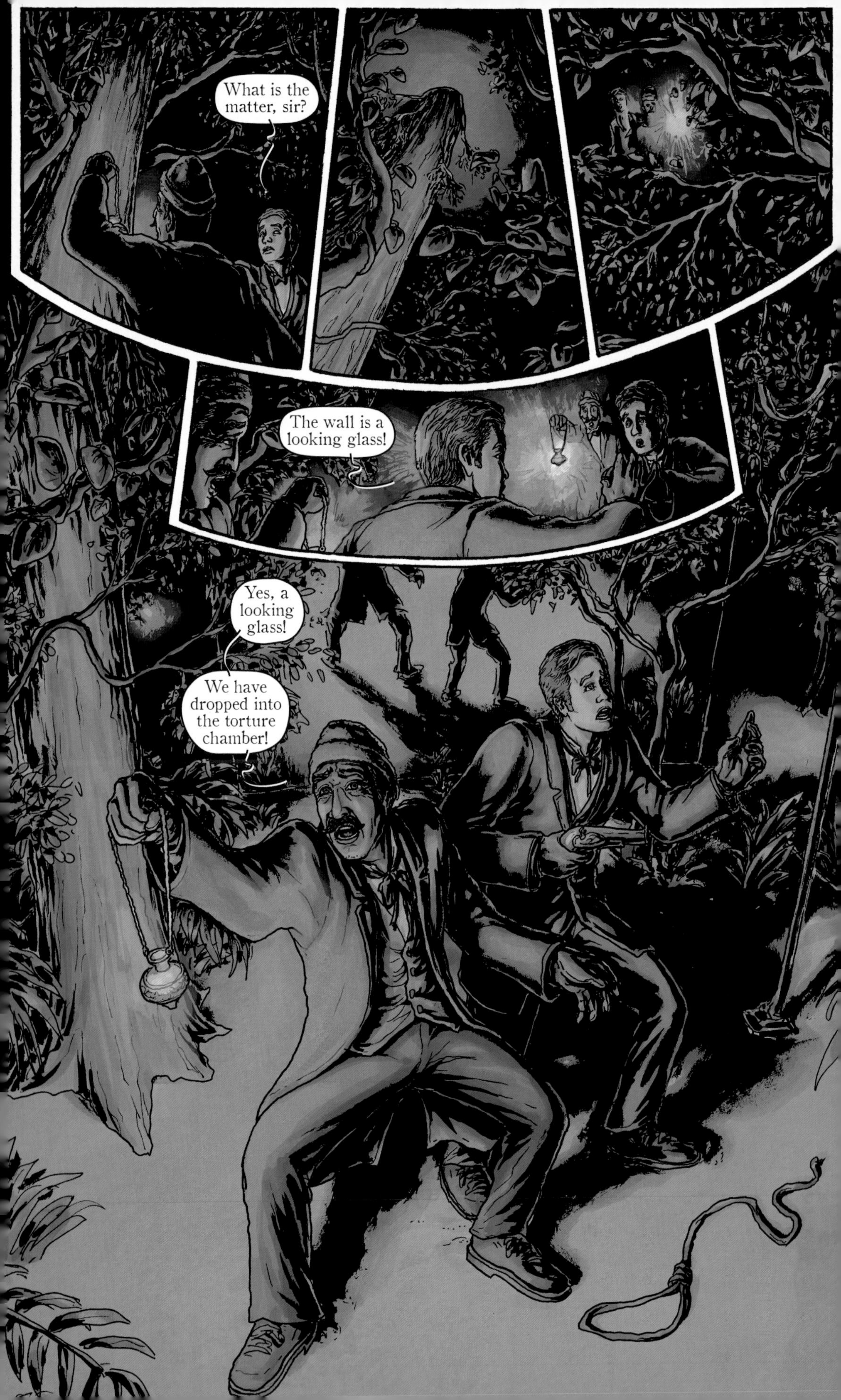
What is the matter, sir?
The wall is a looking glass!
Yes, a looking glass!
We have dropped into the torture chamber!

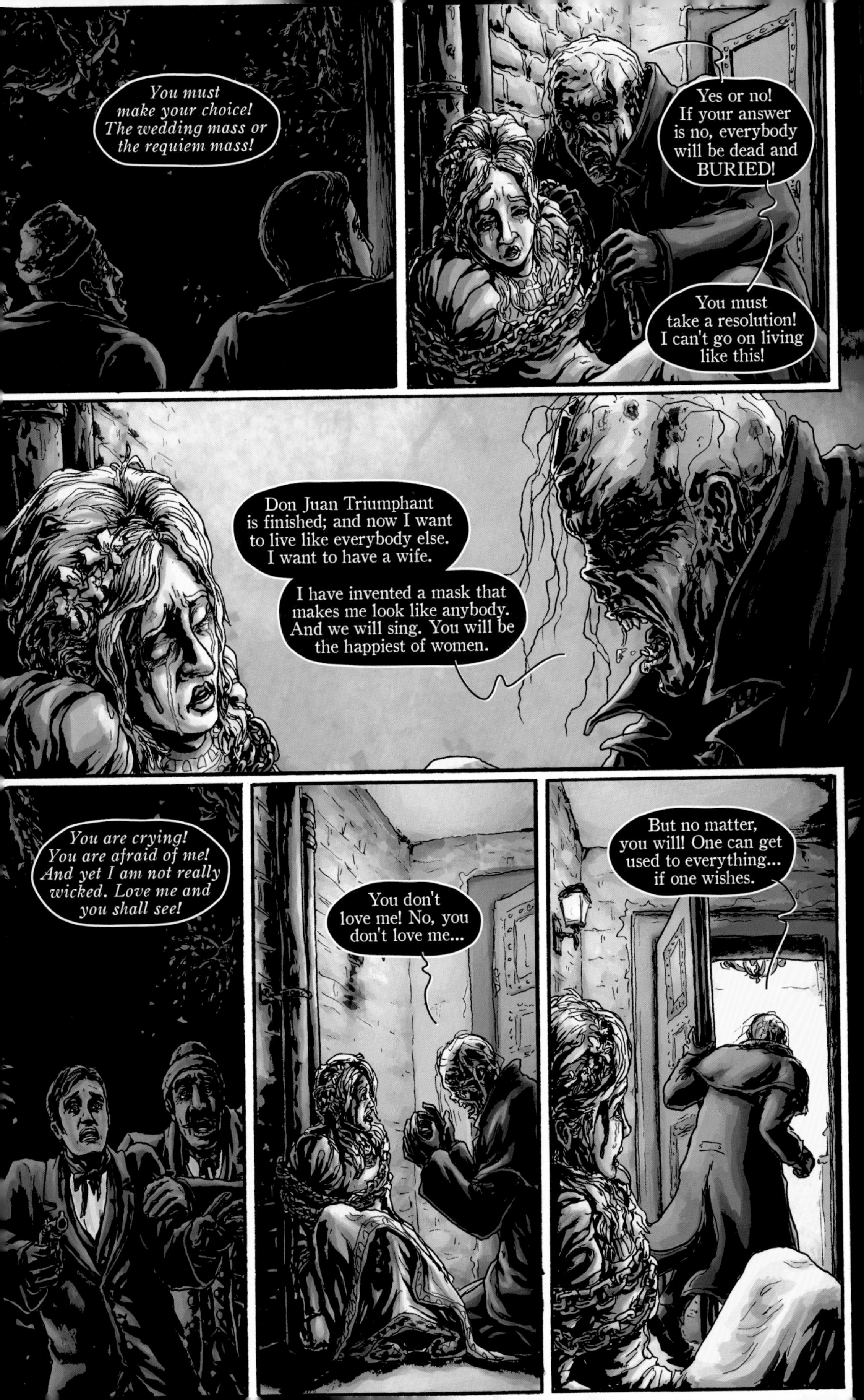

You must make your choice! The wedding mass or the requiem mass!
Yes or no! If your answer is no, everybody will be dead and BURIED!
You must take a resolution! I can't go on living like this!
Don Juan Triumphant is finished; and now I want to live like everybody else. I want to have a wife.
I have invented a mask that makes me look like anybody. And we will sing. You will be the happiest of women.
You are crying! You are afraid of me! And yet I am not really wicked. Love me and you shall see!
You don't love me! No, you don't love me...
But no matter, you will! One can get used to everything... if one wishes.

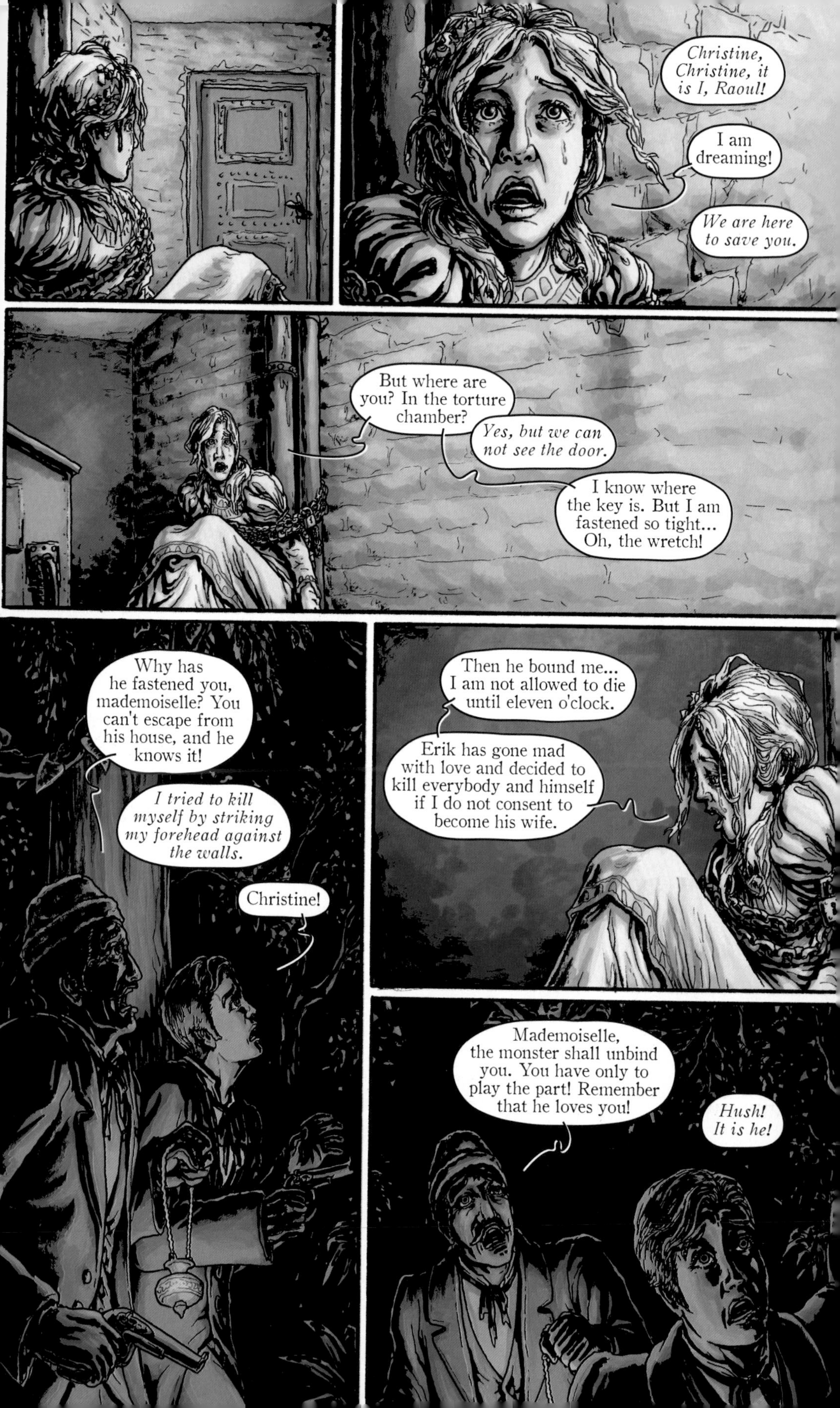
Christine, Christine, it is I, Raoul!
I am dreaming!
We are here to save you.
But where are you? In the torture chamber?
Yes, but we can not see the door.
I know where the key is. But I am fastened so tight... Oh, the wretch!
Why has he fastened you, mademoiselle? You can't escape from his house, and he knows it!
I tried to kill myself by striking my forehead against the walls.
Christine!
Then he bound me... I am not allowed to die until eleven o'clock.
Erik has gone mad with love and decided to kill everybody and himself if I do not consent to become his wife.
Mademoiselle, the monster shall unbind you. You have only to play the part! Remember that he loves you!
Hush! It is he!

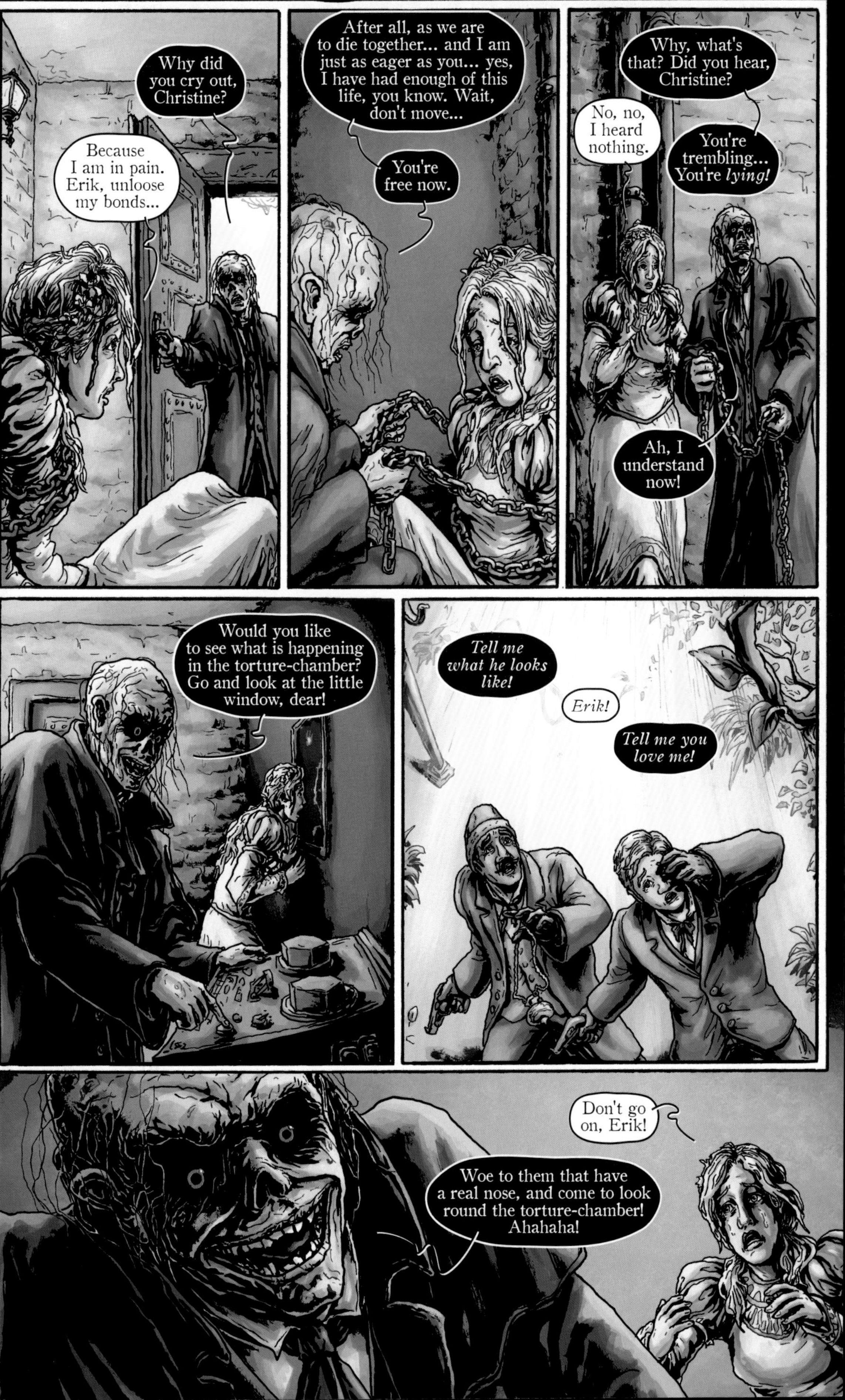
Why did you cry out, Christine?
Because I am in pain. Erik, unloose my bonds...
After all, as we are to die together... and I am just as eager as you... yes, I have had enough of this life, you know. Wait, don't move...
You're free now.
Why, what's that? Did you hear, Christine?
No, no, I heard nothing.
You're trembling... You're *lying!*
Ah, I understand now!
Would you like to see what is happening in the torture-chamber? Go and look at the little window, dear!
Tell me what he looks like!
Erik!
Tell me you love me!
Don't go on, Erik!
Woe to them that have a real nose, and come to look round the torture-chamber! Ahahaha!

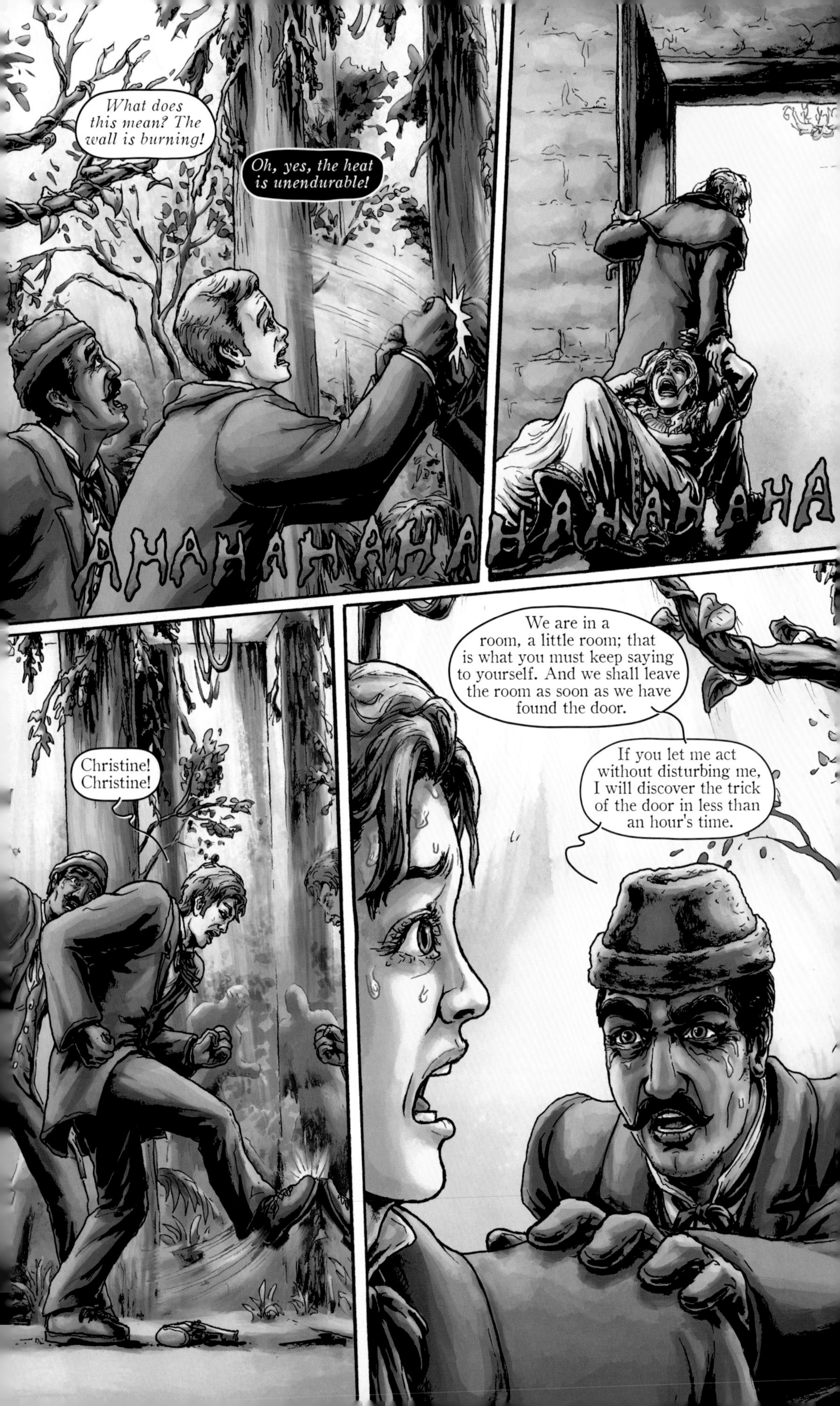
What does this mean? The wall is burning!
Oh, yes, the heat is unendurable!
AHAHAHAHAHAHAHAHAHA
Christine! Christine!
We are in a room, a little room; that is what you must keep saying to yourself. And we shall leave the room as soon as we have found the door.
If you let me act without disturbing me, I will discover the trick of the door in less than an hour's time.

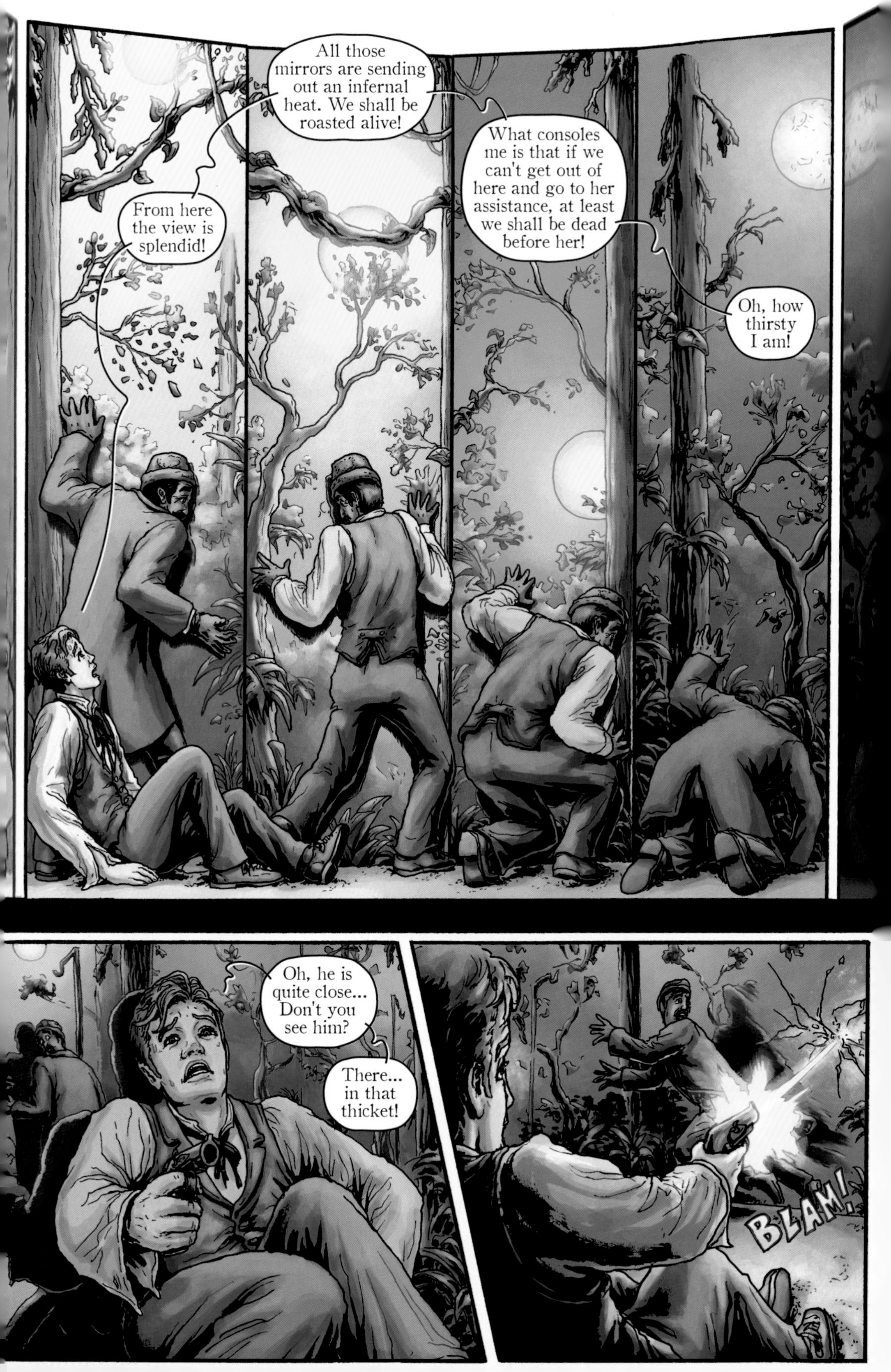
All those mirrors are sending out an infernal heat. We shall be roasted alive!
From here the view is splendid!
What consoles me is that if we can't get out of here and go to her assistance, at least we shall be dead before her!
Oh, how thirsty I am!
Oh, he is quite close... Don't you see him?
There... in that thicket!
BLAM!

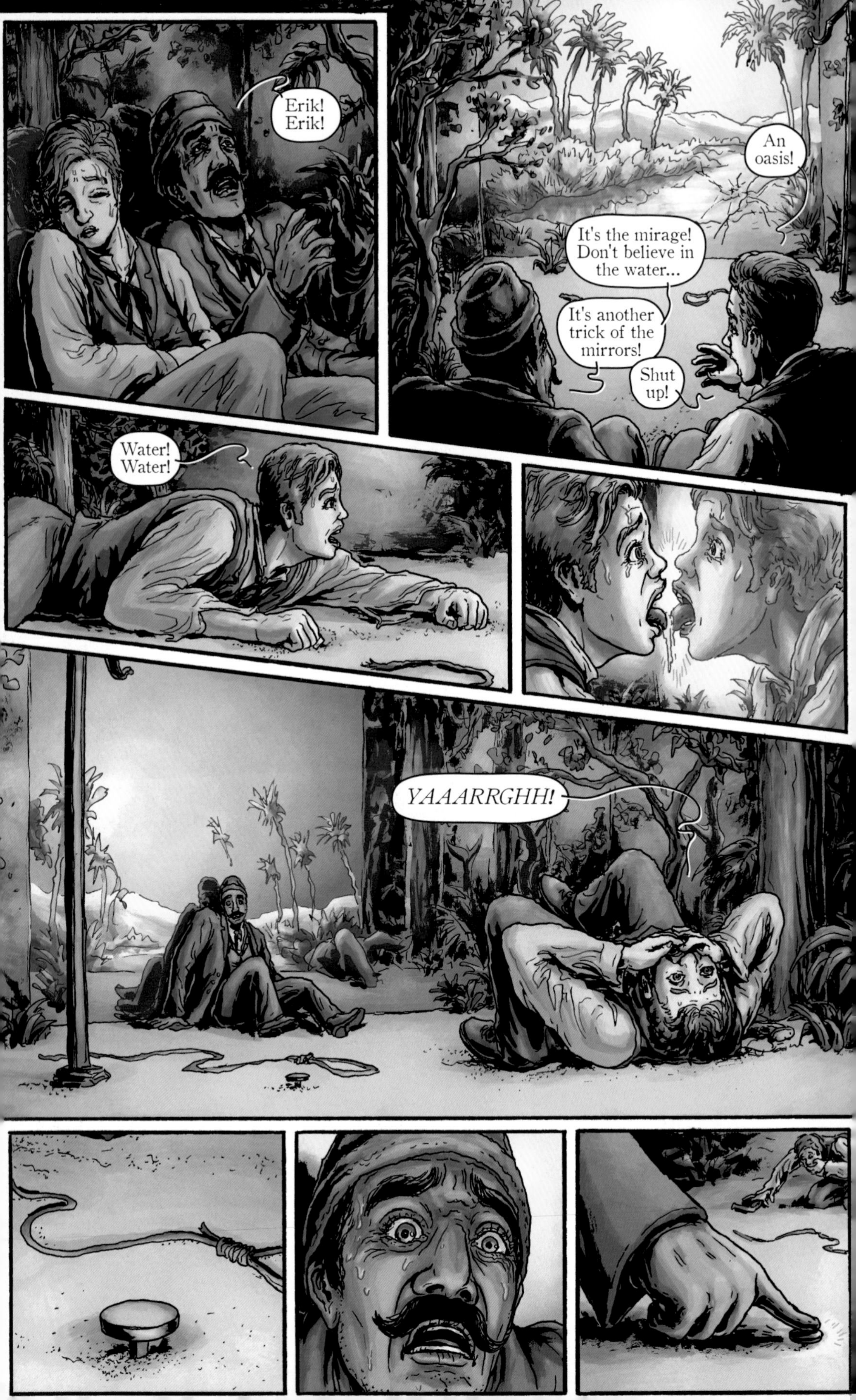
Erik!
Erik!
An
oasis!
It's the mirage!
Don't believe in
the water...
It's another
trick of the
mirrors!
Shut
up!
Water!
Water!
YAAARRGHH!

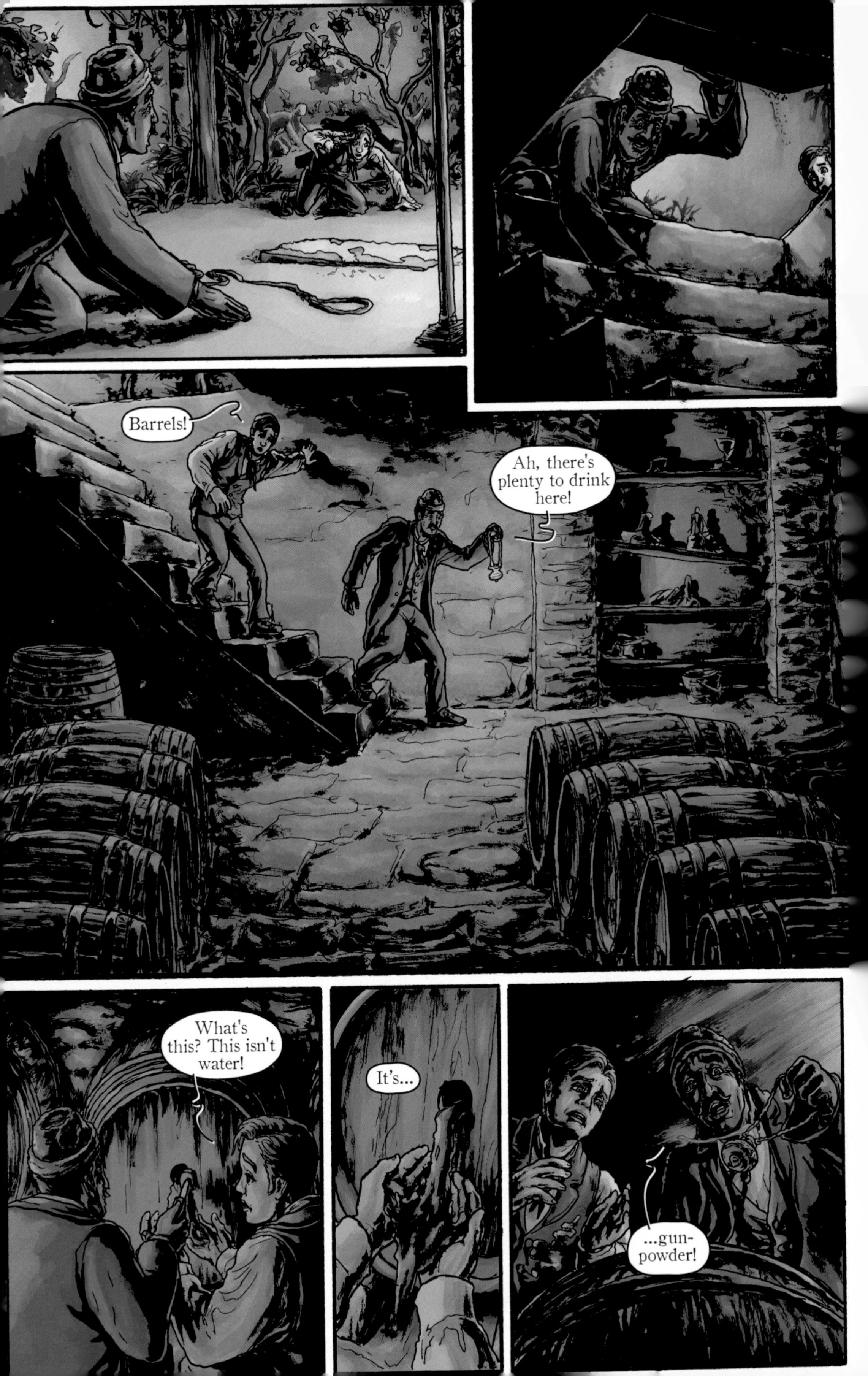
Barrels!
Ah, there's plenty to drink here!
What's this? This isn't water!
It's...
...gun-powder!

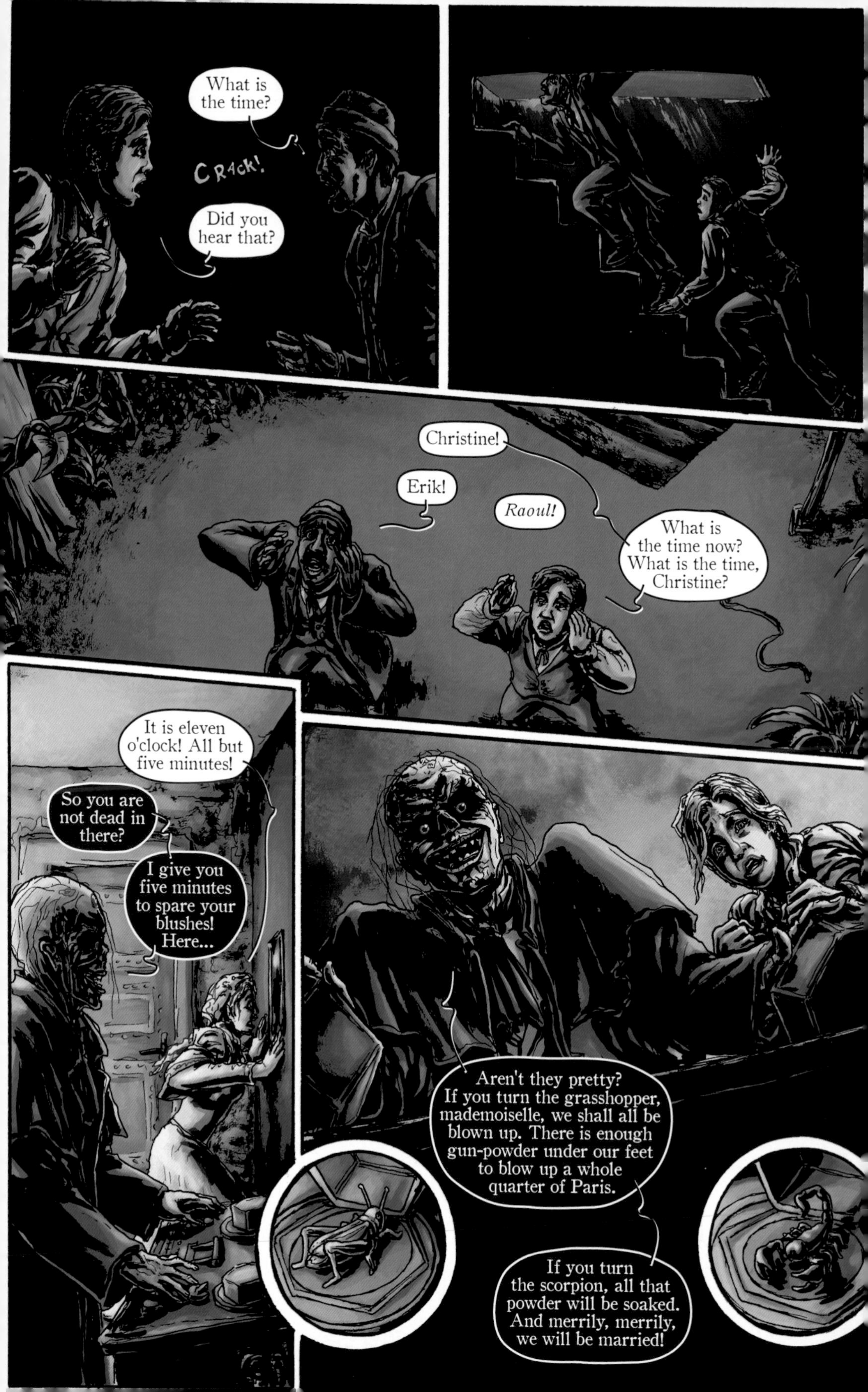
What is the time?
CRACK!
Did you hear that?
Christine!
Erik!
Raoul!
What is the time now? What is the time, Christine?
It is eleven o'clock! All but five minutes!
So you are not dead in there?
I give you five minutes to spare your blushes! Here...
Aren't they pretty? If you turn the grasshopper, mademoiselle, we shall all be blown up. There is enough gun-powder under our feet to blow up a whole quarter of Paris.
If you turn the scorpion, all that powder will be soaked. And merrily, merrily, we will be married!

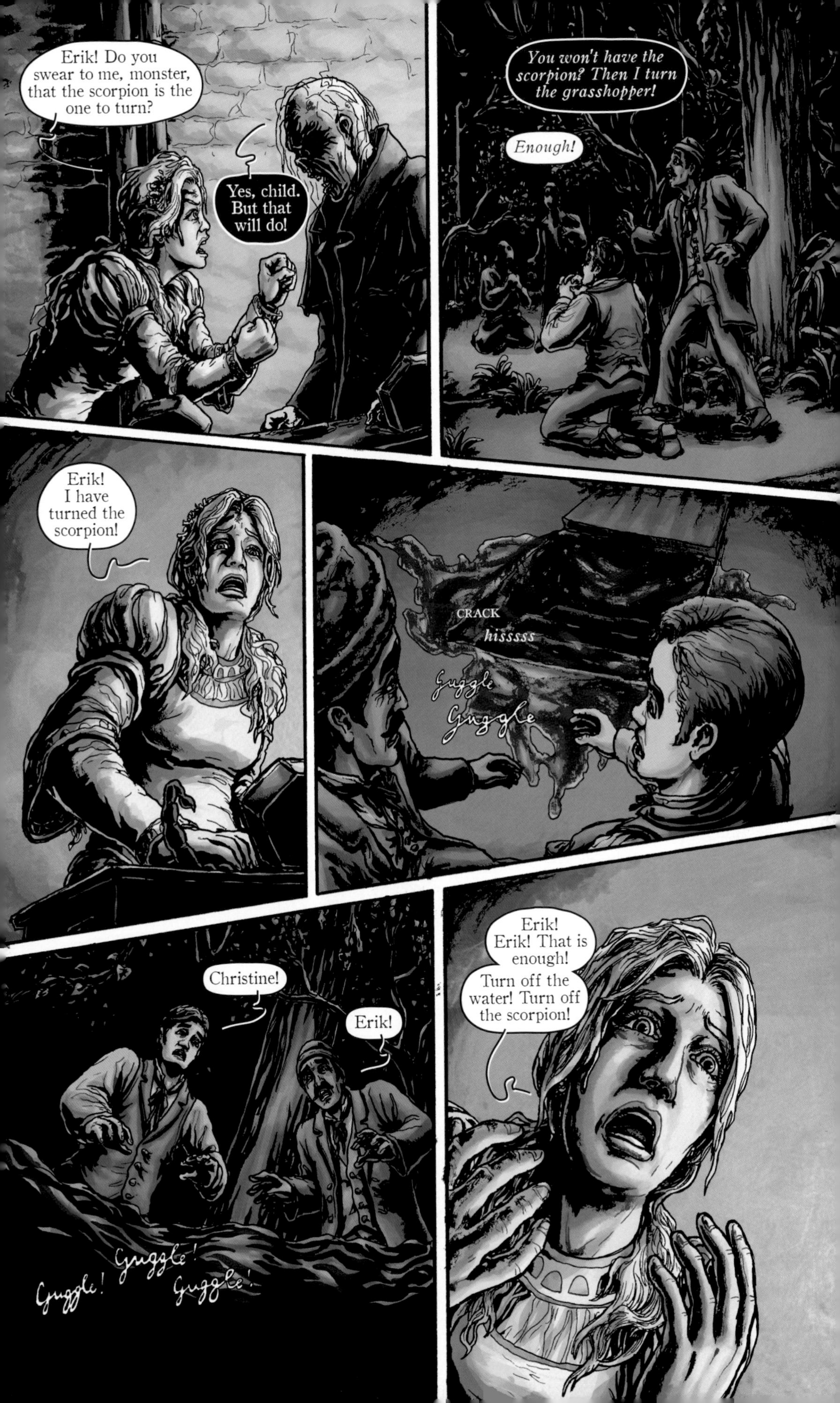

Erik! Do you swear to me, monster, that the scorpion is the one to turn?
Yes, child. But that will do!
You won't have the scorpion? Then I turn the grasshopper!
Enough!
Erik! I have turned the scorpion!
CRACK
hisssss
Guggle
Guggle
Christine!
Erik!
Guggle!
Guggle!
Guggle!
Erik! Erik! That is enough!
Turn off the water! Turn off the scorpion!

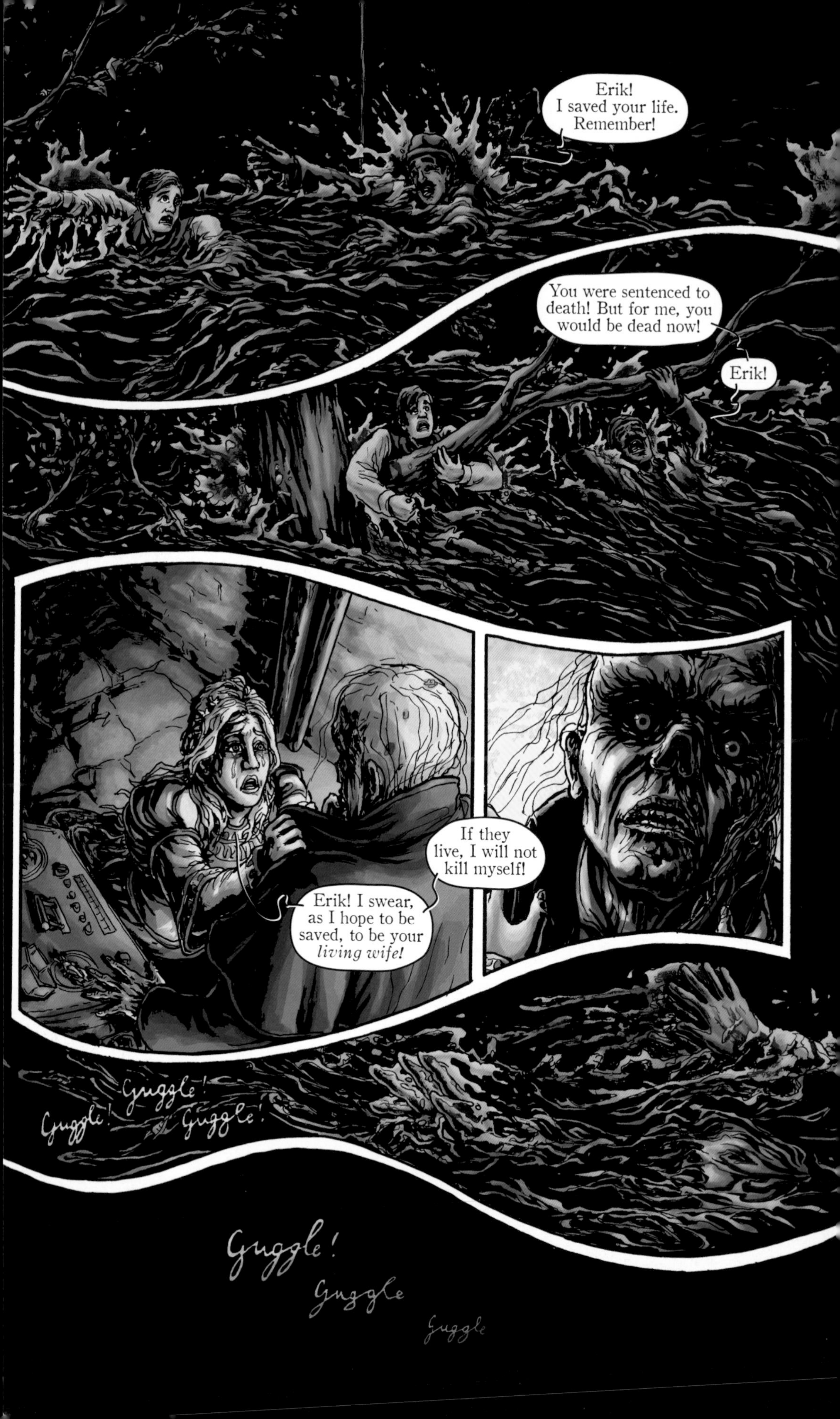

Erik! I saved your life. Remember!
You were sentenced to death! But for me, you would be dead now!
Erik!
Erik! I swear, as I hope to be saved, to be your *living wife!*
If they live, I will not kill myself!
Guggle! Guggle! Guggle!
Guggle!
Guggle
Guggle

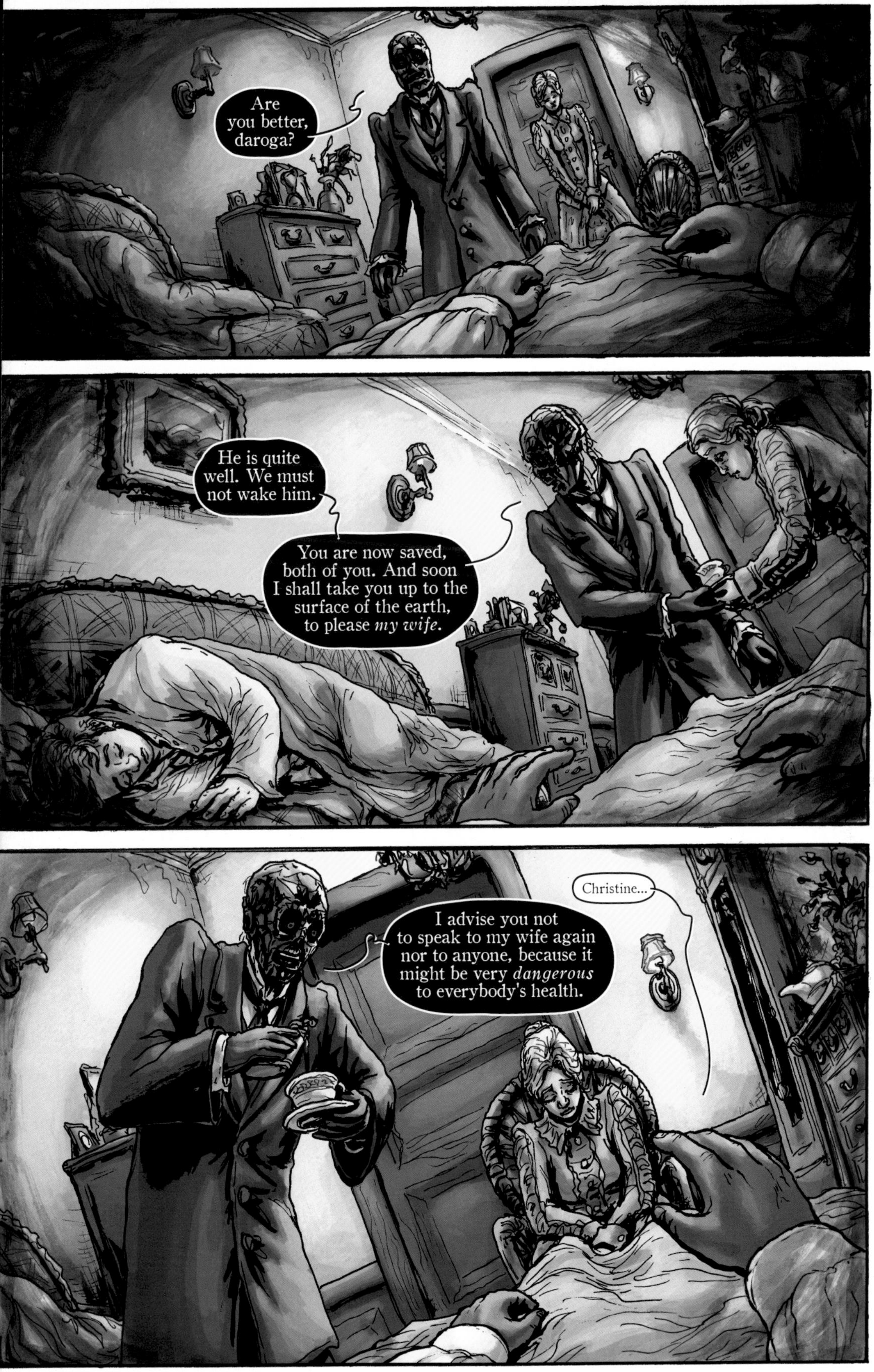
Are you better, daroga?
He is quite well. We must not wake him.
You are now saved, both of you. And soon I shall take you up to the surface of the earth, to please *my wife*.
Christine...
I advise you not to speak to my wife again nor to anyone, because it might be very *dangerous* to everybody's health.

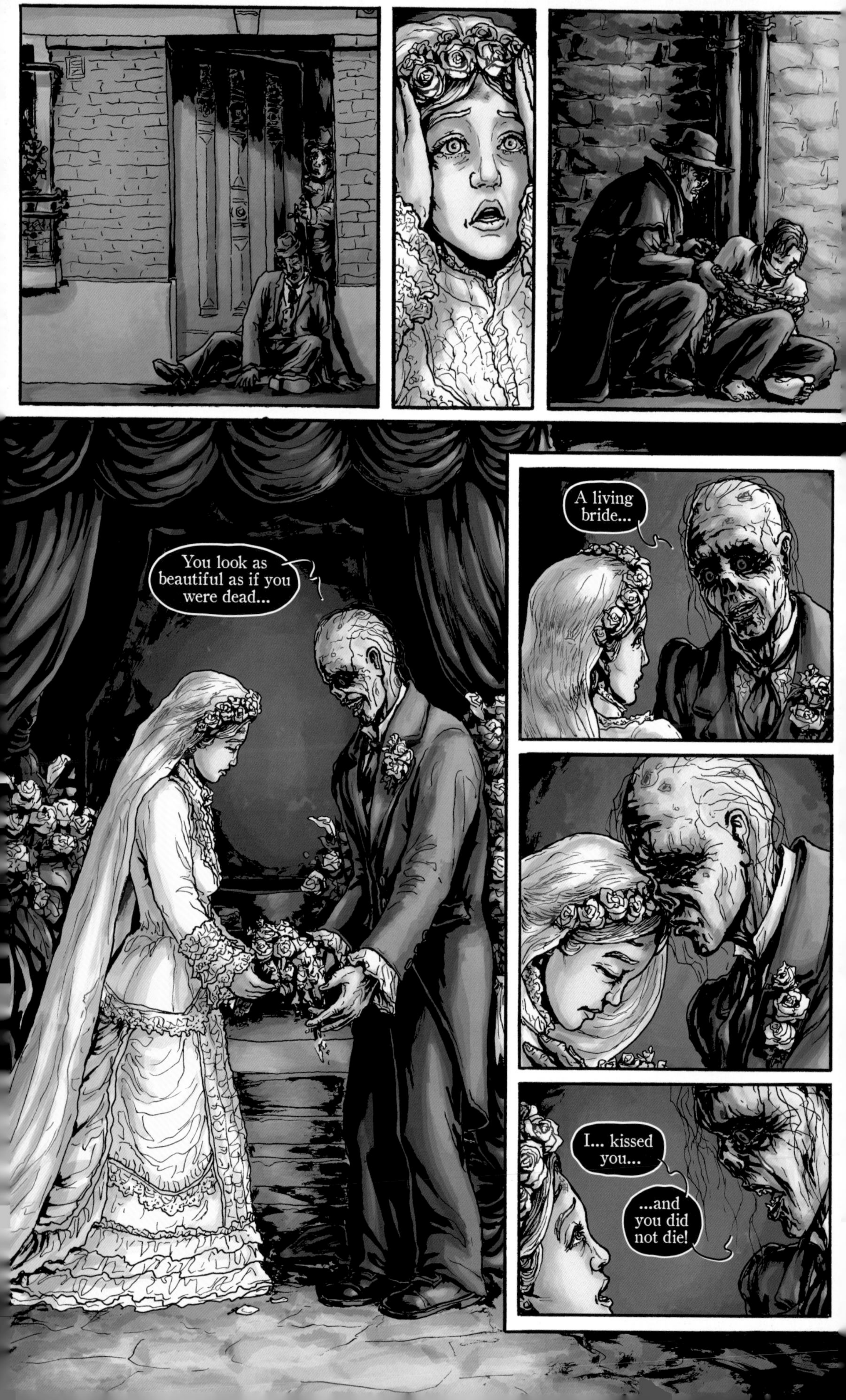
You look as beautiful as if you were dead...
A living bride...
I... kissed you...
...and you did not die!

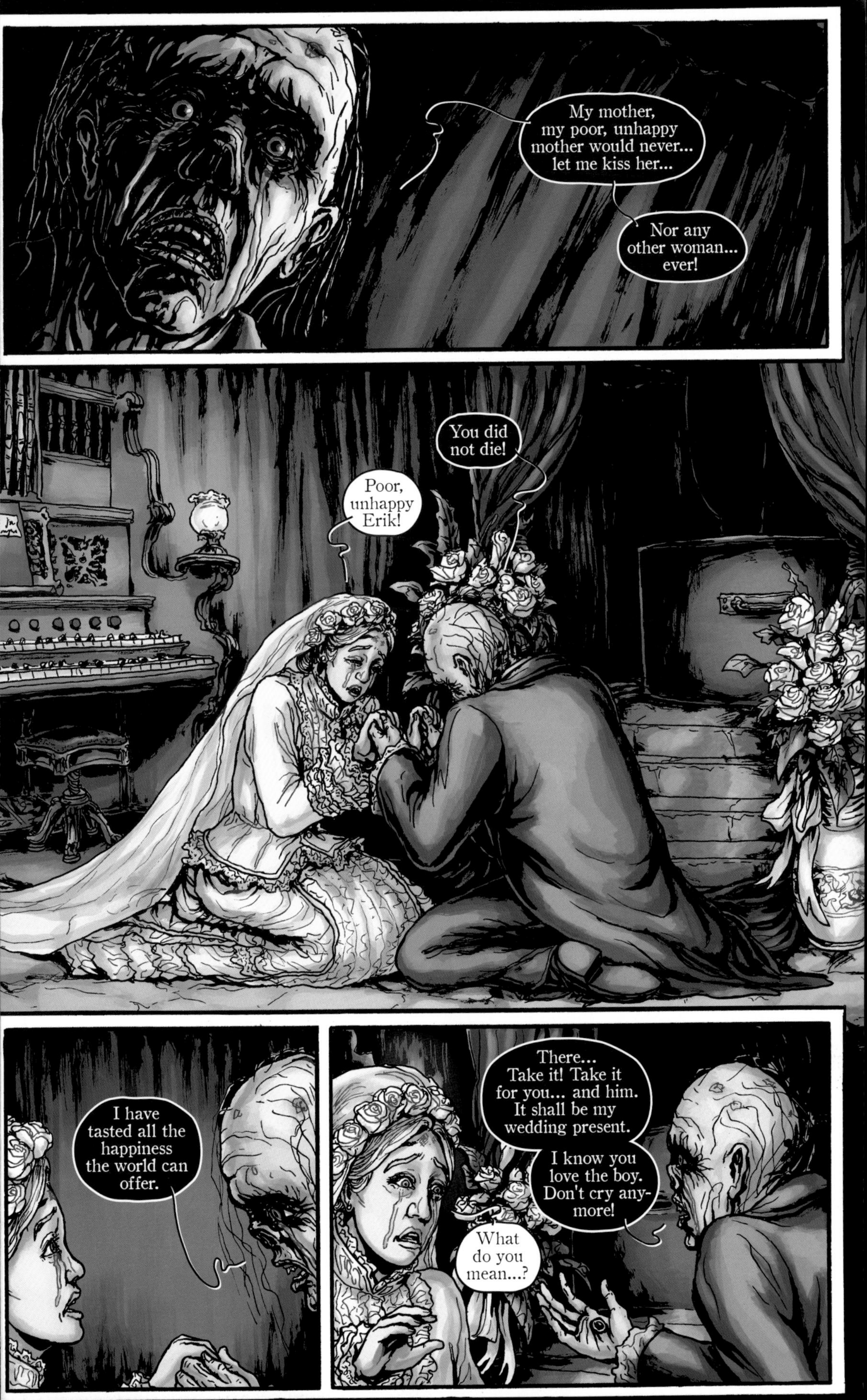
My mother, my poor, unhappy mother would never... let me kiss her...
Nor any other woman... ever!
Poor, unhappy Erik!
You did not die!
I have tasted all the happiness the world can offer.
There... Take it! Take it for you... and him. It shall be my wedding present.
I know you love the boy. Don't cry any-more!
What do you mean...?

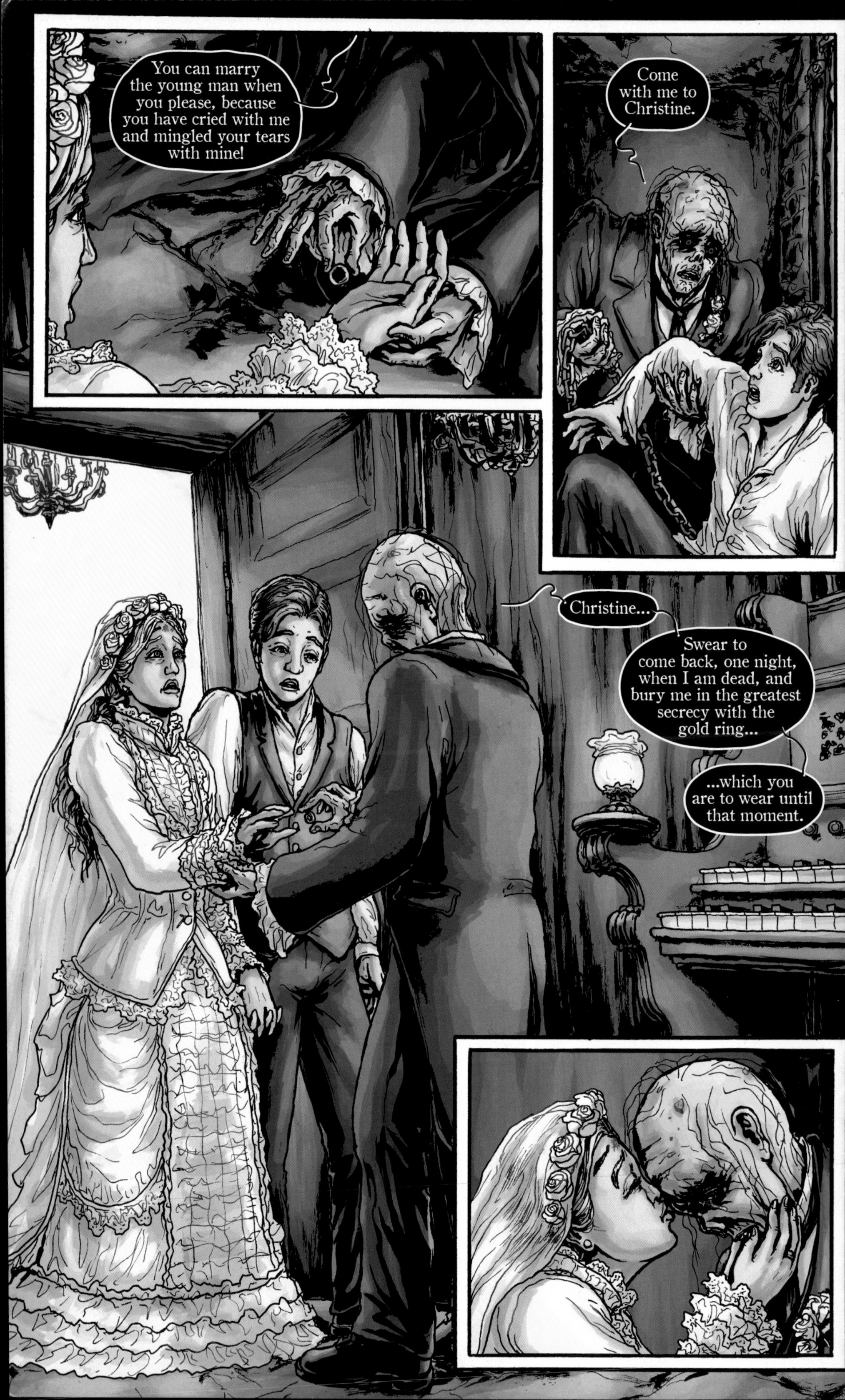

You can marry the young man when you please, because you have cried with me and mingled your tears with mine!
Come with me to Christine.
Christine...
Swear to come back, one night, when I am dead, and bury me in the greatest secrecy with the gold ring...
...which you are to wear until that moment.

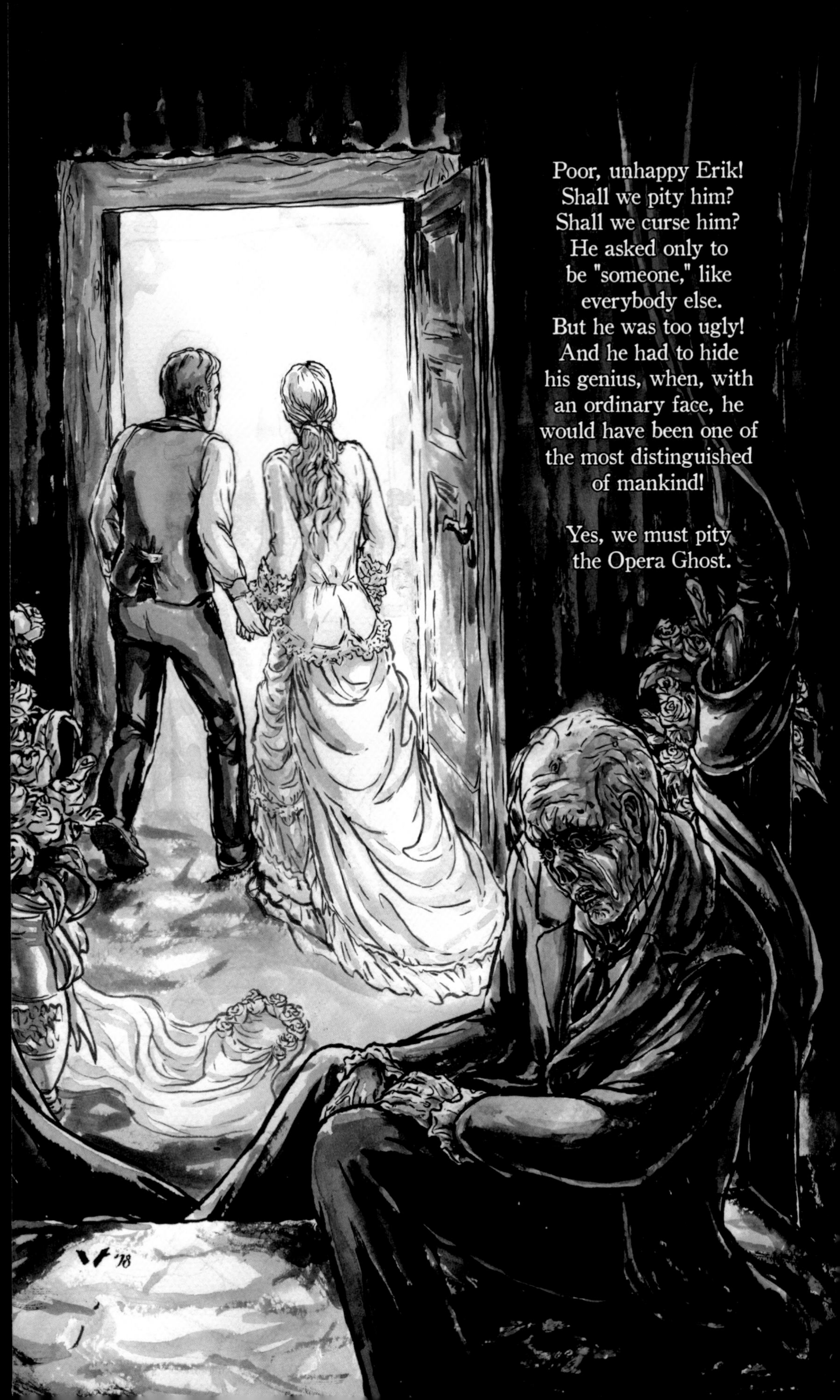
Poor, unhappy Erik!
Shall we pity him?
Shall we curse him?
He asked only to
be "someone," like
everybody else.
But he was too ugly!
And he had to hide
his genius, when, with
an ordinary face, he
would have been one of
the most distinguished
of mankind!
Yes, we must pity
the Opera Ghost.

Acknowledgements

This book was a labor of love (and hate and all the emotions in-between), that wouldn't have been possible without the following people:

First of all, I'd like to say thank you to CHRIS RYALL, who gave me my first job in the industry and was the first person to encourage me to work on this story. I owe my life as I know it to you.

TYLER CHIN-TANNER: you gave this book a chance, allowed me to make a lifelong dream of mine come true and held my hand through the process. Words can't describe how grateful I am to you for your generosity, patience and support.

KEVIN EASTMAN: thank you for letting me tag along on your crazy adventures and for going out of your way to promote this book to your fans. I never expected to one day be able to call you, a living legend, a friend – you're awesome.

ROD OLLERENSHAW: without your support and encouragement I probably wouldn't have started coloring comics, and then none of this would have happened. You're one of the coolest teachers I've ever had and I hope this book makes you proud.

PATRICK THOMPSON and NOVELLA LOCRITANI: the unsung heroes of this book. You two worked endless hours painstakingly flatting my pages, trying to figure out my squiggles and I am so grateful and sorry.

All my friends and family who helped me through the ups and downs while I was working on *Phantom*. I literally wouldn't have survived the experience without you.

ANDREW LLOYD WEBBER: thank you for introducing me and new generations to this story through your music. I'm sure my neighbours are grateful, too.

And most of all, GASTON LEROUX: for writing this timeless masterpiece. I can only hope I was able to retell it in a way that did it justice.

Vanya Tomi
2020

Varga Tomi

The Palais Garnier in Paris, France.

VARGA TOMI is a Hungarian artist and colorist. He graduated from The Kubert School in Dover, NJ in 2015. Since then he's worked with a number of publishers and high-profile creators, most notably IDW and KEVIN EASTMAN on *Teenage Mutant Ninja Turtles,* and A Wave Blue World and MARGUERITE BENNETT on the *Broken Frontier Anthology* and *Ghastly Tales.*

Backstage Access

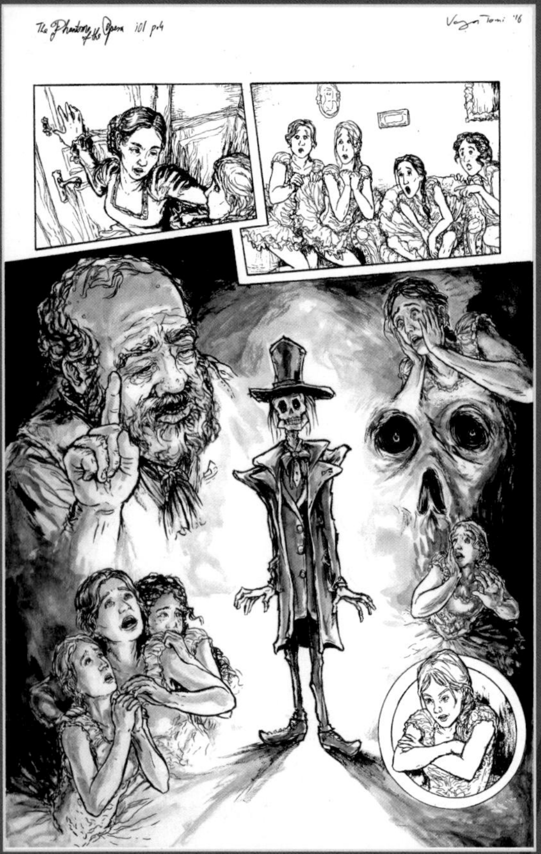

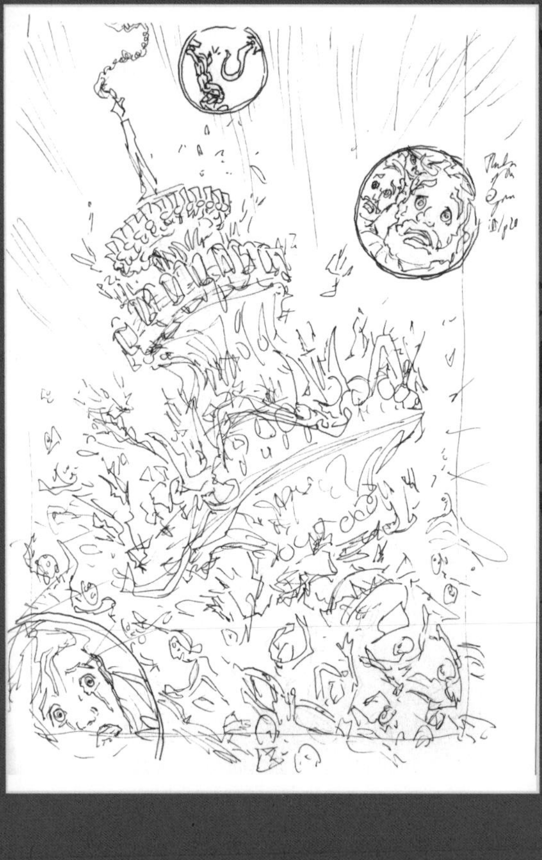

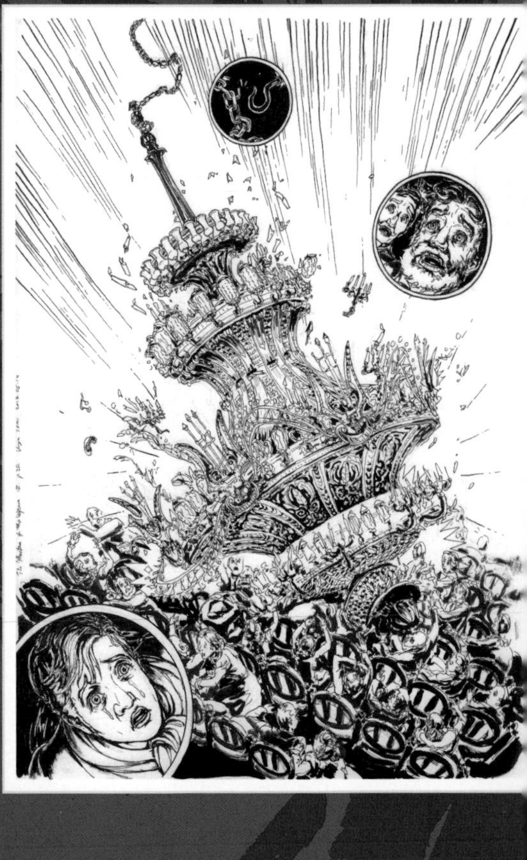

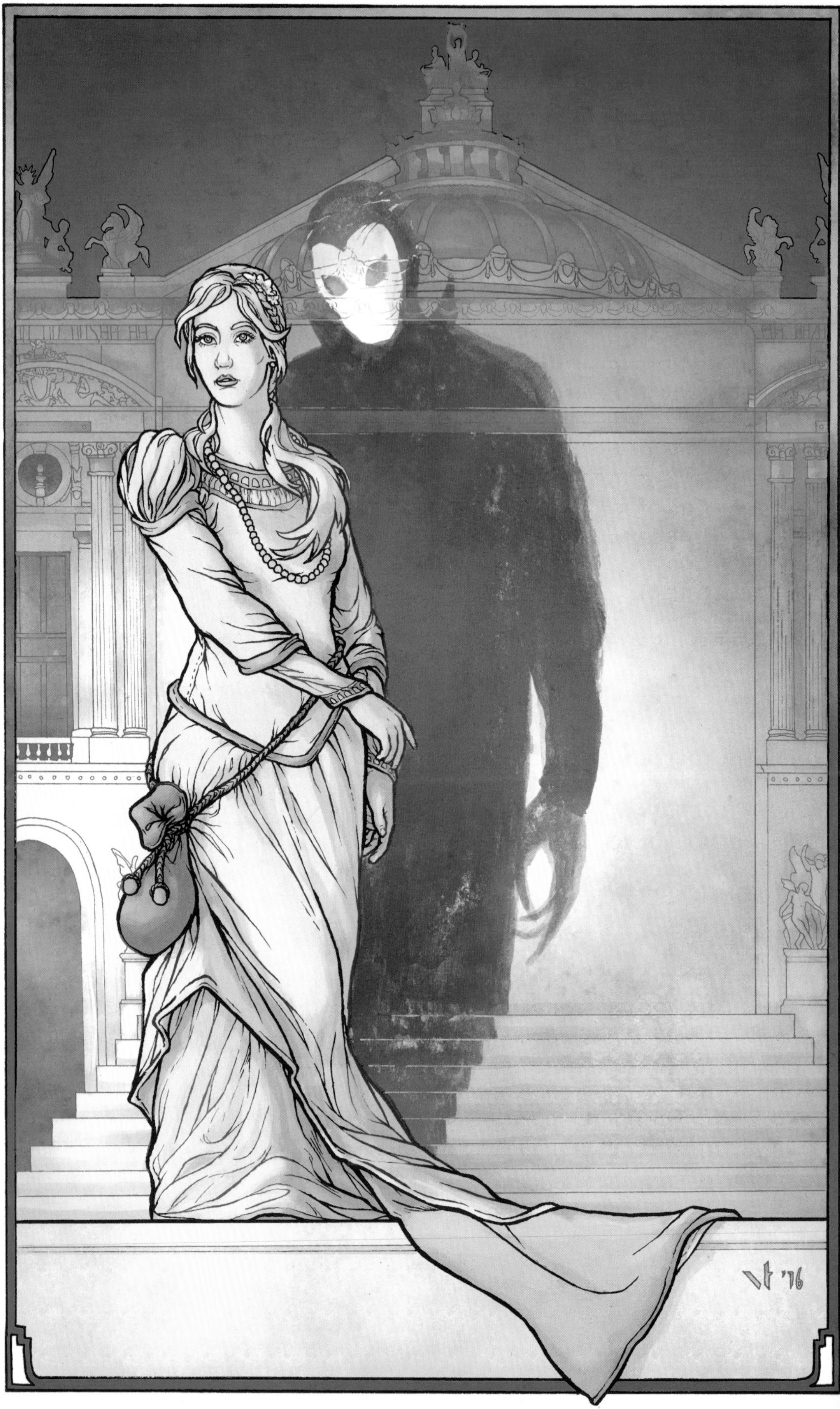
vt '76

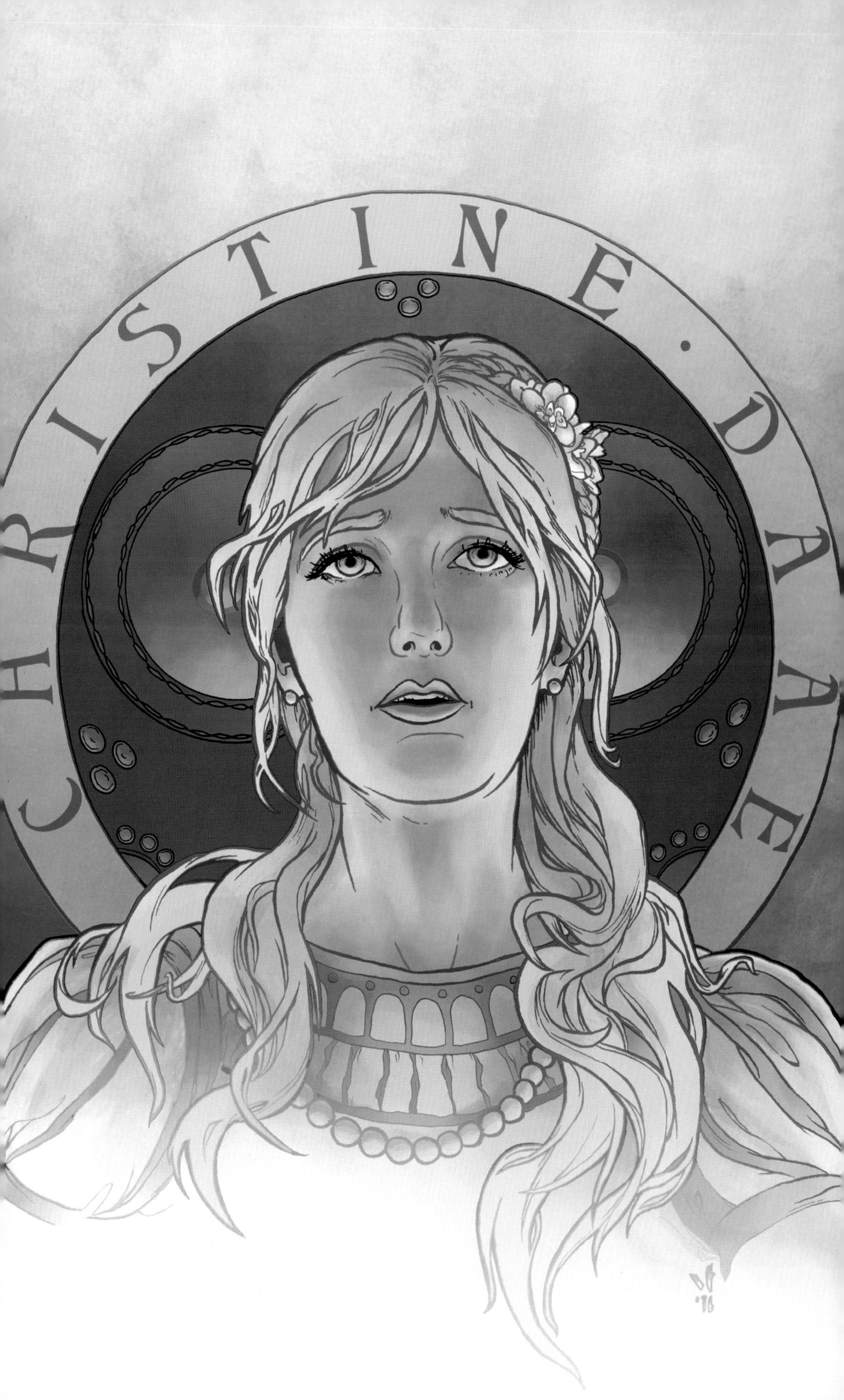
CHRISTINE · DAAE

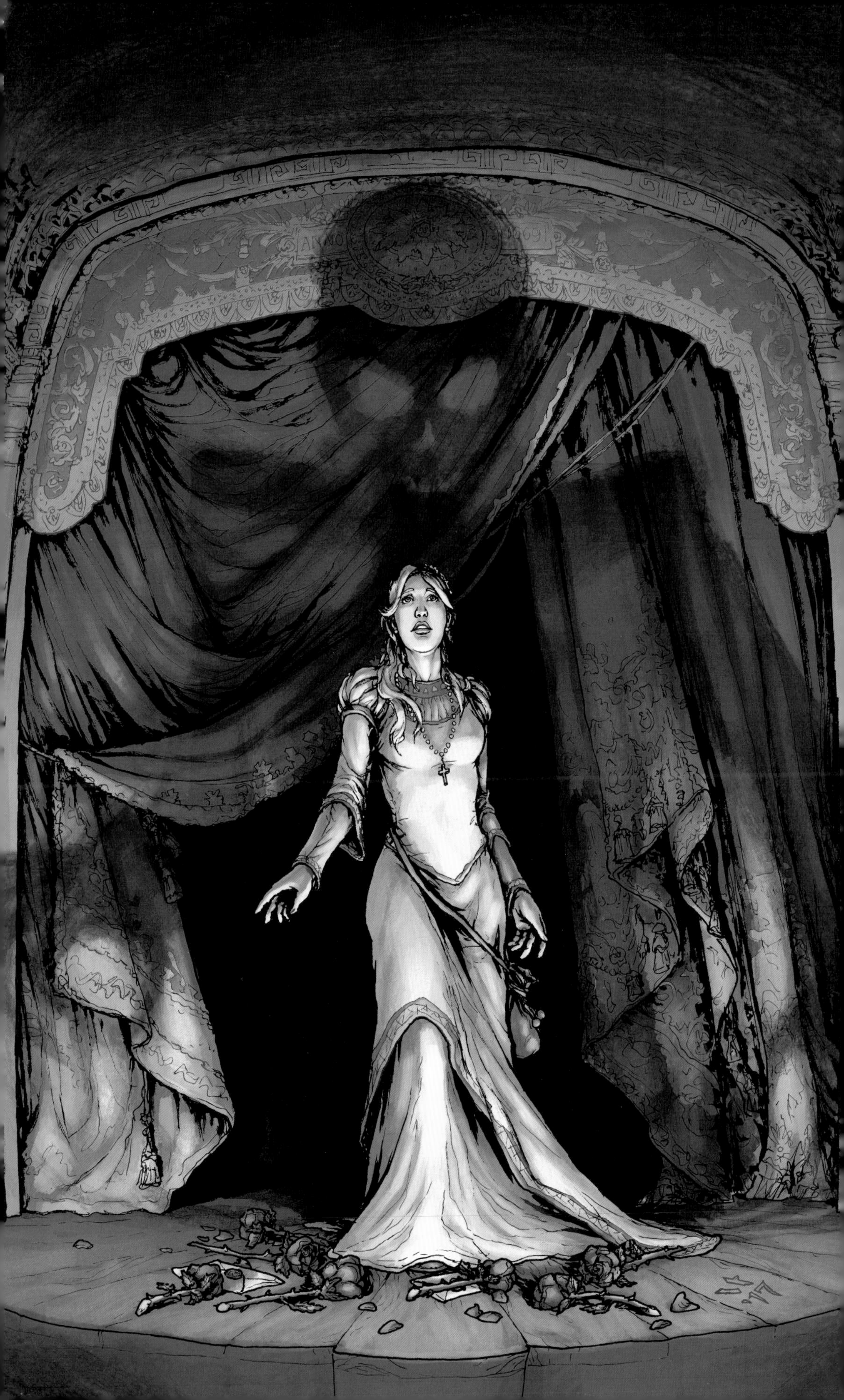
ANNO